Pour Nigel,

Have a nice trip with Toussaint Charbonneau!

The Lost Guide

The Man Behind the Lewis and Clark Expedition

Richard Hétu

Translated from the French
by
Bianca Zagolin

East Village Press

The Lost Guide
Richard Hétu

Originally published in French in Canada under the title *La route de l'Ouest*, by VLB éditeur in 2002.

We gratefully acknowledge the financial support of Quebec's Société de développement des entreprises culturelles (SODEC) in the translation of this book.

For more information about this title please contact:
www.eastvillagepress.com

Book design by:
The Floating Gallery
www.thefloatinggallery.com

Printed in Canada

Richard Hétu
The Lost Guide
1. Author 2. Title 3. Novel
Library of Congress Control Number: 2004104477
ISBN: 0975330705

Prologue

Meeting the Americans

November 1804. Funeral scaffolds lay scattered everywhere on the white frosted prairie. Toussaint Charbonneau and his two Indian women were nearing the Mandan villages, whose dead were exposed to the wind, according to tradition.

Such a mournful sight reminded Charbonneau of old Ménard, who had been killed a few days earlier on the trail to the Assiniboine River trading post. He had been the first White man to settle permanently among the Indians of Upper Missouri, and now the old trader didn't even have a proper burial. Hunted down by a band of Assiniboines, his men had been forced to leave his body riddled with arrows on the plain. "The wolves must have devoured him," Charbonneau said to himself, shuddering at the idea.

Bird Woman drew him out of his morbid thoughts. She was riding behind him and, pointing upward, she called out:

–Look, Toussaint!

A huge flock of geese was flying over them, darkening the sky. Charbonneau's eye followed the birds' flight to the South.

–I wouldn't mind a duck in my pot! Charbonneau shouted merrily, having cooked many a memorable feast on the Great Plains.

–And I in my belly, added Otter Woman, who followed on her own horse and led another one that pulled a *travois*[1] loaded with buffalo skins.

Toussaint Charbonneau had a stocky build; he was thirty-five[2], the sun and wind had dried out his skin, but he hardly showed his age. As for his companions, two Shoshoni slaves he had bought from a Hidatsa chief, they were not even twenty. They had started at daybreak on their way to meet the Americans who were camped on the north shore of the Missouri River, downstream from the Mandan villages. The day before, Toussaint had gotten wind of their arrival. Just back from hunting, he had been summoned by Caltahcota, one of the chiefs of Metaharta, the Hidatsa village where he had been living for many years.

At nightfall, Caltahcota had welcomed Charbonneau in his spacious lodge. He was surrounded by the members of his family, not to mention his dogs and horses that he kept indoors at night to protect them from Assiniboine thieves. He was sitting by the fire, with a white buffalo skin on his shoulders, a somber look on his face. Four days earlier, along with Mandan and Arikara chiefs, he had attended a meeting convened by the Americans.

In an incensed tone, Caltahcota had said to Charbonneau:

–They announced that we have a new Great Father. They have engraved his face. Look.

The chief had held out a silver coin. On one side was the raised profile of a man with aristocratic features. Charbonneau could not read and so was unable to make out the inscription around the effigy: TH. JEFFERSON PRESIDENT OF THE U.S. 1801 A.D.

–He looks like one of our *bourgeois,* had remarked Charbonneau, turning the coin in the palm of his hand.

On the other side was engraved a handshake under a peace pipe and a tomahawk crossing each other. The words PEACE AND FRIENDSHIP appeared between the images.

–They also gave us this flag, Caltahcota had continued as he unfolded on the floor the star-spangled banner of the young American republic. They want us to trade with them and to make peace with the Arikaras, those scoundrels. If One Eye had been there, he would have walked away with their scalps!

Caltahcota had taken back the coin and put away the flag. Staring at Charbonneau straight in the eye, he had declared:

–Go and see those impudent foreigners and offer your services. You will be our eyes and ears among them.

The French-Canadian trader had agreed to set out for their camp the very next day. He wasn't especially gifted for diplomacy or spying, but he could spot a good deal. According to Caltahcota, the strangers were planning to spend the winter with the Mandans, close neighbors of the Hidatsas, whom the French-Canadians called *Gros-Ventres*[3]. In the spring, the Americans would continue their journey to explore the Missouri River. They had left St. Louis in mid-May in search of a navigable passage between the Mississippi and "the great salted lake," the Pacific.

"Indeed!" Charbonneau said to himself as he left Caltahcota's lodge. "They will need an interpreter to talk with the Big Bellies, buffalo skins to get through the winter and maybe even one of my Shoshonis to cross over the Rockies!"

Around 8 o'clock in the morning, they arrived in the vicinity of Mitutanka, the first Mandan village, on the banks of the Missouri. Many of the inhabitants were swimming in the river as they usually did almost all year long.

Charbonneau silently shook his head.

–They'll never catch me doing that, he whispered as he watched men, women and children splashing about in the freezing water, screaming and laughing.

He just couldn't understand the appeal of such morning ablutions. It's not that he was particularly sensitive to the cold. During his many winter expeditions, he would often sleep out in the open, wrapped in a buffalo skin, and he would sometimes wake up under an extra blanket of snow. Of course, his tolerance of the cold did not match that of the Upper Missouri Indians. When the icy winter winds swept across the plains, he always wore an undervest and a shirt under his traveling cloak. But the Indians were often bare-chested under their buffalo coats, even in 30° below weather. No wonder they enjoyed frolicking in the near-freezing river!

In fact, Charbonneau was afraid of the water. In spite of his countless travels on the waterways of Canada, Louisiana and the United States, the man did not know how to swim.

–Good shot!

The exclamation came from the shore where a group of young women were playing with a leather ball. They threw it in the air and tried to keep it up as long as possible, using their feet and their knees. They were lacking neither skill nor charm. One of them in particular drew Charbonneau's attention and he felt a hardening in his corduroy pants. Her body still streaming with water, the Mandan girl had joined the game without taking the time to dress.

"Damn the Americans," Charbonneau said to himself. "If it weren't for them, I could stop and do a little frolicking myself with that little number!"

The young woman noticed the trader. She bore his look without feeling in the least embarrassed. Like the other Indian women of Upper Missouri, who often had two or three lovers or even more, she wasn't at all prudish. One day, she would no doubt have the chance to ascertain in person the veracity of one of the five names given to Toussaint Charbonneau by the Mandans and the Hidatsas: the Great Horse that Came from Afar, the Chief of the Little Village, the Man Who Possesses Many Gourds, the Forest Bear, and finally, One Whose Man-Part Is Never Limp. Each one of these names contained equal parts of admiration and irony, except for the last one, in which clearly admiration prevailed over irony.

Toussaint Charbonneau had earned the most daring of these nicknames shortly after his arrival in Upper Missouri in 1796. On a winter evening, the Mandans had invited him to join them in the buffalo dance. The ceremony had started in a lodge in Ruptare, the second Mandan village. In the middle of the dwelling, some elderly men, squatting on skins, had formed a circle around a figurine representing a woman. A young man had invited Charbonneau to sit among them; he had then lit a pipe and offered it to the trader and the other members of the group.

Charbonneau and the elderly sages had smoked in silence. After a while, the young man had come back to the middle of the lodge with other Mandans of his own age. Each one was accompanied by a young woman dressed only in a buffalo skin wrapped around her body.

Each young man had addressed one member of the circle with the same theatrical flourish.

–This is my wife! I beseech you to pass on your medicine to her!

Charbonneau was only too pleased to oblige. In a flash, he rose to his feet and followed outside the pretty Mandan who had just been offered to him. Not quite as frisky, some of the old men had required help to get up. In the end, each member of the circle had found himself outside with a woman who, away from the others, had lain on her buffalo skin and offered her quivering body to him.

This ritual, performed on the eve of a hunting expedition, was meant to infuse into the young men, through their wives, the experience and powers of the wise elders. The sexual act had to be carried out on a buffalo skin in order to convey to the herd that it was time to come near.

Charbonneau was neither old nor wise. But, in the eyes of the Indians, he possessed great powers as a White man. That night, he had passed on his "powers" in quick succession to six women, gladly taking over from the old men who had been unable to perform. Thus, he had made his contribution to one of the most successful hunts in the history of the Mandans, who called themselves the People of the First Man.

That's how he got his naughty nickname and his reputation, which explained the lust in the eyes of the Mandan girl on the banks of the Missouri. She paid the price for allowing herself to be distracted: the leather ball hit her in the forehead.

Toussaint Charbonneau's two women, who had not missed a thing, burst out laughing.

–Never lose sight of the ball! commented Bird Woman in a mocking voice.

–You'd better cover up or you'll catch cold! continued Otter Woman in the same tone.

–Shut up, you two! interrupted Charbonneau; for a moment, he had completely forgotten the Shoshoni women.

They both fell silent. They didn't want to arouse the man's anger. But they kept on smiling to themselves.

Part one

Winter at Fort Mandan

Chapter one

The Corps of Discovery

A great lover of travel stories, Thomas Jefferson received, on August 1802, on the eve of his departure for Monticello, Alexander Mackenzie's book, *Voyages from Montreal on the River St. Laurence through the Continent of North America to the Frozen and Pacific Oceans in the Years 1789 and 1793.* In the torrid heat of the South, the President of the United States and his private secretary, Meriwether Lewis, devoured the story by the Scottish explorer who was the first man to cross the continent north of Mexico. Toward the end of the book, both men felt a twinge of sorrow as they read the words that Mackenzie had inscribed on a rock facing the Pacific: "*Alexander Mackenzie, from Canada, by land, the 22nd of July, One thousand seven hundred and ninety-three.*"

–Mister President, allow me to become the first American to go up the Missouri and down the Columbia! exclaimed Lewis to Jefferson after reading the book. I promise you that I will succeed where Mackenzie failed. I will find the Northwest passage!

By way of an answer, Jefferson merely smiled, while examining Lewis, who was built like a soldier but had the look of a poet. The President's heart was beating as fast as his secretary's. He wanted to get to the Great Plains and Oregon before the British, the French, or the Spanish. Since his youth, he had seen in the West the very destiny of the American nation.

On May 3, 1803, he came closer to fulfilling his vision by purchasing French Louisiana, a vast territory that extended from the Canadian border to the Gulf of Mexico, for the sum of fifteen million dollars. With this single transaction, he succeeded in doubling the size of his country.

A few months earlier, Jefferson had granted his secretary's wish when he had entrusted him with the mission of exploring the Missouri River up to its source and then to sail down the Columbia as far as its mouth. In the president's eyes, Meriwether Lewis, a twenty-eight-years-old captain, was perfect to lead the first American expedition across the continent. He came from a good Virginia family who lived on the farm next to Monticello, in the hills of Albemarle County. After his studies in Richmond, he had taken over the family plantation, an estate of about two thousand acres and two dozen slaves.

But running a plantation bored him. As soon as he had been able to hand over his responsibilities to his younger brother, he had joined the army. Over the next four years, he had discovered what his fellow countrymen called the "frontier" as he traveled all over the new territories of the United States, Indiana, Kentucky, Ohio, Missouri, where some Indian chiefs were still resisting American law.

In 1796, he was assigned to a company of elite riflemen where he met a man with whom he would have a lifetime association, William Clark, another Virginian from Albemarle, an army captain. In early 1801, after having been promoted to the rank of captain, he had proudly accepted the position of secretary to the new President of the United States, Thomas Jefferson.

For two years, Meriwether Lewis lived in the presidential residence, at 1600 Pennsylvania Avenue, in Washington, and in Monticello. He had all his meals with the President , at whose table he met the most important figures of his times, and enjoyed the finest French wines to which the President had grown accustomed during his stay in Paris. In the company of the philosopher of the American Revolution, Meriwether Lewis added to his practical experience an impressive intellectual store. The President had detected only one flaw in him, a tendency to be melancholic.

When the time came to organize the exploration of the West, Jefferson decided that the Corps of Discovery would be under the joint command of Lewis and his friend Clark, whose family he knew well. The President left nothing to chance. Before the start of the expedition, he gave the two captains a long questionnaire drawn up in collaboration with his colleagues of the American Philosophical Society, an organization from Philadelphia dedicated to the advancement of human knowledge. During their trip, Lewis and Clark were expected to take copious notes on the language, customs, occupations, illnesses and beliefs of the Indians they would meet.

The expedition was financed by the United States Congress and it reflected Jefferson's boundless intellectual curiosity. A worthy representative of the Age of Enlightenment, the third American President had an encyclopedic mind. He could pride himself on being a meteorologist, a phrenologist, a geographer, a cartographer and a botanist. He also had a passion for astrology, ethnology, paleontology and natural history. Hoping to make Lewis an extension of his own self, he sent his protégé to perfect his education with the scholars in Philadelphia. He wanted to get the most accurate descriptions, not only of the Indian nations, but also of the plants and animals of the West that were unknown to Americans. He wished to receive detailed accounts describing the new territories, maps indicating their watercourses, records of winds, temperatures, longitudes and latitudes. He attached great importance to commerce and diplomacy, but he did not exaggerate when he wrote that the goal of the Lewis and Clark expedition was also "scientific and literary."

M'en revenant de la jolie Rochelle
M'en revenant de la jolie Rochelle
J'ai rencontré trois jolies demoiselles

C'est l'aviron qui nous mène, qui nous mène
C'est l'aviron qui nous mène en haut.[4]

On May 14, 1804, shortly after four o'clock in the afternoon, the song known to all voyageurs from Canada and Louisiana rang out at the mouth of the Missouri. The Corps of Discovery was setting off on a great adventure, ascending a river whose source was unknown to the White man. On the shore, the wives and children of the French-Canadian *engagés* were waving their handkerchiefs and holding back their tears. From Lachine to St. Louis, it was the same thing every spring: descendants of the settlers of New France, heirs to the *coureurs de bois*, would leave their families to go West, striking up a cheerful song. In Lewis and Clark's troop, about ten Frenchmen, as the American soldiers called them, sang in unison:

J'ai rencontré trois jolies demoiselles
J'ai rencontré trois jolies demoiselles
J'ai point choisi, mais j'ai pris la plus belle.

C'est l'aviron qui nous mène, qui nous mène
C'est l'aviron qui nous mène en haut.[5]

Twenty-nine men and a dog were heading up the river aboard a sixty-foot keelboat. Seven soldiers and six *engagés* followed in two canoes, one red and the other white.

Each craft was heavily loaded. The expedition had gotten its equipment from the French merchant Auguste Chouteau, the emperor of the fur trade and co-founder of St. Louis. The supplies included, among other things, three thousand four hundred pounds of flour, five hundred and sixty pounds of biscuits, fifty pounds of coffee and a hundred and twenty gallons of whisky. The troop also carried numerous presents for the Indians, among which were four thousand six hundred sewing needles, one hundred and thirty plugs of tobacco and eight copper pots.

On that day, pushed along by a gentle breeze, the Corps of Discovery covered a short distance of sixteen miles before setting up camp on the upper tip of the first island. In the evening, around the fire, the members of the expedition spoke gravely of their situation. Attentive to everything that was being said, Private Patrick Gass, a twenty-four-year-old soldier from Pennsylvania, expressed the state of mind of the group in his journal. By the light of the fire, he wrote:

"The best authenticated accounts informed us that we were to pass through a country possessed by numerous, powerful and warlike nations of savages of gigantic nature, fierce, treacherous and cruel; and particularly hostile to white men. And fame had united with tradition in opposing mountains to our course, which human enterprise and exertion would attempt in vain to pass."

The next day, the troop stopped in St. Charles, a village of about four hundred and fifty inhabitants, most of who were born of French-Canadians from the St. Lawrence Valley. In his journal, Lewis did not hide the low esteem in which he held these settlers. He wrote: "A great majority of the inhabitants are miserably poor, illiterate and when at home, excessively lazy."

And indeed, the residents of St. Charles refused to practice agriculture seriously because they considered it a "degrading" occupation, as had noted Captain Lewis. The men preferred letting their wives and children starve to changing their way of life. From father to son, they were hunters, trappers, voyageurs. The most skillful set up their own businesses, but the great majority worked for the French and Spanish merchants of St. Louis. They were the *engagés,* the hired men of the fur trade, and they could be away from their families for periods of six, twelve or even eighteen months. In this life, rich in adventures and hardships, they showed remarkable drive and endurance.

Thus, in spite of Lewis' reservations, Clark hired two residents of St. Charles as soldiers, François Labiche and Pierre Cruzatte, two boatmen of mixed race who knew the Missouri intimately over more than four hundred and fifty miles. Cruzatte, whose mother was Omaha, took care to pack, along with the rest of his gear, the fiddle of an old French-Canadian friend.

The members of the Corps of Discovery were ready for anything, except boredom. For almost three months, they traveled up the

Missouri without seeing a single Indian. On the banks of the river, all the villages were deserted. It was the season of the buffalo hunt, the major event in the lives of the Plains Indians. Moving away from the Missouri, they followed the herds that provided them with everything they needed, food, clothing, weapons, etc.

On the morning of July 23, eager to announce to the Indians the identity of their new Great Father, Lewis sent for Pierre Cruzatte, the boatman, and Georges Drouillard, the hunter. He gave them some tobacco and dispatched them to look for the Otos and the Panis. Although they knew the region, the two men didn't find anyone. On August 1st, Clark celebrated his thirty-fourth birthday in a brooding mood. Where could the Indians be?

The next day, at sunset, six Indians finally appeared at the camp. They claimed to be Oto and Missouri chiefs. They were immediately invited to participate in a conference that would take place in the morning.

American diplomacy was set in motion under a canopy that had been pitched on the riverbank to protect the participants from the sun. Drouillard acted as interpreter. He knew the sign language used by the Great Plains Indians, being the son of a French-Canadian father and a Shawnee mother. He proclaimed American sovereignty, announced the arrival of new traders and promoted peace among nations.

Little Thief, an Oto chief, immediately responded to Meriwether Lewis's harangue.

–Dear brothers, we have always traded with the White man, French, Spanish or English. We care little about the color of the flag, as long as the price and the quality of the merchandise is good.

Big Horse, a Missouri chief, continued:

–Our new Great Father must prove his good intentions by offering us generous gifts.

–Why not begin with a spoonful of your milk? asked Little Thief.

The Oto chief was using a euphemism for whisky.

Captains Lewis and Clark did not appreciate the way the meeting was going. Alcohol was not supposed to serve as diplomatic lubricant. It was fully sober and in a solemn atmosphere that the Plains Indians were supposed to accept American sovereignty.

But the chiefs kept on harassing the captains with their incessant requests. One of them said:

–Do not leave bad memories behind. Give us gunpowder and whisky!

The captains tried to calm down the chiefs by distributing a few harmless gifts. The Indians were quick to denounce their mediocrity.

–The White man takes us for little children!

For the sake of peace and quiet, the captains gave in to the chiefs' demands and provided them with alcohol and gunpowder. Greatly vexed, they ended the conference with a demonstration of their air gun, an American novelty, after which they left the site of the meeting, which they had named Council Bluffs. The first attempt at American diplomacy on the Missouri had failed. But Captain Clark was careful not to admit defeat. Knowing that Jefferson would be the first to read his journal, he wrote[6]: "Those Chiefs all Delivered a Speech acknowledging Their approbation to the Speech and promising to prosue the advice & Derictions given them. They wer happy to find that they had fathers which might be depended on.

"We gave them a Cannister of Powder and a Bottle of whiskey and delivered a few presents to the whole after giving a breech cloth Some Paint guartering & a Meadele to those we made Cheifs. After Capt Lewis's Shooting the air gun a feiw Shots (which astonished those natives) we set out and proceeded on…"

The Corps of Discovery continued to advance along the Missouri, chased by clouds of mosquitoes, overwhelmed by unbearable heat.

Speaking on behalf of the French-Canadian *engagés*, François Rivet complained to Captain Clark about the diet to which the Americans subjected them.

–When we travel, we are used to eating six times a day, said the Montreal native.

Clark remained inflexible.

–If you don't find two meals a day sufficient, you are free to go back to St. Louis, he answered.

On August 18, Captain Lewis found a way to earn the appreciation of the men. On his twenty-ninth birthday, he ordered that each member of the expedition get a glassful of whisky. Cruzatte pulled out his violin and played rigadoons for the occasion. Under heavy skies streaked with lightning, the men danced, sweating profusely. By eleven o'clock, the rain was pouring down in buckets, forcing the fiddler to put away his instrument.

Two days later, the Americans suffered the loss of their first man, Sergeant Charles Floyd, who succumbed to peritonitis. Patrick Gass was elected by the men to the rank of sergeant.

On August 28, at the mouth of the James River, an Indian swam up to the boat and informed the men on board that there was an important Yankton Sioux camp about twelve miles away.

The Sioux... Jefferson couldn't have been clearer in his instructions to Meriwether Lewis on the way to behave with this people of warriors whose reputation bordered on legend. "On that nation, we wish most particularly to make a favorable impression, because of their immense power," had explained the President of the United States.

When he wrote these lines in June 1803, Jefferson was still hoping to succeed in cajoling the Sioux and thus opening the way to American commerce in Upper Missouri, a country rich in furs; the Northwest Company, founded in Montreal twenty years earlier, enjoyed a virtual monopoly in that region. Opening up this new territory would silence the critics of the Louisiana purchase. According to Jefferson himself, the United States were still "miserably weak" in their newly acquired western lands.

But the author of the Declaration of Independence had an interest in the Sioux and the other nations of the Great Plains that went beyond mere considerations of trade. As many cultured men of his time, he liked philosophizing about the Indians of the West, those "noble savages" still untouched by civilization. He dreamt of integrating them fully as citizens of the United States. "I believe the Indian to be in body and mind equal to the white man," he wrote in 1785, when he was Ambassador of the United States in Paris.

Jefferson would never have made such remarks about the Negroes whose inferiority was written into the Constitution of 1787: according to this revered document, a Black slave was only worth three-fifths of a White citizen. But the Indians of the Prairie held a special place in the President's heart and mind. Since his early childhood, he fantasized about the people and the territories of the West, the *Terra Incognita* of his days. In Philadelphia, educated people would speculate endlessly about the presence, in the Great Plains, of white-skinned Indians, mammoths, unicorns and giant beavers measuring six feet from the tip of the nose to the end of the tail. Thanks to the explorations of the Corps of Discovery, Jefferson would finally be able to distinguish myth from reality.

The Sioux, at last! Lewis and Clark dispatched three members of the expedition to the village to invite the Indians to a conference. The next morning, the emissaries came back with five chiefs, seventy warriors and Pierre Dorion, a French-Canadian trader who had been living for years with the Yanktons, of the Dakota family, whom the French named Sioux, a Chippewa word meaning enemy.

In spite of the precarious situation of their tribe, the Yankton dignitaries were stunningly elegant. Tall and slender, they wore dazzling clothes made of skins and decorated with feathers, beads and porcupine quills. "Barbarian splendor," Captain Clark thought to himself, impressed by the scene.

The Americans and the Yanktons settled down under an oak tree, near which flew an American flag. Pierre Dorion acted as interpreter. He was married to a native woman and had six children of mixed race; he was fluent in the Sioux language. Thanks to him, the captains were able, for the first time, to communicate with the Great Plains Indians with precise words rather than approximate signs.

Captain Lewis made his usual speech, which aroused great interest among the Yanktons. For years, they had tried in vain to put an end to the economic dependence in which they were kept by the Tetons, their Sioux big brothers.

When Lewis had finished speaking, Weucha, the most important of the Yankton chiefs, asked the Americans for a day to prepare his answer.

–I must discuss your proposals with the other chiefs, he said solemnly.

The Americans agreed, but before they left, they distributed gifts to the Yanktons.

The next morning, preceded by four musicians, the Yankton dignitaries came back and took their place under the oak tree. Each chief held his best peace pipe. Weucha, named the Liberator by the French-Canadians, started to speak, his gaze fixed on Lewis and Clark.

–I see before me two sons of my Great Father. You can see me, as well as our other chiefs and our warriors. We are very poor. We have no gunpowder, no bullets, no knives, and our women and children in the village have no clothes. I wish that my brothers, who have offered me a flag and a medal, give something to those poor people or allow them to trade with the first boat that will come up the river.

Dorion translated the Liberator's words in French and Georges Drouillard conveyed them to the captains in English.

Weucha continued.

–I will bring together the chiefs of the Panis and the Omahas, and I will make peace between them. It is better that I do it rather than the sons of my Great Father, for they will be more willing to listen to me. I will also lead some of the chiefs to your country in the spring.

Lewis and Clark couldn't believe their ears. They were witnessing the realization of their diplomatic objectives. Weucha, esteemed chief of the Yankton Sioux, had accepted an alliance with the Americans!

The chiefs lit their peace pipes and passed them around. Lewis and Clark were overjoyed as they inhaled the smoke. They named the site of the meeting Calumet Bluffs. The rest of the day brought more delights. After the morning conference, some Yankton youths gave a demonstration of their skills with bow and arrow. In the afternoon, the women arrived to prepare the evening meal. They wore tunics made of skins and the members of the expedition found them most alluring. In the evening, men with painted bodies sang and danced around the fire, proclaiming their war or hunting feats. They were accompanied by musicians who beat on drums and shook various rattles.

During the show, the women roasted nice plump dogs, a delicacy among the Sioux.

At Dorion's suggestion, the Americans thanked the Yanktons by throwing gifts at them –tobacco, knives, ribbons, string. Under a starry sky, they enjoyed the best evening of the journey.

The euphoria of the celebration continued for several days. Beyond the Niobrara River, every day the expedition discovered animals and plants unknown to Americans up until then. Lewis gave the pretty name of "barking squirrel" to the prairie dog. Clark spotted a coyote and called it "prairie fox." On September 14, Private John Shields shot a type of hare which he rudely named jackass rabbit. Two days later, another hunter brought back to the captains a black-beaked magpie, a bird whose existence in North America was still unknown to the White man.

The region was truly a living Eden. A few weeks earlier, fire had set the prairie ablaze. As the expedition sailed by it, a new, spring green grass covered the plains that stretched as far as the eye could see. Lewis went ashore many times and took long walks, rejoining the rest of the troop at the location of the night camp. On September 17, after one of these hikes, he wrote one of the many beautiful pages of his journal:

"Before sunrise I set out with six of my best hunters… One quarter mile in rear of our camp, which was situated in a fine open grove of cotton wood, passed a grove of plumb trees loaded with fruit and now ripe… The plain is entirely occupied by the burrows of the *barking squiril…* this anamal appears here in infinite numbers, and the shortness and virdue of grass gave the plain the appearance throughout its whole extent of a beautiful bowling green in fine order…

"This scenery already rich, pleasing and beautiful was still farther hightened by immense herds of Buffaloe, deer, Elk and

Antelopes which we saw in every direction feeding on the hills and plains. I do not think I exaggerate when I estimate the number of Buffaloe which could be compreed at one view to amount to 3000."

Following President Jefferson's orders, Lewis and Clark fulfilled their duties as botanists and zoologists. They collected specimens, preserved skins and skeletons, wrote descriptive notes. But the excitement of discovery was soon replaced by a gnawing anxiety.

The Sioux… Lewis and Clark knew that the decisive encounter with the Teton Sioux was near. And what they knew about them was hardly reassuring. President Jefferson had given them the journal of Jean-Baptiste Truteau, a French merchant from St. Louis, who had gotten into trouble with the Tetons in 1794. After his unfortunate experience, Truteau had given this piece of advice to those who traveled to Upper Missouri: "Avoid this tribe, for the sake of your goods as well as the safeguard of your own lives."

After the conference in Calumet Bluffs, Half-Man, one of the Yankton chiefs, had also warned them in no uncertain terms:

–I fear that the nations upstream will not open their ears.

The first contact with the Teton Sioux took place at the mouth of the Bad River, on September 23. In the evening, three young men swam up to the boat to tell the Americans that some Tetons had their camp not far from there. The captains received them kindly and sent them back with two tobacco plugs for their chiefs and an invitation to a conference.

Two days later, around eleven o'clock in the morning, two Teton chiefs, Black Buffalo and the Partisan, accompanied by fifty warriors, arrived at the site of the meeting, on an island in the middle of the Bad River. The Americans put up a pole for the United States flag and a tent where everyone gathered at noon.

After a military parade, Lewis addressed the assembly. His speech was brief. Since Pierre Dorion had refused to go to the Teton country with the rest of the expedition, the American had to fall back on Pierre Cruzatte as interpreter. He knew a few words of Sioux. But Lewis soon started to notice on the chiefs' faces signs of lack of understanding and displeasure. He decided to cut short his harangue and proceed immediately to the distribution of gifts.

He gave Black Buffalo, who seemed to be the most important of the chiefs, a medal bearing the effigy of President Jefferson, an American flag, a uniform jacket with stripes on it and a three-cornered hat. The Partisan had to be content with a medal and a flag.

Lewis had just made a diplomatic blunder. Humiliated in front of his warriors, the Partisan leapt up indignantly.

–These presents are ridiculous, he protested. If you wish to get through, you'll have to leave us a canoe full of goods!

Surprised by the Partisan's vehemence, Lewis resorted to his usual diversion, a demonstration of his air gun.

But the Tetons were not at all impressed. That's when Clark tried to ease the tension by making a proposal to the chiefs:

–Why don't you come on board, he said.

The Americans showed the chiefs the keelboat, their air cannon and all the strange things likely to amuse them. They also offered them a quarter glass of whisky. Black Buffalo and the Partisan immediately snatched the bottle from them and emptied it.

The Partisan became very difficult, and so did Black Buffalo. Clark had a lot of trouble convincing them to get off the boat. He finally succeeded by inviting them aboard the white canoe.

Cruzatte and Labiche went along as interpreters. They paddled towards the shore where warriors, women and children had gathered. As soon as the canoe touched land, three men grabbed its towrope. At that very moment, the Partisan, suddenly sober, turned to the Captain and announced defiantly:

–We are the rulers of this land! You shall go no further!

Cruzatte translated. Clark's face turned crimson. No Indian had ever spoken to him in that tone.

–We will pass, whether you like or not, he answered. My men are not squaws, but warriors.

Black Buffalo sniggered:

–I also have warriors. And if you attempt to pass, they will hunt you down, one after the other.

Clark had heard enough.

–On my boat, I have what it takes to kill in a single day twenty tribes like yours! he shouted, pulling out his saber.

Seeing the weapon, the warriors gathered on the riverbank reached for the arrows in their quivers and drew back their bows. Clark and his interpreters were surrounded. If the chief had given the signal, they would have been pierced by arrows. But, from the corner of his eye, Black Buffalo saw the red canoe drawing near. A dozen soldiers were on board with their rifles aimed at the Sioux on the shore. The confrontation could well have turned into a massacre of women and children. Black Buffalo wisely ordered his men to let go of the canoe rope.

Clark remembered President Jefferson's instructions. Before leaving for the expedition's camp, he held out his hand to Black Buffalo, stifling his anger. But the chief refused to shake it.

The following day, as if nothing had happened, the Teton chiefs behaved most politely toward Lewis and Clark. Some warriors came to fetch them at their camp and transported them on white buffalo skins to Black Buffalo's village.

The Americans were treated to a Sioux feast: prairie turnips, grilled dog and pemmican, a dish made from sun-dried buffalo meat mashed with melted fat into a solid paste.

They only ate a very small amount of the dog.

Everyone made a speech, but given the absence of a competent translator, no one was able to break through the wall of incomprehension that stood between the Tetons and the Americans.

Late in the evening, Lewis and Clark were offered women by Black Buffalo. They refused this gesture of hospitality.

For two days, tension was replaced by a rather forced cordiality. Lewis and Clark took advantage of the situation to carry out their ethnological mission. They asked questions to the Tetons and took notes on their vocabulary, clothing, architecture, music, cooking and system of justice. In his journal, Sergeant John Ordway gave a description of one of the Sioux villages: "Sergt Gass informed me as he was at the village to day that he counted 80 Lodges (of the Teton Tribe) which contain ten persons each... about 2 thirds are women and children. The women are employed in dressing Buffalo Skins for clothes and lodges…"

Despite the reduced tension, the members of the expedition did not let down their guard altogether. An Omaha prisoner of the Tetons had told Cruzatte that the Sioux chiefs still intended to prevent Lewis and Clark from going further.

The Americans set the date of their departure for September 28. On that day, after breakfast, four Teton chiefs came visiting on the keelboat. Black Buffalo was among them and he insisted on accompanying the expedition for a short distance. Rather than getting involved in a discussion with him, the captains agreed, only too happy to see the other three chiefs go ashore.

A rope tied the boat to the riverbank. When it was time to leave, several Teton warriors seized hold of it, putting on the same act as before. A crowd of Tetons closed in around the Americans. The Partisan was right in front.

As he watched the maneuvering, Lewis started losing patience. Furious, he issued a first warning to Black Buffalo:

–If your men don't let go of the rope, I will order my soldiers to shoot into the crowd.

Black Buffalo stretched out his arms to Lewis.

–My men only want tobacco, he said, casting a worried look at the Partisan. Give them some and we will let you go.

–That's out of the question, retorted the Captain. Tell your men to let go of the rope, or else...

Black Buffalo hesitated. He was facing a dilemma. In order to keep his influence on the Partisan and the other Tetons, he had to get something out of the Americans. But he did not want to put at risk the lives of the women and children of his nation.

He said to Lewis:

–I see that my brother is angry. I see that he is ready to shed blood for a plug of tobacco. I, too, am angry.

Lewis took a plug of tobacco from his bag and threw it at Black Buffalo.

–You stated that you were a great man and that you had influence, said the Captain scornfully. Prove it! Order your men to let go of the canoe rope and we will leave without further ado.

Black Buffalo raised his head and turned his back to Lewis; he got off the boat and gave the tobacco to his warriors. Then, getting hold of the rope, he threw it on the boat.

The Americans immediately headed off and made their way under a south-eastern breeze.

Their coming had done nothing to lift the blockade of Upper Missouri. The trappers and merchants who would venture there next, fewer in number than the members of the Corps of Discovery and not as well armed, would have a taste of Sioux revenge.

This time, Clark did not censure his words. In his journal, he called the Tetons "the vilest miscreants of the savage race" and "the pirates of the Missouri." Jefferson was going to be disappointed.

Chapter Two

Fort Mandan

Christ! swore Toussaint Charbonneau as he caught sight of Fort Mandan, a log structure the likes of which had never been seen in Upper Missouri. It will stand, not only against drafts, but also cannonballs!

Located on low-lying land planted with tall poplars, the buildings, still under construction, consisted of two rows of cabins, with slanted roofs, at right angles to each other, with a palisade on the river side. About forty men were working on the fortifications and building canoes. From the way they were dressed, Toussaint could tell that about a dozen of them were French-Canadians.

Otter Woman grumbled, showing her displeasure.

–I don't trust these people, she said, pointing to the American soldiers.

Bird Woman, on the contrary, seemed delighted to see the Americans. She whispered in Charbonneau's ear:

–Fate has brought us here.

–Did you have a dream? asked the trader.

–No, just a vision.

In the middle of the yard, two men in uniform were talking to each other. A Negro with an impressive build was standing behind them and stroking the head of a black Newfoundland. Toussaint made his way toward the three men.

Captain Meriwether Lewis looked the newcomer up and down; he was dressed like a typical voyageur, red scarf around the neck, blue greatcoat on his back, deer skin leggings and moccasins. The tips of his belt hung down his left side, as was customary. Lewis was not impressed. "Another French-Canadian," he thought. "There is no doubt about it; the country is full of them."

The former secretary to President Jefferson had not changed his mind about the descendants of the settlers of New France. He couldn't even remember the names of the French-Canadians who were part of his own expedition, François Rivet, Jean-Baptiste Lajeunesse, Paul Primeau, Charles Hébert and the others, all natives of Montreal, Ste. Rose, Chateauguay, Ste. Genevieve and other places. Most of them would go back to St. Louis in the spring on the keelboat. For the time being, they were building canoes or helping the Americans to complete the construction of their fort before winter.

While the women stayed back on their horses, fascinated by the sight of the dark-skinned giant, Toussaint dismounted and walked up to the leaders.

–Who are you and what do you want? inquired Captain Lewis.

The French-Canadian did not appreciate the tone of the American, nor the way he looked at him, but he was careful not to show it, wishing to make a good impression. René Jusseaume, a French-Canadian trader and interpreter, whom Charbonneau knew well, soon joined them.

–He wants to know who you are and what you want, Jusseaume translated for the benefit of his fellow countryman who didn't understand a word of English.

–I am Toussaint Charbonneau, interpreter and free trader with the Big Bellies, he said, raising his tuque. I've heard that you will spend the winter among us and I've come to offer my services. You won't find a more trustworthy man in the entire country!

Jusseaume conveyed Charbonneau's words, but omitted the last sentence. A week earlier, he had been hired by the Americans to act as interpreter with the Mandans, among whom he had been living for more than ten years with his Indian wife and their two children. He and Charbonneau competed with each other as traders, unfairly most of the time.

–Are these skins for sale? asked Captain Clark, pointing to the pelts on the *travois*.

–Yes, they are, answered Charbonneau to the American who had flaming red hair. My women can bring you more, if you wish. And he added in a confidential tone:

–They are Shoshonis. They come from the Rockies.

In an aside to Jusseaume, he said:

–You'd better translate that, or I'll cut your throat!

When they heard the complete translation of Charbonneau's words, the two Americans looked at each other wide-eyed. Clark then asked the trader:

–Would you be willing to accompany us to the Pacific with one of your women?

–It depends on your conditions, replied Charbonneau with detachment.

–Do you think you can stand the rigors of an expedition for several months into wild country? asked Lewis a moment later.

It was Charbonneau's turn to eye the Captain scornfully. He did not try to hide his feelings. Looking offended, he said:

–I'll have you know that I covered on foot the distance from Grand Portage, on the North shore of Lake Superior, to Montreal, on the St. Lawrence River. And all that to bring a letter to a company boss! I have eaten cat's tails roots so as not to starve; I have killed a bear in the forest with my bare hands; I have braved more rapids than all your men put together. Do I look like a cowardly *mangeur de lard*[7]?

The Americans looked at each other again. They had learned to be wary of the bragging of French-Canadians. Had not René Jusseaume, for example, boasted about his supposed participation in the American Revolution? By his account, he had been a spy on behalf of George Clark, Captain Clark's brother and hero in the War of Independence. Jusseaume might have seen him in Illinois or Kentucky, but he certainly did not fight with him. He wasn't even able to describe a single battle against the English or the Indians, not even the one fought against the Panis with Daniel Boone! He was obviously lying.

But this Toussaint Charbonneau might just be telling the truth about the two Shoshonis. Before the end of the winter, they would find a way to get to the bottom of it.

–When the fort is completed, you can settle here with your women, said Captain Clark to the trader. While waiting to start on our journey, we will be relying on you to be our interpreter with the Big Bellies. By the way, do you know Le Borgne?

–Of course, I do, answered Charbonneau, with an enigmatic smile. He has just left to wage war on the Shoshonis.

Furious kicking awakened Bird Woman, who was seven months pregnant. She opened her eyes and stroked her round belly. The baby inside immediately calmed down. "Did he have the same nightmare as I," she wondered, staring at the ceiling.

It was still dark in the room set aside for the interpreters of Fort Mandan where Toussaint Charbonneau and René Jusseaume had moved in with their women a few days earlier.

Bird Woman tried to forget about her nightmare. But to no avail: the images had long been imprinted in her brain. They arose from the depths of her sleep and brought her back suddenly to her first year in Upper Missouri.

She was then twelve years old, which among the Indians meant she had reached womanhood. The year before, the Hidatsas had abducted her during a raid on her Shoshoni village. She now belonged to Le Borgne, the most powerful chief of the Menetarra village. He had named her Sacagawea, or Bird Woman. Three other Shoshoni slaves lived in his lodge. To cheer them up, Sacagawea would often sing them songs from their country. She had a happy disposition, but one day, she fell silent, and her silence lasted a long time.

Her recurring nightmare always began the same way, with a scene she had actually lived, the visit of a British trader at Le Borgne's lodge.

All the members of the chief's household are present. After the usual polite exchanges, Le Borgne says to his guest:

–Last spring, when you were away, I went to war. I killed a Shoshoni chief, two youths and many women and children. In the end, I saved a young woman's life. I brought her back and I treated her kindly, because I wanted to offer her to you. Unfortunately, three days ago, she fled in the middle of the night on one of my best horses.

–Where did she go, asks the visitor, visibly puzzled.

–She went back to her people, on the other side of the mountains, Le Borgne answers. It's the third time that she has run away. The last two times, she had nothing but the clothes on her back. But this time, she is properly dressed and well armed. She has a bow, arrows and two knives.

After a pause, Le Borgne continues in a dreamy voice:

–She is very beautiful. None of our women can match her beauty. In fact, there is no greater beauty among all Indian nations. We know the White man would like her and that he would pay a generous price to have her. That's why I saved her life.

From the back of the lodge, an old blind woman's voice is heard.

–You were much too good toward her, my son. You should have killed the bitch. She stole my knife, which I had for three winters. It was a good knife. Only the handle was broken!

–That's right, says another woman who sits not far from Sacagawea. That bad slave also stole my knife. I wish she were dead!

In her corner, Sacagawea makes herself as inconspicuous as possible. That night, when she can't sleep, she thinks about the beautiful slave who dared to flee three times. Did she manage to reach the Three Forks? Did she make it to the Shining Mountains?

The answer comes a few days later. Four young men who were chasing the fugitive return to the village with her head on a pole, which they drive into the ground in front of the chief's lodge before giving him back the horse stolen by the slave. Without any further formalities, they retreat to their respective huts to rest from their efforts.

They had followed the tracks of the Shoshoni woman by the holes that she had dug in the ground to pull up the roots on which she fed. When she had reached the mountains, the young girl had taken her time, thinking she was out of danger. She had stopped to kill a buffalo with her bow and arrows. She had built a shelter with green branches and started to dry the buffalo meat to stock up on supplies for the last leg of her trip.

Her pursuers had lost her trail. They had wandered for days in the mountains before giving up the chase. On their way back, they had chanced upon the Shoshoni girl as she was about to resume her journey home. They had put an end to her life by spearing her through her bosom.

In Meneterra, the men do not deign to look up at the gruesome trophy brought back by the warriors. The scalp or the head of a woman, no matter how beautiful, is not worthy of their attention. However, the women of the village gather around the pole and start to dance, noisily celebrating the capture of the slave girl.

One of them pulls on the hair and sends the head rolling on the ground. The other women immediately grab it and use it as a ball, kicking it from lodge to lodge.

–Here comes the enemy, shout some when they get the ball.

–Take good care of her! scream the others, giving it another kick.

Sacagawea is now standing at the entrance of Le Borgne's lodge. She looks on in horror as the head goes around the village three times before it is turned over to the children who use it as target practice.

Four years later, Sacagawea was still haunted by those images. In the interpreters' room in Fort Mandan, she wondered again, stroking her belly: "Does he have the same dreams as I?"

–Charbonneau! Jusseaume! Get up! You're late! called out Sergeant John Ordway, knocking on the bedroom door.

Startled by the wake-up call, the two men reluctantly got out of bed, dressed in a hurry and went out without a word to their women. Captain Lewis was waiting in the middle of the yard with a reproachful look; armed men were replacing those who had mounted guard during the night. The Corps of Discovery was more than two thousand miles from the mouth of the Missouri and the captains found it prudent to post sentries all the time.

–Let's go, ordered Captain Lewis just as the sun rose on Fort Mandan, over which flew the United States flag.

The American and his two French-Canadian interpreters rode along the Missouri in the direction of the Knife River, on whose banks were the Hidatsa villages. Sergeant Ordway followed them in a canoe together with four armed soldiers. The day –November 25, 1804 –promised to be warm and pleasant, in contrast with the bitter cold of the previous days. Trees were no longer covered with frost. On the water, swans lingered, in less of a hurry to go South.

And Charbonneau was singing:

Sur mon chemin j'ai rencontré
Deux cavalières bien montées
Lon, lon, laridon, daine
Lon, lon, laridon, don.[8]

Jusseaume joined in his countryman's song.

In spite of his worries, Captain Lewis couldn't help smiling. These French-Canadians were always ready to break into song. For them, any trip was an opportunity for a recital. "If only the Big Belly chiefs were as good-natured," he thought. Unfortunately, ever since old Caltahcota's visit in late October, he had not heard from them, and they refused to come to Fort Mandan. Their absence concerned the Captain and so he had decided to go and meet them. He wanted to set out before them his "Great Indian Plan," on which, he believed, depended the expansion of the United States to the West.

Charbonneau and Jusseaume stopped singing when they saw, on the north bank of the Missouri, the Assiniboine camp from where rose the smoke of several bivouac fires. The women of the band were busy taking down the tepees.

–They are getting ready to leave, said Jusseaume to Lewis. You'll see, the squabbling will start again in no time at all.

Two weeks earlier, close to seventy Assiniboine families, along with a few Crees, had come from the North to trade with the Mandans and the Hidatsas. Once or twice a year, these enemy nations would forget their differences and engage in bartering.

Before the start of the exchanges, they would hold a ceremony during which they invented relatives for themselves by adopting one another. For the next few weeks, they thus lived in harmony, long enough to acquire what they needed in the way of food, clothing, travel and arms. Shortly after, the Assiniboines would begin stealing horses all over again, an activity for which they often suffered deadly reprisals.

Captains Lewis and Clark could not have chosen a more strategic spot for wintering in the Great Northern Plains. Despite the smallpox epidemic of 1781, which had reduced their numbers and favored a reconciliation between them, the Mandans and the Hidatsas still played a vital role in Upper Missouri. They lived in five villages whose population of four thousand inhabitants was greater than that of St. Louis. Besides hunting buffalo, they grew cereals, corn, beans, squash, pumpkins and tobacco, crops that contributed to their influence.

For the bands of nomads of the Great Northern Plains –the Assiniboines, the Crees, the Crows and the Cheyenne, among others –the Mandan and Hidatsa villages represented an essential meeting place, a crossroads where trade flourished and cultures intermingled. In the spring and fall, these nations all gathered there to get their food supplies. In exchange, they brought Spanish horses, British rifles, luxurious leather garments, colored feathers, furs, metal objects and fabrics.

For three-quarters of a century, Canadians had also been traveling to the Mandan and Hidatsa villages. In the days of New France, Pierre Gaultier de Varennes de La Vérendrye and his sons had shown them the way. If Thomas Jefferson had known the history of this great family of explorers, merchants and soldiers from Three-Rivers, he might have named the expedition led by Lewis and Clark the "Corps of Re-discovery." For, on the way to the Rockies, Lewis and Clark merely followed in the footsteps of La Vérendrye.

Deux cavalières bien montées
L'une à cheval et l'autre à pied
Lon, lon, laridon, daine,
Lon, lon, lari...[9]

Charbonneau and Jusseaume stopped singing again when they saw, not two well-mounted women riders, but seven horsemen, one of whom wore the typical arrow sash from L'Assomption, recognizable by its flame and lightening patterns. The two groups were about to meet, halfway between the Mandan and Hidatsa villages.

–Who are they? asked Captain Lewis, turning to Jusseaume.

–They are men from the Northwest Company, answered the interpreter, who had recognized the employees of this leader in the fur trade, which had its warehouses on St. Gabriel street, in Montreal.

Indeed, Jusseaume knew Charles McKenzie and Baptiste Lafrance. The former was a clerk at Fort Pembina, on the Red River; the latter, an interpreter. Apart from French, he spoke Assiniboine, Cree and Mandan. He was the devious type.

Four more voyageurs rode behind them, Joseph Azur, Jean-Baptiste Turenne, William Morrison and Alexis Kay, with whom Jusseaume had worked in the past. But the trader had never seen the man with the arrow sash who rode at the head of the group.

–Do you know the young fellow? Jusseaume asked Charbonneau.

–I don't know him from Adam.

The man couldn't have been older than twenty. He had an aura about him, a strange combination of authority, distinction and casualness. He wore a beaver hat, a social necessity in London or Paris, but an unusual occurrence in the Great Northern Plains. Unlike the raccoon bonnet, the beaver hat did not have the look of fur. Made out of down from the animal, the headgear favored by dandies was of felt. On his, the young man from L'Assomption had stuck an Indian feather. For the rest, he was dressed in the voyageur style.

When he was within a few steps of Captain Lewis, the stranger pulled on the reins of his horse, raised his hat and addressed the American in English with a slight French-Canadian accent.

–Allow me to introduce myself. I am François-Antoine Larocque, chief of brigade. Mr. Charles Chaboillez, the *bourgeois* in charge of the Department of the Assiniboine River, has sent me on a trade mission. The gentleman on my right is my assistant, Mr. Charles McKenzie.

McKenzie had an ironic look; he bowed without saying a word.

Turning to the captain's interpreters, Larocque said in French:

–Mr. Charbonneau, Mr. Jusseaume, it's both an honor and a pleasure to make your acquaintance.

–Likewise, the two men answered in unison.

Captain Lewis was surprised. François-Antoine Larocque reminded him of Joseph Gravelines, a French-Canadian he had met a few weeks earlier among the Arikaras and whom he had sent to Washington with two chiefs of that nation from Upper Missouri. Gravelines was going to translate for them to President Jefferson. Lewis had to admit that some of the descendants of the settlers of New France certainly cut a fine figure, especially this Larocque.

Having gotten over his surprise, the Captain returned the young man's greetings:

–Mr. Larocque, I am delighted to meet you. Allow me to introduce myself. I am Captain Meriwether Lewis, commanding officer of the Corps of Discovery, and I was instructed by the President of the United Stated to find a navigable passage between the Mississippi and the Pacific Ocean.

These words took Larocque's breath away. Without being aware of it, the Captain had just described Larocque's own life ambition, the dream he was pursuing in the Northwest in the footsteps of La Vérendrye and especially of Alexander Mackenzie, his role model. The great Mackenzie had given him his first chance in the fur trade by hiring him into the XY Company. Larocque was only seventeen then. Three years later, he was leading his first trade mission on behalf of the Northwest Company, which had just taken over the XY Company.

Larocque was very eager to see Lewis again.

–Your mission seems to me of the greatest interest, he said to the American. Will we have the chance to discuss it further?

–I would be most happy to welcome you at Fort Mandan, Captain Lewis answered cordially. Come the day after tomorrow with Mr. McKenzie. You will meet Captain Clark, who shares with me the command of the expedition.

–I'll be there! said Larocque.

Lewis could see that his invitation had overjoyed the young employee of the Northwest Company. He took advantage of the situation to get some information out of him.

–You have just left the villages of the Big Bellies, haven't you?

–Yes, answered Larocque. We arrived three days ago after a very trying journey. We have just rented a lodge from White Wolf, in Menetarra. We are on our way to Black Cat's lodge, in the first Mandan village.

–Tell me, do you know if Chief Le Borgne is at home?

McKenzie spoke up for the first time; he had a heavy Scottish accent.

–We saw him briefly yesterday. He was just back from an expedition in Shoshoni country.

–Very good, said Lewis. We shall invite him to our conference.

–Good luck, said McKenzie with a half-smile.

Lewis thought he detected a hint of mockery in his tone. He took an instant dislike to McKenzie.

Charbonneau would have liked to interrupt Lewis's speech. He had heard enough. He knew that the Captain's "Great Indian Plan" had no chance of ever becoming a reality. But he dutifully continued in his role as interpreter and translated as best he could the words that Jusseaume was communicating in his native tongue. He did not want to humiliate the haughty American in front of the chiefs and warriors assembled in the lodge of Horned Weasel, one of the dignitaries of Meneterra, the biggest of the three Hidatsa villages with its one hundred and fifty lodges and five hundred warriors.

–Your French and Spanish Fathers have pulled back beyond the eastern sea and they will never come back, declared Captain Lewis to the Hidatsas through his interpreters. From now on, you are under the authority of the Government of the Great Knives; it will protect you and fulfill all your needs, as long as you behave as respectful children. Your new Great Father lives in Washington, capital of the seventeen nations. He invites you to visit him and see for yourselves the power of his people.

After Charbonneau had finished translating this part of his speech, Lewis continued:

–We have come here to calm the Missouri's troubled waters, open the way to trade and discover the rivers, plants and animals that can be found on our new territories. Make peace with your neighbors and soon, all kinds of goods will flow upriver.

The Hidatsas listened to Captain Lewis's words in complete silence. Sitting in the first row, the host of the conference was speechless, as were the other chiefs and the warriors.

Horned Weasel was impressive in appearance. In his long black hair, he had tied little wooden sticks –four yellow ones, a blue and a red one –that symbolized the wounds received in combat. On the right side of his head, he had fastened a wooden knife painted in red, which meant that he had stabbed to death a Cheyenne chief. A big tuft of owl feathers rose from the back of his head, indicating that he belonged to the band of the Dog. Eagle feathers radiated from his head. One of his eyes was circled in yellow paint, the other in red. His wizened body was covered with reddish-brown stripes that told of his many feats in war, and a yellow hand on his chest showed that he had captured many prisoners.

Captain Lewis tried to read a reaction in the faces of the chiefs, but was unable to detect anything. Without a doubt, these Hidatsas stirred up more trouble than the Mandans. The day before, he had stopped by the lodge of Le Borgne to invite him to the conference, but the great Hidatsa chief had a young man tell him that "he wasn't home." Offended by this behavior suited to an English lord, Lewis had almost ordered Sergeant Ordway to force his way into the Indian's lodge. But he had managed to contain his anger. He would surely find another opportunity to teach this coarse chief a lesson in civility.

A boy finally broke the silence in Horned Weasel's lodge. He innocently asked Captain Lewis the question that concerned all the young warriors:

–If we don't make war on our neighbors anymore, how will we choose our chiefs?

–That's right, what shall we do? asked another young man more insistently. Our chiefs are old and will die soon. The Hidatsa nation cannot exist without chiefs.

A third warrior added scornfully:

–The man with the great knife is making fun of us. We have not finished avenging our dead, and he wants us to make peace with our enemies! My dogs are more sensible than he is!

Charbonneau translated the objections of the young warriors, but he omitted the last remark. If only Captain Lewis had taken the trouble to talk to him, he could have explained the obvious flaws of his "Great Indian Plan." War, much more than hunting or trading, determined the standing of men in the Great Plains. It allowed them to distinguish themselves, to rise in the community, to become chief. A man like Le Borgne owed his power and influence to the courage and fierceness he displayed in the face of his enemies. A durable peace was unthinkable in Upper Missouri. Charbonneau couldn't get over the naivety of the American Captain. "Such arrogance," thought the French-Canadian, sensing the rising discontent in the lodge.

But the novice diplomat was determined to reorganize relations between the tribes of the West according to the interests of the United States. His Great Indian Plan aimed at bringing about an alliance between the sedentary nations of the Great Plains, the Hidatsas and the Mandans, and their common enemy, the Arikaras. Through this union, Lewis was pursuing an ambitious goal: isolating the Teton Sioux with whom the expedition had almost come to blows.

For several years, the Tetons had been keeping out American trappers and traders, terrorizing them, holding them for ransom and robbing them at will. By so doing, they protected the interests of Montreal merchants. They were excellent trappers and sold beaver skins of superior quality to the representatives of the Northwest Company that had established two trading posts in their territories, one on the Des Moines River and the other on the St. Pierre. In exchange, they got the weapons and other manufactured goods they needed to trade with their neighbors and, depending on circumstances, to go to war against them. Thus, all that threatened the status quo was a challenge to their supremacy in the region.

The lodge rang out with loud voices. Sweating profusely under his shirt, Toussaint Charbonneau had trouble keeping up with the translation of all the blunt questions, malicious accusations and more or less convincing replies. He even found himself involved in the debate between Captain Lewis and the Hidatsas.

–Why did the Chief of the Little Village go and live with the White man? asked a chief nicknamed Bullet in the Neck.

–Who? said Captain Lewis.

–He's talking about me, explained Charbonneau, sticking out his chest.

Lewis smiled faintly.

–The Chief of the Little Village, as you call him, will accompany us as far as the great salted lake. While we wait for the thaw, we want him at our side.

The Captain's answer did not reassure the Hidatsas.

–We believe the White man is two-faced, said the Pheasant, a fearsome warrior. He speaks of peace, but he is getting ready for war behind the bulletproof walls of a fort.

–That's not true, protested Lewis.

The Pheasant stuck to his opinion.

–We believe the Whites will attack us during the winter with the help of the Sioux and the Arikaras. That's why the Chief of the Little Village has left us. He has taken refuge with his White brothers before the storm.

Lewis didn't have time to contradict the chief. A young warrior, Porcupine Head, echoed another rumor, which Charbonneau immediately translated:

–They say that the Whites will kill us if we go anywhere near their fort.

Lewis became alarmed.

–Who has spread these lies? he asked.

No one answered. A heavy silence fell on the lodge. Lewis was beginning to understand why the Hidatsas had not yet visited Fort Mandan. He insisted once more:

–Who has filled your heads with such nonsense?

A long silence ensued. Finally, Horned Weasel answered:

–Our Mandan friends have warned us against your intentions.

Lewis couldn't help looking incredulous. What the Hidatsa chief was saying made no sense. The Mandans had just agreed to his "Great Indian Plan." They had committed themselves to forming an alliance with the Hidatsas and the Arikaras. Why would they sabotage the whole thing by setting the Hidatsas against the Americans?

The last conference in which the Mandan and Arikara chiefs had participated was still fresh in Lewis' mind. The Mandans themselves had been delighted at the thought of a durable peace among the nations of Upper Missouri.

–We'll be able to hunt without fear and our women will work in the fields without having to watch for the enemy every moment, had said Black Cat to Captains Lewis and Clark.

–We'll make a good peace, had added Great Man, another Mandan dignitary.

The Arikara chiefs had also promised to cease their raids on their Mandan and Hidatsa neighbors. They too lived on the banks of the Missouri, upstream from the territory defended by the Tetons, with whom they had complex relations that the Americans understood poorly. In the captains' eyes, the Arikaras were no more than the "gardeners of the Sioux," a role they would no longer play after the implementation of the "Great Indian Plan."

Lewis and Clark had it all figured out: if they prevented the Tetons from having access to the Arikaras' agricultural produce, these Sioux would then be forced to trade with the St. Louis merchants and accept American sovereignty. It was as simple as that.

But in whose interest was it to sow discord between the Hidatsas and the Americans? In Horned Weasel's overheated lodge, Lewis thought about the traders from the Northwest Company whom he had met the day before. Wasn't their place on the commercial scene of the Great Plains threatened by the arrival of the Americans? They must be the ones spreading false rumors.

Before taking his leave from the Hidatsas, Lewis heard a comment that confirmed him in his opinion.

–According to Lafrance, the French are the only true friends of the Hidatsas, said the Pheasant.

The warrior was referring to Baptiste Lafrance, the most devious member of François-Antoine Larocque's brigade. He added:

–Lafrance also says that you have to be a real dead dog to trust the Arikaras.

–The dead dog is he who makes fun of the United States! replied Lewis, vowing to admonish Lafrance's boss who was to visit him the next day at Fort Mandan.

Disappointed by the turn the conference was taking, Captain Lewis invited the chiefs and the warriors to follow him outside Horned Weasel's lodge, where he asked Sergeant Ordway to do another demonstration of the air gun.

Bullet in the Neck merely shrugged at the sight.

–If the Whites had come with kind intentions, they would have loaded their big canoe with objects needed by the Hidatsas, he said. It is true that they have a lot of gunpowder, but they prefer wasting it to giving a single charge to a poor Hidatsa.

For his part, Horned Weasel severely criticized the imperious tone in which Lewis had given his speech.

–If his White warriors came to my higher plains, my young horsemen would kill them like wolves.

He made a sign to Charbonneau not to translate his last remark.

At any rate, Lewis had heard enough. He gave his men the signal for departure. As he was mounting his horse, he said to Jusseaume and Charbonneau:

–Mr. Larocque will hear from me!

But Lewis had the wrong culprits. The men from the Northwest Company had nothing to do with the Hidatsas' obstructive attitude. It was the Mandans who had spread the malicious rumors about the American expedition. Their goal was simple: to keep the Hidatsas away from Fort Mandan in order to have the monopoly on trade with the Americans. Providing for more than thirty Whites, feeding, clothing and amusing them was the opportunity of a lifetime.

But the Virginian preferred blaming the French-Canadians or the British. He had no idea that a Mandan chief, Big Man, had called the Arikaras "liars," after having personally agreed to ally himself with them.

And neither did he know that Black Cat had shown himself to be just as cynical. He had said to his countrymen:

–I will make peace with the Arikaras just for the pleasure of proving to the Whites that those crooks can't keep a promise.

The Great Indian Plan of Lewis and Clark had gotten off to a bad start.

Chapter Three

The Northwest Company

A fierce gale was sweeping the snow in gusts, blurring everything on its path, the plain, the river, the trees. Wrapped up to his ears in a buffalo skin, Toussaint Charbonneau barely managed to keep his eyes open in the middle of the blizzard. He was standing outside Fort Mandan, watching out for François-Antoine Larocque to arrive. He wanted to warn him about Captain Lewis' anger, which had barely subsided since his return from the Hidatsa villages, two days earlier.

Although he had not worked for the Northwest Company for several years, Charbonneau still cared about the interests of the empire's employees. That hardly meant that he was fond of the company bosses. He merely wanted to continue trading with his countrymen. He dreaded the thought that one day he would have to trade with the Americans, those presumptuous invaders whose language he did not know.

In more than fifteen years of trekking across the North American continent, Toussaint Charbonneau had never learned English, just as he had never learned to swim. He wasn't the only one. Within the Northwest Company, the working language was French. Even the Scots had to have a command of that language; they had no choice. If they wanted to become clerks or partners, they had to be able to communicate in the language of the French-Canadians who held all the subordinate positions as *engagés*, guides and interpreters.

According to a British observer of the day, many "very good fellows" had to give up the fur trade because they didn't speak French, the language of the *mangeurs de lard* and of the North men.

They used to call *mangeurs de lard* the novice voyageurs as well as those who had never gone further west than Lake Superior. They owed their nickname to the salted pork they ate during their travels, a diet they completed with dried peas, beans and sea biscuits. They were hired from May to October to take the merchandise to the Great Lakes and come back to Montreal with the furs that had been brought there by the wintering partners.

The North men traveled west of Lake Superior to the *Pays d'en Haut*[10], a territory known for its myths and legends. They thought of themselves as infinitely superior to the *mangeurs de lard.* They freed themselves from the constraints of laws and religion, braved all dangers and rubbed shoulders with the so-called "savages" whose food and women they shared. They would sometimes sink into servitude, but they preferred not to elaborate on the subject.

The North men received their honorary title on the occasion of a "baptism" in Lake La Pluie. Toussaint Charbonneau had himself been "baptized" in July 1791. True to tradition, he had offered a libation to all his companions to celebrate the event. He himself had hardly drunk.

Thirteen years later, Charbonneau was still pushing back the frontiers of America. His very presence in Upper Missouri attested to his bold character and to the reach of the Northwest Company.

In the early 1800's, the Northwest Company employed up to thirteen hundred of the five thousand French-Canadians who lived west of Lake Superior. It had succeeded in dominating its great rival, the Hudson Bay Company, by following the routes opened by La Vérendrye and taking over the forts deserted by the French. It owed a great deal of its success to the fact that the French-Canadian voyageurs knew the territory very well and were familiar with the peoples of the North and the West.

After the Conquest, the sons of New France had not all been relegated to subordinate roles in the fur trade. In Montreal, many had become prosperous as traders, as in the case of Gabriel Cotté, founding member of the Beaver Club, the very select meeting place for the merchants who had spent at least one winter in the *Pays d'en Haut.* Étienne Augé, Pierre Guy, Jacques Duperon Baby, Maurice-Régis Blondeau and Étienne Campion were among the French-Canadians who had done well in Montreal in the fur trade.

But none of them could compete with Jean-Baptiste Cadot, one of the most famous traders of his day. He had built a real empire in Sault Ste. Marie, where he owned a beautiful house, huge warehouses and farmlands. In 1765, Cadot had formed a partnership with a young and ambitious Scottish merchant, Alexander Henry, who had won exclusive rights to trade on Lake Superior. So great was his reputation as a merchant and an adventurer that Henry was received in France, at Marie-Antoinette's court, ten years later.

Upon returning to Canada, Henry had looked up Cadot and formed an association with other Scottish merchants from Montreal, which would lead, a few years later, to the establishment of the Northwest Company. Among the partners were James McGill, Simon McTavish, Peter Pond and the Frobisher brothers, who had caused a sensation in Montreal by bringing from Lake Athabaska a load of furs worth 50,000 dollars.

And so, in the course of time, Scottish, English and American immigrants and businessmen took over the fur trade. In Toussaint Charbonneau's days, Charles Chaboillez, the man in charge of the Assiniboine River Department, was one of the few French-Canadians among the top men at the Northwest Company.

Chaboillez was born in Montreal in 1772. He was known as a "wintering partner," and in that capacity, he lived all year long west of Grand Portage, the Northwest Company's headquarters. Once a year, the directors of the Montreal empire would meet at this trading post, situated on the north shore of Lake Superior, to settle their business. After the meeting, some would go back to their post in the North Country, the others returned to Montreal, where they acted as financiers, wholesalers and suppliers.

Grand Portage had been the stage of many memorable scenes. During the summer of 1790, the explorer Alexander Mackenzie, then twenty-five-years-old, had experienced there one of the most bitter disappointments of his life. A year earlier, together with four French-Canadians, one German and two Indians, he had set out in a light bark canoe in search of the famous Northwest Passage that was supposed to lead him to the Pacific and to fame.

He had started from Lake Athabaska, gone as far as Great Slave Lake, then followed a river named Dehchoby by the Indians. The expedition was perilous. No White man had ever attempted it, and the Indians they had met throughout the journey had taken a malicious pleasure in reinforcing the fears of Mackenzie's troop.

–Many winters will pass over your heads before you see the ocean, said an Indian of the Dene tribe.

–You will have white hair when you come back, added another.

A third one laid it on even thicker:

–Downstream from a river that flows north, you will find a race of men who will devour you.

Paddling tirelessly in the foaming waters of the river, the explorers had to perform amazing feats to keep the canoe from being smashed on the rocks. Mackenzie had chosen the best voyageurs from Fort Chipewyan, his trading post on the southern shore of Lake Athabaska, which, for the duration of his absence, had been left in the charge of his cousin, Roderick. These dauntless men were François Barrieau, Charles Doucette, Joseph Landry, Pierre Delorme and John Steinbruk. On some evenings at their camp, the members of the expedition had had to resign themselves to boiling lichen, for lack of game or fish. Not without humor, the explorers had named this pathetic meal "rock tripe."

At the end of a forty-day journey, they had reached the big islands at the mouth of the river. Mackenzie named them Whale Islands. Icebergs were floating all around them: the expedition had arrived, not at the Pacific, but at the Arctic Ocean!

Although this failure disappointed him, Mackenzie remained nonetheless convinced that he had contributed to the greatness of the Northwest Company. After all, he had just explored one of the four largest rivers of the American continent. But the following summer, the account of his expedition to the land of the midnight sun had fallen flat at the annual meeting of the company heads in Grand Portage.

The fur barons barely listened to Mackenzie. They just couldn't see what benefit they could derive from the trek of this fiery Scotsman across the tundra. And nothing was more important to them than profit.

In a condescending tone, one of them had said to the explorer:

–My poor chap, it's the Northwest Passage we're interested in, not the passage to the Polar Sea!

In a letter to a friend, dated July 16, 1790, Mackenzie tried to hide his disillusionment. He wrote: "They barely talked of my expedition, which I expected."

Despite the wind that whipped his face, Toussaint Charbonneau would not budge. His frozen feet were telling him to go inside, but in his head he knew he had to wait for Larocque. In the Great Plains, a man's survival often depended on a good piece of information or advice. He knew it well; although still relatively young at thirty-five, he was already one of the great survivors of his times.

How many voyageurs had he seen dying at the bottom of a river, in a brawl with traders, at the bend in a path where they came face to face with a bear?

How many fellow countrymen had he seen sinking as low as slaves, trapped by the Northwest Company, which kept in check a good part of its personnel by selling them alcohol at exorbitant prices?

The system was immoral. The Company bought its rum in Montreal for a dollar a gallon. It resold it to its men in the *Pays d'en Haut* for four dollars a pint, that is, sixteen dollars a gallon. At the end of those endless northern winters, the voyageurs had often gambled away their year's pay and would start drinking on credit, thus becoming ensnared in a system from which they could never free themselves.

A European visitor, Count Andreani, had stopped at Grand Portage. He had been deeply shocked by the dissoluteness of the voyageurs and the rapaciousness of their bosses. In the account of his travels, he described the situation thus:

"The Company's employees are for the most part libertines, drunks and spendthrifts, and that's just the kind of men the Company wants. Such is the speculation on their vices that any employee who is thrifty and sober is assigned to the most tiring chores, until, as a result of ill treatment, he is won over to drunkenness and the love of women, which boost the sale of rum, blankets and adornments. In 1791, nine hundred employees owed the Company more than ten to fifteen years worth of future wages."

The French-Canadian voyageurs were not the only ones to be under the yoke of alcohol. The Northwest Company also used hard liquor in its exchanges with the Indians, who now hunted beaver just so they could get drunk in orgies that sometimes degenerated into quarrels and killings.

Charbonneau had managed to avoid the trap laid by the Northwest Company. He was no saint, far from it, but he didn't trust alcohol. He had never forgotten the lesson from his first expedition.

He was only eighteen. Up until then, he had never gone further than Montreal where his mother had sent him at twelve to learn a trade. His family lived in poverty in Boucherville. A few years earlier, his father had left to get into the fur trade around Fort Detroit on Lake Michigan. He had never come back.

For six years, young Toussaint had worked with trowel and square for a master mason from Montreal, someone by the name of Larochelle. Daring by nature, he could not be satisfied with such monotonous work. He certainly didn't want to set stones with a line for the rest of his life. Like many young people of his age, rich or poor, he dreamt of leaving for the *Pays d'en Haut*, from where voyageurs returned full of cock-and-bull stories, but also with an aura of prestige, wearing embroidered moccasins and *ceintures fléchées,* the typical arrow sashes. These men from the North were very careful not to say anything about the slaves of the trade.

When spring came, near the time when the canoes were getting ready to leave for the Great Lakes and the North Country, young Toussaint shared in the excitement that swept the streets of Montreal. All around the big fur warehouses, the voyageurs would gather to prepare the loads and the supplies for the trip. At the same time, recruiting agents would comb the city and its suburbs in search of novices.

–I want to be a *voyageur*! called out Charbonneau, year after year.

One spring, when he was fifteen, one of the agents had answered:

–We don't need a *mangeur de lard*: we're looking for real men.

The following year, another one had said:

–You look pretty skinny to me. Eat your soup, we'll see next year.

Two years later, he attracted the attention of a recruiting agent. Jean-Baptiste Perrault had been hired as a clerk by Alexander Kay, a Scotsman newly-arrived in Montreal with the idea of making his fortune in the fur business.

Perrault was barely older than Charbonneau; he came from a respectable family. His father had been an employee at the St. Maurice ironworks at the time of the French. He had later become a fur merchant in Rivière-du-Loup.

In 1783, after studying at the *Petit Séminaire de Québec*, young Perrault had traded with the Illinois on behalf of a Montreal merchant by the name of Marchesseau. A year later, upon setting out with Alexander Kay, he had decided to give a chance to Charbonneau, who had approached him on the street.

–I am warning you, you might never see your mother again, Perrault had said to him.

–I know. My father went to Fort Detroit and never came back!

Perrault had Charbonneau put his mark at the bottom of a contract. At the end of the year, the young recruit would get one hundred dollars, a real fortune for him.

On a lovely morning in May, they had sailed from Lachine, the starting point of all journeys to the Great Lakes, Louisiana and the *Pays d'en Haut*. The village of Lachine was three miles from Montreal, upstream from impassable rapids. It got its name from the fact that French explorer Robert Cavelier de La Salle was obsessed with finding a sea passage to the riches of China, something he pursued in vain all his life. Still, he did explore the Mississippi and, on

April 9, 1682, in the name of King Louis XIV, he took possession of a territory he named Louisiana.

Perrault had outfitted two "bastard" canoes for sixteen men –fourteen voyageurs, a boss and a clerk. They were each loaded with merchandise in ninety-pound bundles, with rifles and ammunition, wool blankets, supplies, small barrels of liquor and vast quantities of miscellaneous objects: glass beads, combs, mirrors, rings.

Perrault would have preferred a little more food and a little less alcohol, but he had no say in the matter. Kay was the boss and he never missed a chance to remind everyone.

The two boats were part of a flotilla of fifty canoes on its way to Michillimakinac, a famous trading post situated at the confluence of Lakes Huron and Michigan. Thousands of French-Canadians, of Hurons and *Outaouais* earned their living there with the fur trade.

–Hurrah! Hurrah!

On the Lachine quay, the crowd cheered and applauded as the canoes pulled away. And from the river rose one of the voyageurs' favorite songs:

En roulant ma boule en roulant,
En roulant ma boule.

Derrière chez nous y a un étang
En roulant ma boule,
Trois beaux canards s'en vont baignant
Rouli roulant.[11]

According to tradition, the members of the brigade, Scotsmen included, had gone ashore about fifteen miles further, at the tip of the island of Montreal, to pray in St. Anne's church. Toussaint had lit a candle to the patron saint of the voyageurs, thinking of his mother, Marguerite Charbonneau, née Deneau, who had broken down and wept upon learning of her son's decision to leave.

–Not another one! she had cried out.

–Don't worry about it, I'll be back with a hundred dollars, Toussaint had replied.

Other voyageurs had put offerings in the collection box to have masses said for travel companions who had died. Still others had hung up commemorative objects to give thanks for wishes granted. The next day, Charbonneau had turned his back on Canada and taken the route opened by the *coureurs de bois* of New France.

They traveled up the Ottawa River and reached Michillimakinac on June 28. From there, Kay's troop had continued toward the Illinois, stopping briefly at Green Bay and at Prairie du Chien. Young and vigorous, Charbonneau had had no trouble keeping up with the rhythm of the paddles or carrying the ninety-pound loads during the portages. But he had suffered sheer agony because of the millions of mosquitoes and blood-thirsty gnats. This torture was hardest on the newcomers whom time and weather had not yet toughened.

But you couldn't complain; whiners were called *mangeurs de lard*, an insult even among *mangeurs de lard*. A man, a real one, was supposed to withstand anything.

On a day of scorching heat, Charbonneau had walked through a cloud of mosquitoes that sucked almost all his blood. Sancharité, a member of the troop, had tried to comfort him:

–Think of the deer and moose. The gnats get into their nostrils and choke them. You can at least defend yourself!

In the evening, only thick smoke would keep the mosquitoes away. To protect himself from their bites, Charbonneau had grown a beard.

But mosquitoes were not the only thing he had to endure. As the rest of the group, he had to put up with Kay's atrocious personality. The sour-tempered and arrogant Scotsman was never wrong about anything and would not accept advice, even though he had no experience of the fur-trading business. He was all the more difficult to bear as he drank all the time.

In the fall, just when beaver fur is the silkiest, Kay had decided to venture into the woods in the hope of finding Indians, who had not been seen yet. With his usual lack of foresight, he had left Fond du Lac on the western shore of Lake Michigan without bringing the supplies needed for the expedition. His men soon started complaining that they were hungry, game being harder to find than expected. For days, they had to feed on water plants that they boiled. They had to find them at the bottom of a lake or under the snow that covered a marsh.

Charbonneau had learned to utter the ultimate insult of the voyageurs:

–Damned dead dog! he whispered behind Kay's back, and so did the other members of the troop.

They had spent the winter at the portage of La Savane, where Perrault had had a log cabin built. The Indians from the region had paid numerous visits, attracted by the brandy that Kay would serve them in order to get as many skins as possible from them. The meetings led to drunken orgies that often turned violent. And that is how, at the end of the winter, an Indian woman Kay had insulted became indignant and thrust a knife into his heart.

Before collapsing, Kay had cried out in bad French:

–*Je suis tué!*[12]

The next day, Perrault described in his journal what had followed: "In a moment, everybody armed themselves with knives, rifles, tomahawks and sticks, with *pagamaganes,* spears, etc. and, never having found myself in such a situation, I was quite disconcerted."

Toussaint Charbonneau was just as stunned. And Perrault had said to him:

–If you don't want to end up like him, go easy on the liquor.

Charbonneau had begun working for the Northwest Company in 1793. While passing through Grand Portage, he had made the acquaintance of Alexander Henry Junior, the person in charge of the Pembina post on the Red River. He had "signed" a three-year contract with him. The attribute "Junior" had been added to Henry's name to differentiate him from his legendary uncle, Alexander Senior, the very same who had made his fortune at Jean-Baptiste Cadot's side. When he met Charbonneau, Alexander Junior was looking for a clerk to take charge of the Pine trading post on the Assiniboine, not far from the mouth of the Souris River. From there, the Montreal empire spread its tentacles all the way to Mandan and Hidatsa villages in Upper Missouri.

Charbonneau didn't know how to write, but he succeeded in convincing Henry that he was perfectly able to keep the Company's books.

–Give me something to write with, he had said to him in French, a language that the Scotsman spoke quite well.

Armed with paper and quill, Charbonneau had started to draw in a column the animals most sought after by trappers: beaver, fox, lynx, mink, wolf, bear and buffalo. Across this column, he had drawn some of the goods exchanged for the skins: a pair of trousers, a fishhook, a tuque, a gun, a cooking pot, a sewing needle.

On the front of the sheet, he had illustrated his knowledge of the comparative value of the pelts and goods by drawing ten beavers for a rifle, one beaver for a cooking pot, half a beaver for a cotton shirt. In the fur trade, the most valuable animal, the beaver, was the standard of exchange. Charbonneau had continued drawing: three bears for a beaver, four wolves for a beaver, ten mink for a beaver.

When the time came for him to append his mark to the bottom of the document Henry had presented him, Charbonneau was beginning to anticipate a new life. At the expiry of his contract, he would be a "free man," the situation the *mangeurs de lard* dreamt of when they first left Montreal. A free man could engage in trading in his own name, provided that he was no longer bound by contract to another trader or to a company. He also had to have paid all his debts.

Toussaint Charbonneau did not owe anything to anyone. He was proud to be a free man. And it was to preserve his status that he was waiting for François-Antoine Larocque in the middle of the snowstorm.

The next day, François-Antoine Larocque made out a figure on the riverbank. He squinted as he tried to identify the person who was waving to get his attention, but to no avail. He was blinded by the reflection of the sunlight on the snow.

–Can you see who it is? Larocque asked, turning to Charles McKenzie, who followed right behind.

McKenzie shook his head.

It had stopped snowing during the night. In some spots, the snow came up to the chests of the horses whose breath turned to a white vapor.

As he drew near, Larocque recognized Charbonneau and made his horse come to a halt. In a cheerful voice, he called out:

–Well, well, Mr. Charbonneau! You're just the man I wanted to talk to! I need an interpreter for a few days among the Big Bellies. Would you work for me?

–I have no objections, but you'll have to speak to the Americans, answered Charbonneau. I work for them.

–Until when?

–Until their return.

Larocque opened wide his eyes.

–Their return from the sea?

–That's right.

–I must leave with you!

Charbonneau knew it was time to bring young Larocque down to earth.

–I've waited for you here to let you know that Captain Lewis is furious. He thinks that you have been sowing discord among the Big Bellies. Yesterday, a Mandan even swore to him that you were handing out medals and English flags to the chiefs. If it's true, he will force you to leave the country.

–It's not true, replied Larocque very seriously.

–I can vouch for that, added McKenzie.

–That's good, said Charbonneau, making a sign to Larocque and McKenzie to follow him inside Fort Mandan.

He knocked on the captains' door. York, Clark's servant, opened the door and showed in the men.

Bent over a table, Lewis and Clark were drawing a map of the territory covered by the Corps of Discovery since it had left St. Louis. From the Mississippi to the James River, all the tributaries of the Missouri were already marked out. In the spring, the map would be sent to St. Louis on the keelboat with all the other documents and specimens–journals, animal skeletons, plants, etc. –intended for President Jefferson.

Without interrupting his work, Lewis said sternly:

–We waited for you all day yesterday.

–We are truly sorry, answered Larocque, removing his beaver hat. The bad weather prevented us from getting here sooner.

Lewis looked up, put his quill down and looked straight at the French-Canadian.

–We were about to send one of our men to fetch you. We have been told that you give medals and flags to the chiefs. In the name of the United States, I must strictly forbid you to continue doing so. Our government considers these objects as sacred emblems of the Indians' attachment to their country. As you know, Louisiana is now an American territory.

–I'm not likely to disobey your orders, answered Larocque in an ironic tone. I have neither flags, nor medals, nor attestations of good behavior. We have come here solely to trade furs.

Larocque paused before continuing with a smile.

–As you undoubtedly know, England and the United States signed a treaty ten years ago, according to which the merchants of each nation have the right to trade on the territory of the other...

–Provided they obey the laws and regulations in force, Captain Lewis said, cutting him off. In our country, that means that it is forbidden to give out medals and flags, and also to exchange alcohol for furs with the Indians. I know for a fact that the English do not hesitate to engage in this deplorable practice in their territories.

McKenzie felt obliged to defend British honor.

–I can assure that such a practice is discouraged in the territories of the Crown, he declared.

Lewis was about to reply, but Larocque spoke first.

–Could I borrow Mr. Charbonneau for a few days? he asked the Captain. I need him as an interpreter.

Lewis took Clark aside. After a few moments, he came back and said to Larocque:

–Tell Mr. Charbonneau that he can work for you, on the condition that he will not utter a single word to the Indians that might cause harm to the United States and their citizens, even if you gave him the order to do so, which surely you wouldn't do.

–It goes without saying, replied Larocque.

–Would you be so kind as to pass on the message to your friend Lafrance, added Lewis.

And with these remarks, the war of the flags came to an end. Changing tone, Lewis invited Larocque and McKenzie to spend the night at Fort Mandan. After a meal of buffalo steaks, wild rice and corn prepared by York, the Americans offered the visitors a glass of whisky. Alcohol helped to ease the strained atmosphere, but could not completely overcome Lewis' Anglophobia. In the course of the evening, Captain Lewis asked the Scotsman point-blank:

–Tell me, Mr. McKenzie, if you had lived in the colonies at the time of the American Revolution, on which side would you have fought?

McKenzie pulled a wry face.

–You know, Captain Lewis, politics is not my strong point.

–My dear McKenzie, the American Revolution was not about politics, but about liberty!

Captain Cark intervened between the two men.

–A little more whisky, Mr. McKenzie?

Meanwhile, Larocque was dying to talk about the expedition. He was grateful that chance had led him to Upper Missouri at the same time as Lewis and Clark. The Americans were flattered by the interest the young man showed in their adventure, and answered all his questions and requests, except one.

First, they showed him their travel documents: passports and letters of recommendation signed by the French, Spanish and British ambassadors in Washington. These letters, written a few months prior to the Louisiana Purchase, provided assurances that the Corps of Discovery's objectives were "purely scientific and literary."

Of course, the Americans were not only interested in science and literature, readily admitted the two captains to Larocque, who had no doubts about it. The expedition was also intended to set the borders with the British territories and to announce to the Indians the identity of their new Great Father.

–And how did the Indians receive the news? Larocque asked with obvious curiosity.

–With the exception of the Teton Sioux, they are very happy, replied Captain Clark. Unfortunately, the Tetons have tried to block our way. We had to resort to threats.

–What are you going to do about them?

–We have a plan.

And Clark proceeded to lay out in detail the plan to bring about an alliance between the sedentary tribes of the Great Plains. In his presentation, he omitted only the recent troubles that Lewis had had with the Hidatsas. To hear him talk, one would have thought that he was in the process of transforming relations between the Indian nations of the West.

Larocque was surprised by Clark's optimism. In spite of his youth, he was sufficiently familiar with the Indian country to know that the Captain was probably deluding himself about the success of American diplomacy. As a matter of fact, he wrote in his journal: "During the time I was there, a very Grand Plan was schemed, but its taking place is more than I can tell although the captains say they are well assured it will."

But on that evening, Larocque was careful not to reveal what he really thought. While he was asking the captains questions, he worked out in his mind his own plan to get the Corps of Discovery to hire him. He was determined that he, François-Antoine Larocque, would accompany Lewis and Clark all the way to the Pacific. It was his destiny!

He came from a great Canadian family. His paternal grandfather, Antoine Larocque, had been a scribe to the king in Quebec City, in the days of New France. His paternal grandmother, Catherine Guillemot, had among her relatives a certain Abraham Martin, who had given his name to the Plains of Abraham, where the French suffered defeat at the hands of the English in 1759.

After the Conquest of New France, Antoine Larocque had moved to L'Assomption, a prosperous village twenty-four miles from Montreal, where he had gone into business, an activity he kept up until he died at age seventy. At his funeral, the *Quebec Herald* wrote that there were "more than thirty carriages" in front of the L'Assomption church. According to the paper, "It was the most important funeral ever seen in that town."

François-Antoine Larocque's uncle, Laurent Leroux, was one of the giants of the *Pays d'en Haut*. In 1786, this intrepid relative of his had become the first White man to explore the region between Lake Athabaska and Great Slave Lake, on the shores of which he had founded a trading post named Resolution. Three years later, he had accompanied his friend Alexander Mackenzie on part of his first journey of exploration, stopping at the mouth of the Yellow Knife Bay, where he had built Fort Providence.

At age twenty-seven, with his wealth of adventures and wide business experience, Leroux had returned to L'Assomption, where he had taken control of the manufacturing of arrow sashes, an industry in full expansion. He had married a local girl, Esther Loiselle, and proceeded to fill his nephew's head with dreams of unexplored horizons.

In the captains' room, François-Antoine Larocque couldn't restrain himself anymore.

–I want to leave with you! Give me a chance to finish my trading and settle my business with Mr. Chaboillez, my boss, and I'll be back when the thaw comes, ready to accompany you in this exploration worthy of Christopher Columbus!

Lewis and Clark smiled at each other, without interrupting the French-Canadian.

–My uncle, Laurent Leroux, used to say to me: 'You'll see, François-Antoine, the Americans will reach the Pacific by going up the Missouri River and down the Columbia.' My uncle was an explorer, you know. His friend Alexander shared his views. Do you know Sir Alexander Mackenzie? His explorations of the Arctic and the Pacific have earned him a knighthood from King George III. He gave me my first chance in the fur trade.

–We know him very well, declared Captain Lewis as he got up.

He walked toward a small bookcase at the foot of his bed. He brought back a book and placed it on the table. Larocque recognized the title of the fantastic account published in 1801 by Mackenzie: *Voyages from Montreal on the River St. Laurence through the Continent of North America to the Frozen and Pacific Oceans in the Years 1789 and 1793.*

–As soon as President Jefferson heard about the publication of this book, he ordered a copy, said Lewis.

–How about that! exclaimed Larocque. Do you realize that we are standing here together because of the same man! By the way, did you know that Mackenzie was born on an island called Lewis, off the coast of Scotland? It's fate!

"It certainly is," Lewis thought as he remembered the impact the book had had on the President of the United States, and consequently, on himself...

He briefly leafed through Mackenzie's book, then looked up at Larocque.

–I would like you to tell us what you know about Mackenzie.

Larocque relaxed, only too happy to seize this opportunity to make himself better known to the captains.

–In fact, it all goes back to the time when I was seven. Whenever I asked my uncle to tell me about Mackenzie's trip to the Pacific, he would sit me on his knee. Often, the visitors who were present would interrupt their conversations to listen to this eloquent storyteller. I know the story by heart, word for word. My uncle always began with the same question:

"You remember Alexander's journey to the Arctic, don't you, François-Antoine? Well, that misadventure did not discourage him for very long. A year later, he went to London in order to learn more about astronomy and cartography. He was twenty-seven at the time.

"After his stay in England, he came back to Montreal, armed with his new knowledge and equipped with new instruments, more determined than ever to discover the Northwest Passage. From Lachine, he returned to the North Country, where he made preparations for his journey.

"Many months went by before everything was ready. Finally, on the afternoon of May 9, 1793, he set off from the Forks post, on the Peace River, a hundred miles west of Lake Athabaska. He was accompanied by a clerk, Alexander Mackay, six voyageurs –Joseph Landry, Charles Doucette, François Beaulieu, Baptiste Bisson, François Comtois and Jacques Beauchamp –and two Indians. You will remember that Landry and Doucette had traveled to the Polar Sea with Alexander. From Lake Superior to the Rockies, they knew the lakes and rivers of the Northwest like the back of their hands.

"If you could have seen their bark canoe, my dear François-Antoine. A masterpiece, as light as a feather, in spite of its twenty-five feet in length, and so well proportioned that the men were able to load it with three thousand pounds of baggage, supplies, ammunition and gifts for the Indians.

"I won't go into all the dangers that they had to overcome while going up the Peace River, because what awaited them was much worse. Indeed, in its last few miles, the river became a torrent. Hemmed in between steep mountains, it towered before the members of the expedition like a wall. Towing the canoe was out of the question.

"The men had to carry through the forest and the rocks the baggage, supplies and the craft made heavy by the many repairs. After two full days of portage, they were exhausted, yet their troubles were far from over.

"If you can believe it, a few days later, their precious canoe was smashed to pieces in the rapids. The men had to hold on to the floating fragments so as not to drown.

"Sadly, Alexander had lost half his equipment. He feared he might have to abandon his expedition. Instead, he decided to build another canoe, smaller than the first, on which he succeeded in reaching, on the other side of the Rockies, 'the river that flows west,' the famous river that would lead him to the Pacific at last.

"The Indians from the region tried to dissuade him from continuing on his journey. They said to Alexander that the river was impassable in many places. Furthermore, the tribes that lived on its banks would make short work of the explorers! They were so nasty, so barbaric!

"Alexander refused to lend credence to these old wives' tales that reminded him of the exaggerations he had heard from the

Plats-Côtés-de-Chien on his journey to the Polar Sea, and decided to carry on. But first, he had to boost his men's morale. Some of them did not want to go on. They had no strength left; they had just gone up a wild river and crossed the Rockies, an unheard of feat.

"'My dear friends,' said Alexander to them, 'together, we have overcome overwhelming hardships. Are you going to belie the great reputation that makes the voyageurs proud? Are you going to lay yourselves open to shame by going back, you, brave among the brave, without seeing the Pacific?'

"The men gulped down a glass of rum and promised their leader to follow him to the ends of the earth.

"Alexander had to stop again a few days later. According to the information provided by the Indians and his own observations, the river he was sailing, the Tacoutche Tesse, was supposed to flow into the sea a great distance further south. By traveling deeper inland, he ran the risk of not being able to come back before the river froze over. He did not wish to expose his men to such a danger. He consequently decided to go by land, following a straight line to the sea. To those who hesitated, he said:

"'If you leave me, I shall continue alone.'

"The voyageurs stayed with him, as you can well imagine. They buried the canoe and part of their equipment in a cache and set off again. Each voyageur carried a bundle of about ninety pounds, on top of a rifle and ammunition. Alexander and his clerk carried a sixty-pound load, apart from the rifle and ammunition. Alexander was considerably hampered by his telescope, which he carried slung across his shoulder.

"Even though they only ate two meals a day, their pemmican reserves were dwindling dangerously fast. Finally, after sixteen days of grueling efforts and extreme fatigue, François Beaulieu cried out:

"'Sea!'

"It was indeed before them, a vast expanse of water. The men had tears in their eyes, François-Antoine. On a rock, using vermilion mixed with bear fat, Alexander wrote these simple words that would ensure possession of these territories for his country: *Alexander Mackenzie, from Canada, by land...*

"The next day, without waiting, Alexander started on his journey home. Realizing that the route he had explored could not be used for trading, he sank into a deep depression. The following spring, he went back to Grand Portage and never returned to the North Country."

The two captains had listened religiously to Larocque's story. Lewis had a dreamy look as he stroked the cover of the book by Mackenzie, a little distressed at the fate that its author had met. If he and Clark were not the first to cross the continent from east to west, they could still dream of finding the Northwest Passage. Larocque thought the moment favorable to bring up his request again:

–You understand, gentlemen, why it's so important for me to come along with you as far as the Pacific. It's my destiny.

–That may be so, Mr. Larocque, answered Lewis with a smile, but you must understand that your presence would put us in a rather delicate position. A subject of the British Crown cannot possibly take part in an expedition financed by the United States Congress.

–Haven't you already hired Toussaint Charbonneau? objected Larocque.

–Mr. Charbonneau is a free man and there is no danger that he will write a travel guide for your fur companies, replied Captain Lewis sharply.

Larocque took the blow without a word. Lewis seized the opportunity to change the subject.

–Mr. Larocque, let me congratulate you on your excellent English. Where did you learn?

–I beg your pardon? said Larocque who had not paid attention to Lewis' question.

–Your English, where did you learn it?

–Ah! my English, responded Larocque in a sullen tone. Well, before he died, my father sent me to study in Boston. He had just been elected member for the district of Leinster to the first Parliament of Lower Canada. He was very anxious for me to learn the English language and the political system of the United States.

–I find that surprising, said Lewis. I thought that French-

Canadians were taught to mistrust Americans. Didn't your priests and your lords discourage you from taking up arms on our side during the War of Independence? We sent the illustrious Benjamin Franklin to Montreal in the hope of spreading some revolutionary fervor over there, but all in vain. Just think: if the French-Canadians had fought the English with us in 1776, today your province would be part of the United States and you could join us on our expedition to the Pacific!

–French-Canadians did not trust you, struck back Larocque. At your side, they would be losing their language and their faith.

–What good are your language and your faith if you remain under English domination? asked Lewis.

Charles McKenzie broke his silence:

–French-Canadians got what they wanted in 1774. You remember the Quebec Act? It was one of the causes of your own revolution, if I am not mistaken...

–I thought politics did not interest you, Mr. McKenzie, interrupted Lewis.

Chapter Four

The White Buffalo

Sacagawea saw York bending down over her. In her feverish state, she wanted to believe that Captain Clark's servant was a medicine man who would relieve her suffering. York made her take little sips of some sweet tea. Sacagawea swallowed the drink, holding the cup with her freezing hands. The weather outside had plummeted to twenty-eight degrees below zero and the fire barely warmed the room of the interpreters.

After the tea, York served her some stewed fruit. He spoon-fed her like a baby. An indescribable smile took form on the lips of the Shoshoni woman. York had never seen anything quite as beautiful.

Sacagawea soon stopped shivering. She looked around and nodded slightly as she noticed Toussaint Charbonneau and Otter Woman who were standing behind York.

She had been delirious all night. At one o'clock, her teeth were chattering; at two, she was drenched with sweat and clutching with both hands her painful, swollen abdomen. Soon after waking up, Charbonneau had gone to fetch Lewis, the expedition's appointed doctor. Unfortunately, he had already gone hunting with fifteen men, among them the other interpreter, René Jusseaume. The day before, the Mandans had reported the presence of a huge herd of buffalo on the southern bank of the river.

In the absence of Captain Lewis, Clark had ordered York to make some tea and stewed fruit for Charbonneau's woman.

–Make her drink and eat something. If she's not better tonight, Captain Lewis will take care of her.

Indeed, the tea and stewed fruit seemed to have a beneficial effect on Sacagawea, who closed her eyes shortly after having taken the delicious medicine the black-skinned man had given her. Otter Woman pulled up the buffalo skins over her companion. York left the room, followed by Charbonneau who was going to join young Larocque for some trading with the Hidatsas.

Before being swallowed up by the cold, Charbonneau said to Otter Woman:

–I'll be back in seven days. If she's still sick, go and see the Red-Haired Man. He is a good White man.

–I know, answered Otter Woman.

When York and Charbonneau had left, René Jusseaume's wife started to hurl insults from the back of the room:

–Filthy bitches!

The Mandan woman was directing the worst abuse at the two Shoshonis, even drawing from the repertoire of her French-Canadian husband.

–Bloody sluts!

Since she had settled in Fort Mandan, nothing was working for *La Jusseaume,* as they called the proud Mandan, mother of two children of mixed race. The Americans ignored her, as if she were the lowest of the low. Charbonneau's Shoshoni women got all the attention, those lousy slaves who were not even worthy of licking the soles of her feet. She would cry with rage about it. York should have been serving her tea and stewed fruit! She was not only the daughter of a chief, but also the wife of a White man, a much-envied status that exempted her from the chores that were the lot of other women. Her man didn't even dare raise a hand to her. He owed everything to her father, his position as a trader with the Mandans, his stranglehold on the finest skins of Mitutanka...

–Vultures!

What she had witnessed that morning had driven her to her wits' end. She knew that York was neither a superior being nor a medicine man, in spite of the extraordinary color of his skin. He was nothing but a slave; her husband had explained everything to her. And now this slave, who belonged to Captain Clark, was serving another slave, Sacagawea, as if she were the first wife of a chief. When her husband returned from the hunt, she would certainly complain. And if this humiliating situation did not change, she would go back to live in her father's lodge.

–Crazy cows!

With her eyes half-closed, Sacagawea could hear the insults from *La Jusseaume*, but she attached no importance to them. She was used to the fits of jealousy of the Mandan woman. Under her mountain of blankets, she thought only of the birth of her child and her return to her native village, two events that would soon transform her life.

She considered herself lucky. Charbonneau could have decided to have Otter Woman accompany him; her tummy was as flat as the plain. Forced by the Americans to choose between his two women, the trader had opted for the one who was seven-months pregnant. And so, when spring came, Sacagawea and her baby would leave with the Corps of Discovery. Once they reached the Shoshonis, the young mother would help the members of the expedition get horses to cross over the Rockies. She would also go down the Columbia River with them as far as the great salted lake. Her presence within the expedition would symbolize the peaceful intentions of the Americans: in Indian country, nobody went to war accompanied by a woman.

Was Charbonneau guided in his choice by amorous or paternal feelings? If that had been the case, the trader would have been the last one to admit it. His decision was based mostly on the fact that Sacagawea was the daughter of a Shoshoni chief. As such, she would surely facilitate the negotiations between the Americans and the members of her nation.

Otter Woman had reached the same conclusion and, as a consequence, she was not jealous of Sacagawea. She merely asked her to bring a message to her family.

–If my parents are still alive, tell them that I think of them every day of my life.

–I'll tell them much more, answered Sacagawea. I'll tell them that their daughter has become the most beautiful and the most generous of Shoshoni women.

The Hidatsas had abducted them both four years earlier during a raid on the Three Forks, a place along the Missouri where the Shoshonis usually gathered at the end of the summer.

They were captured while trying to swim across one of the branches of the river. As fast in the water as she was on land, Otter Woman had almost managed to escape from her pursuers who immediately named her after the web-footed mammal.

In Menetarra, Sacagawea, Otter Woman and another young woman from their tribe had ended up in the lodge of Chief Le Borgne. For two years, they had been reduced to slavery. They worked in the fields, gathered wood, tanned skins and occasionally satisfied the sexual needs of their master's guests.

They also did the cooking, but rarely ate their fill. When they dared to complain, Le Borgne and his wives would answer:

–You cooked the food, now lick your fingers!

In spite of all that, Sacagawea used to sing, simple songs that she had learned on her mother's knee. With a soft and melodious voice, she described the thousand and one transformations of nature, like that of the caterpillar into a butterfly, her favorite: a monarch came out of its chrysalis, dried its wings and flew off, vanishing in the prairie. When they listened to Bird Woman sing, her companions would regain their courage.

The following summer, after another raid, Le Borgne had brought back to his lodge one more Shoshoni woman. She came from a village that Sacagawea and her companions did not know. She was exceptionally beautiful and kept to herself, protected by the Hidatsa chief who forbad his wives to talk to her.

She took advantage of this preferential treatment to run away three times. When Le Borgne's warriors came back with her head on a pole, Sacagawea didn't feel like singing anymore.

However, this horrifying story was not enough to discourage another one of the Shoshoni slaves. A few moons later, during a village celebration, she quietly slipped away and was never seen again.

A whole season had passed before Sacagawea dared to mention the fugitive to Otter Woman.

–From now on, we shall call her Butterfly Woman, she had said to her fellow Shoshoni in their own language.

–Shut up, you two! had ordered one of Le Borgne's wives, who never let the slaves out of her sight.

A few months later, Toussaint Charbonneau was visiting Le Borgne. He noticed the two Shoshoni women in the chief's lodge. Le Borgne had followed the direction of Charbonneau's eyes.

–They're yours for the right price, he had said.

Charbonneau had walked up to the women; they were barely fourteen.

–Can you trap beaver? he had asked them in the Hidatsa language.

–Yes, had lied Otter Woman. Our Shoshoni brothers have taught us how to hunt beavers in the Rockies.

Charbonneau had turned to Le Borgne and said, stroking his beard:

–I can offer you a horse.

–Ah! Now I see why some call you the Man Who Possesses Many Gourds. How dare you make fun of me! Make me a serious offer!

–I would offer you more, but they have *la bougeotte.*

–Speak Hidatsa so I can understand!

–*Bougeotte* is a word in my language that means to be always on the move, if you see what I mean. Unlike you, I don't have any warriors to chase after women across the plain.

–Give me a white buffalo skin and the Shoshoni women are yours.

–A white buffalo skin! You know very well I don't have one...

–I'll give you until the first snow to find one, otherwise you'll owe me two horses, a cotton shirt, a pair of corduroy pants and a box of hooks.

–It's a deal.

Sacagawea and Otter Woman had followed Charbonneau on foot to his house, in Metaharta, the small Hidatsa village. They hadn't looked back.

When they got to his lodge, Charbonneau had pulled out his cooking pots and utensils and asked the women to sit by the fire.

–I'll show you how to make *boudin blanc*[13], he had said to them most seriously. Watch carefully; next time, it will be your turn to serve me.

Later, the women had eaten the *boudin blanc* dripping with fat. They had licked their fingers and cried with joy. Never had they eaten anything so delicious!

That night, they had fallen asleep happy for the first time since they had arrived in Upper Missouri. Charbonneau had woken them up to have sex. After several hours, just as he was coming, he had cried out in pain and ecstasy, before falling asleep between the two women.

On the left buttock of the French-Canadian, the Shoshonis had noticed a horrible red scar. They had wondered what might have caused it. The claw of a grizzly? A hunting knife?

York was soaking his feet in a basin of hot water. Meriwether Lewis was warming his hands over the fire and William Clark was writing at his table:

"The thermometer stood at 12 d. below 0. Capt Lewis took 15 men and went out. They killed 8 buffaolw & one Deer… This day being cold several men returned a little frost bit; one of the men with his feet badly frost bit – my servents feet also frosted & his P__s a little…"

After York had finished giving Sacagawea tea and stewed fruit, Clark had sent him to join Lewis at the hunt. The servant had come back with a frostbitten foot. The Captain had immediately set water to boil.

York was observing his master at the table. He was certain that he was writing about the extraordinary hunt in the snow-covered prairie. He himself had managed to shoot two buffalo, but was only able to bring back one. Like the soldiers, he carried a weapon supplied by the United States army. In the Great Plains, he felt like a new man. He still obeyed Captain Clark's command, but he no longer felt like a slave.

His visit with the Arikaras, at the beginning of October, had completely convinced him of his worth.

Above the territory of the fearsome Tetons, the Arikaras had welcomed the Corps of Discovery with open arms. Two French-Canadians, who had been living in their midst for many years, had facilitated communications with the visitors. They were Pierre-Antoine Tabeau and Joseph Gravelines, and they worked for René Loisel, a fur merchant from St. Louis. One was born in Lachine, the other in Montreal.

Gravelines had translated the captains' speeches to the Arikara chiefs. Lewis liked him a great deal and found him "honest, discreet and an excellent boatman."

Tabeau had played a less official role, but was no less appreciated by the men of the expedition. Thanks to his services, the soldiers and the *engagés* had discovered the charms of the local women who had been most accommodating. Tabeau had also acted as interpreter for York, who had made quite an impression on the Arikaras.

The Arikaras had never seen a man of his color, "as black as a bear," according to Tabeau's description. York was tall and muscular; he enjoyed showing off his strength to the Arikaras by performing all sorts of amazing feats.

The Arikara witnesses had concluded that it was "great medicine." The Indians called "great medicine" anything they could not explain. For the Arikaras, York's strength had to come from the color of his skin and they examined him from head to toe.

The children followed him everywhere, shouting and running about every time the black giant turned around, pretending to be a wild beast.

The women, too, took an interest in York. On October 12, in the golden light of autumn, two very pretty Arikara girls had joined him on the keelboat, where he was alone.

Even a man had asked for his sexual favors; he introduced his wife to him and invited him to lie beside her. The Indian then left the lodge to be on the lookout at the entrance until what he deemed the necessary time had elapsed. When a member of the expedition had come to get York, the Indian had made him wait.

–Great medicine, he had explained.

York was born in Virginia. His father bore the same name, and his mother was called Rose. They had had two other children, Nancy and Juba, the latter being the symbolic link that still bound this family of slaves to Africa.

Juba was the name of two kings who had reigned on Numidia in ancient times. Juba I had espoused Pompey's cause against Rome, with disastrous consequences. Juba II, his son, was reinstated in Mauritania by Augustus. He had written in Greek a *Roman History* and a *History of Africa.*

Juba.

Sometimes, the masters would allow their slaves to name one of their children. When York's father had been granted this privilege, he had, like many slaves before him, given his son an African name.

Juba.

–We haven't always been slaves, he would say to his children.

During his childhood, York had no duties other than to play with William Clark, the youngest son of planter John Clark. York and William became inseparable; they fished, hunted, swam and rode together. They only parted when it was time for the master's son to take his lessons, which York didn't have the right to attend.

When he was twelve, he moved to Kentucky with his and his master's family. At the instigation of his elder son George, the revolutionary hero, John Clark, had acquired a plantation called Mulberry Hill, near Louisville. York had then reached the age when the sons of slaves leave their games and start working. His master could have sent him in the fields to do backbreaking work. But having decided not to separate him from William, he chose instead to make him the servant of his youngest son.

York had moved into the "big house," as the slaves called their masters' residence. He dressed like William and ate the same food.

While he was happy for his son, York's father had warned him:

–Never forget that William Clark is not your friend, but your master, and he has the right of life and death over you.

A year after his arrival in Kentucky, York heard about the trial of a slave from Louisville, someone by the name of Tom, who had stolen less than two yards of batiste and a few ribbons. He had been sentenced to death and executed.

Clark was still writing in his journal. York discreetly observed him; his father's words came back to him: "He is your master... he has the right of life and death over you." That remained true, the black-skinned man knew it; his condition had not changed, but in his head, he did not feel like a slave anymore. And he wondered how he could go back to being one, once their expedition to the Pacific was over. And why he should...

François-Antoine Larocque bent down to count the pelts that Le Borgne had laid at his feet: forty silver fox skins, seventeen wolf skins, eight red fox skins, two beaver skins.

The young trader from the Northwest Company could not hide a disappointed pout. He turned to the chief who was taller than him by a head and said:

–Couldn't your men start hunting beavers a little more vigorously? The Missouri and its tributaries are teeming with these animals that would greatly enrich your nation, if you only took the trouble.

Toussaint Charbonneau translated Larocque's words, the same that all Canadian traders spoke on their first visit to Upper Missouri. The Hidatsa chief listened to the interpreter; his one good eye flashed a furious glance. Hammering out his words, he retorted:

–Hunting beavers is a degrading activity. A Hidatsa man won't get off his horse to kill an animal. He won't search the ground like a badger to satisfy the White man's greed. He has all he needs on the plain and has no use for your metal traps. His horse, his spear, his bow and arrows, those are his weapons to hunt. Consider yourself lucky that our women will occasionally condescend to trap a beaver!

The chief stopped, eying Larocque scornfully.

The native of L'Assomption lowered his eyes. Le Borgne was impressive. He looked freakish with his gigantic build and limbs, his black, frizzy hair that shaded his coarse features.

Larocque was familiar with the classics: the chief reminded him of Polyphemus, the Cyclops in the *Odyssey.* He could well understand why Le Borgne was feared by his men as much as by his enemies. Everything about him was intimidating, his gaze, his size, his ugliness. If you went by what McKenzie and Charbonneau said about him, and they knew him well, he was capable of the worst kind of cruelty in war as in love.

However, Larocque had also been told that Le Borgne was perfectly capable of discussing the finer points of diplomacy and commerce. Therefore, he took the liberty to insist:

–Times are changing, great chief. Nowadays, the Indian nations of the North are walking hand in hand with Whites, and they supply them with beaver pelts. In exchange, they get useful goods they didn't even know existed before our arrival.

Le Borgne shrugged his shoulders.

–White men don't know how to live, he said in a sarcastic tone. They leave their country in small groups; they risk their lives on the Great Lakes and among foreign nations who will take them for enemies. What good is the beaver to them? Does it protect them from disease? Does it follow them after their death?

–Beavers are a precious currency, replied Larocque enthusiastically. If you started hunting seriously, as do your neighbors to the North, you could triple the number of your blankets, rifles and horses.

Le Borgne shook his head from right to left.

–We are not slaves, he said in a contemptuous tone. And neither were our fathers. There were no Whites when I was young and we lacked nothing. We were successful in war; the tips of our arrows were cut out of flint and those of our spears in stone; they inflicted fatal wounds. Our villages rejoiced when the men returned from war; our warriors brought back many scalps.

The chief paused, which allowed Charbonneau to translate, then he continued:

–The White man arrived and brought goods with him, that's true, but he also brought smallpox and firewater. Ever since, the Indians have been dwindling in number and they are not happy anymore.

As if to prove him right, a young woman burst into tears in the chief's lodge. Larocque looked her way and his heart stopped beating for a second. The Indian girl was breathtakingly beautiful.

They bargained over the skins for an hour. In the end, they settled on a price. In exchange for them, Larocque gave the chief some cloth, two blankets from the Hudson Bay Company, a coat, a big ax, some gunpowder, two knives, vermilion powder and glass beads, to which he added ten plugs of tobacco, another knife and fifty bullets.

–These humble presents are a token of my respect, said Larocque to the great chief. As you can see, there is no rum in my merchandise. Believe me, I have seen the ravages of firewater. And I know that the most powerful of the Big Belly chiefs is also the wisest.

Le Borgne preferred inspiring fear to admiration, but he wasn't immune to flattery and so he answered in kind:

–We don't understand the passion of the French for beaver fur, but we like them better than any of the other Whites. We know they wish us no ill. Take for example the One Whose Man-Part Is Never Limp...

–Who? exclaimed Larocque after hearing the translation. One Whose Man-Part Is Never Limp?

–He's talking about me, replied Charbonneau, throwing out his chest.

After this clarification, Le Borgne continued:

–The One Whose Man-Part Is Never Limp doesn't want to live with Whites anymore. He's crazy about our women. I understand him...

Le Borgne smiled faintly and gestured with his hand toward the Indian beauty who was still sobbing.

–You'll always be welcome in my lodge, said the chief to his guest.

Larocque remained silent for a moment, with his eyes riveted on the young woman. At last, he tore himself away from the beautiful sight.

–That's fortunate, he told the chief, because I'm certainly planning to come back. I need your help to achieve a plan my chief is very keen on. You mustn't say a word about it to the Americans.

–I don't even speak to them, said Le Borgne scornfully. I'm listening.

Larocque presented his plan. If he couldn't join the Corps of Discovery, the young French-Canadian intended to lead his own expedition to the Rockies. Two months earlier, his boss, Charles Chaboillez, had already spoken of his intention to entrust him with the mission of heading up the Yellow Stone River as far as its source, which was still unknown to the Whites. After his meeting with Lewis and Clark, Larocque knew that he had to get started as soon as possible. Rumor had it that the Yellow Stone had its source at the foot of the Rockies, in a region teeming with beavers. Larocque wanted to be the first White man to explore this promising territory and to establish there a fort for trading. He would thus follow in the footsteps of his uncle, Laurent Leroux, and of his hero, Alexander Mackenzie, who had made a name for himself by combining exploration and commerce.

But the young adventurer didn't want to meet with the same difficulties as old Ménard, the recently deceased friend of Charbonneau, the last White man to reach the Rockies. In 1795, at the end of a stay among the Crows, old Ménard had everything he owned stolen from him: horses, rifles, knives, slaves and lots of precious beaver furs. On top of losing a fortune, he had nearly lost his life.

François-Antoine Larocque knew he needed help. He said to Le Borgne:

–I have spoken of my plan to other chiefs of your nation, but none want to help me. They told me that the Crows would serve me the same medicine they gave old Ménard. What do you think?

–Don't you worry about it, it's just a pack of lies, answered Le Borgne. An adoptive son of mine is a Crow chief. He'll be here next spring. I'll ask him to accompany you. He'll watch over you like on the apple of my only good eye.

Larocque and Charbonneau smoked one last pipe with Le Borgne, then left his lodge. Outside, they came across a woman who was screaming like a tormented soul.

–One Eye! I'm warning you, your medicine will not prevail against my anger! You will be driven out of your village like Lying Coyote! The Evil One will have your dirty hide!

The woman was standing twenty feet from the entrance to Le Borgne's lodge. With disheveled hair and bulging eyes, she was asking the Evil Spirit of the Great Plains to punish the Hidatsa chief.

"A real shrew," thought Larocque.

Turning to Charbonneau, the young clerk asked:

–Who is she?

–A mad woman. Le Borgne has killed her only son to take his wife, the beauty you heard crying in the lodge. And ever since her son died, the mother shouts the worst insults to the chief, who is in love with that beauty.

–He loves her? asked Larocque, seeing again in his mind the face of the Indian girl who had made his heart leap.

–Well, he likes to possess her anyway, answered Charbonneau.

The woman did not seem to be aware of the two French-Canadians who had stopped before her. Standing barefoot in the snow, she was shouting her head off and pulling at her clothes:

–Ochkih-Hadda will come and tear your other eye out, and he will force you to walk the surface of the earth!

Shivering with cold, Charbonneau and Larocque continued on their way and went to get their horses in a nearby lodge.

–It's like that almost every day, said Charbonneau.

–But why doesn't Le Borgne silence her? asked Larocque.

–He can't, replied Charbonneau. The Big Bellies never raise their hand to mad people. They feel it's their duty to protect them. It's part of their beliefs.

–What about the young woman. What will become of her?

–Are you interested in her?

Larocque did not answer.

Two suns shone in the boundless sky of the Great Plains. François-Antoine Larocque would not have been able to tell the real one from its double.

–There's going to be a snowstorm, said Charbonneau.

This optical illusion was created by the refraction of the rays of the sun through the crystals suspended in the upper layers of the atmosphere. Charbonneau knew that this phenomenon was a sign of impending bad weather. But on that December morning, the sky was still a bright blue. The fake sun did not raise the temperature by a single degree; it was a cold day in Upper Missouri.

After trading for five days with the Hidatsas, Charbonneau had suggested joining the inhabitants of Metaharta on the plain where a buffalo hunt was to take place. Pleased with the pelts he had obtained, Larocque had enthusiastically accepted. He had heard about the hunting feats of the Southern Indians and he was eager to see them in action.

Charbonneau had picked up two of his horses at the lodge of Caltahcota, the old Hidatsa chief who had stayed behind in the village; his rheumatism made it impossible for him to ride to the hunt. He planned to use the extra horses to carry buffalo meat to Fort Mandan, where he would return the next day.

The two French-Canadians had covered about ten miles on the plain when they saw a white cloud rising on the horizon.

–The slaughter has begun, announced Charbonneau to his fellow countryman.

The strong wind of the past few days had swept across the plain. Only a thin layer of snow was left on the ground from the last storm; here and there, tufts of dry grass showed through it. Trampled underfoot by thousands of stampeding animals, the layer of snow rose as a fine powder and formed the cloud that grew bigger as Charbonneau and Larocque got closer.

The two men did not stop at the camp of the Hidatsas, which lay at the foot of a hill called Turtle Mountain. Most of the women were waiting for the end of the hunt in their tepees from whose cone-shaped tops smoke emanated. Children were having fun being pulled by dogs on their sleds, the same transportation that would be used at the end of the day to bring back the meat and robes from the buffalo hunt.

Charbonneau and Larocque covered another mile before they could make out the hunters and the buffalo. They pulled on the reins of their horses to stop and admire the sight before them.

At least a hundred hunters on horseback were galloping flat out in the midst of a huge herd of buffalo. The Hidatsas were incredibly agile riders. They directed their mounts simply by squeezing their knees, so that their hands remained free to shoot fifteen arrows a minute. None used a rifle, a weapon that required no courage.

Charbonneau could read surprise and admiration on Larocque's face.

–It takes months to train a horse for the buffalo hunt, he explained.

The hunter had to teach his horse how to run in the middle of a panic-stricken herd, to gallop as close as possible to the animals, all the while avoiding being gored. A mediocre mount had no chance in this game, since a healthy buffalo could run faster than such a horse.

Larocque felt the ground shaking under the hoofs of the horses and buffalo. On his left, he saw a seasoned Hidatsa hunter cleave his way through the herd to cut off a buffalo. His horse came up on the right side of the animal and pushed it toward the open plain.

The chase continued for half a mile. The hunter managed to get within four feet of his target. He pulled an arrow out of his quiver, bent his bow and, leaning toward the animal, shot him. The arrow went right through the beast, piercing the heart. It collapsed heavily, raising a white cloud.

–Christ! cried out Charbonneau, who had followed the hunt with Larocque. Right in the chest!

Triumphant, the hunter stopped his horse, dismounted and ran to the dead buffalo. He cut open the animal, carved out the liver and ate it on the spot, raw, steaming and dripping with blood. For the hunter of the Great Northern Plains, there could be no greater joy, nor anything more delicious.

Not far from there, another scene caught the attention of the two observers. A young hunter had shot three arrows into the side of a buffalo that kept on running. None of the projectiles had pierced the animal's body.

The hunter risked being humiliated. If the buffalo were found dead with two or more arrows in his body, the young Hidatsa would become the laughing stock of the entire village. That evening at the camp, a woman would give him back his arrows and, in a mocking tone, she would congratulate him for "his courage and his precise aim." Of course, if he had needed three arrows to kill a buffalo, it was because he had lacked courage and not gotten close enough to the beast.

Not wanting to be subjected to such an affront, the young hunter rode up to the right of the buffalo. At the right moment, he bent over, grabbed two of the arrows and ripped them out of its side. The buffalo nearly gored the horse, but the latter narrowly escaped the attempt by stepping slightly out of the way, guided by the rider's instinctive reaction. The hunter and his mount truly moved as one.

The buffalo would probably survive its injuries, but at least the hunter's honor would remain intact.

The men from Metaharta killed about forty animals during the hunt. Within a radius of more than a mile, the big beasts were scattered on the plain, making brown spots on the snow. Attracted by the scent, packs of wolves started coming from all sides.

Before nightfall, the women arrived with the sleds and dogs to carry out the work that fell to them. They cut up about twenty of the animals and took only the skins of the others, which would later be used to make clothes and tepees, or sold to traders.

When the women were done with one animal, the wolves took care of what was left, which could well be the whole buffalo. They feasted on the meat for the rest of the night. The next morning, the carnivorous beasts had such full bellies that they were too heavy to flee from the hunters. Dozens of them would die, riddled with arrows, which meant more skins to trade.

Charbonneau and Larocque themselves did not return to camp empty-handed; they had killed three buffalo with their rifles. They were cutting up the last one, when they heard shouting. They looked up and saw the Hidatsas forming a circle around a buffalo. They were too far to see the animal.

They quickly tied the meat and skins on their horses and went toward the crowd. What they saw took their breath away. An eighteen-year-old hunter had killed a white buffalo, female to boot.

–*Bonne sainte Anne!* exclaimed Charbonneau.

Albino buffalo were extremely rare on the Great Plains. An Indian who owned the robe of such an animal, especially that of a female, couldn't hope for greater medicine. If, in the course of his life, he didn't get the chance to kill a white buffalo, which was generally the case, he was ready to give ten horses to obtain its remains. During a special ceremony, he would offer it up to the Lord of Life or to the Sun, which amounted to the same thing. In a suitable place on the plain, he would roll up the skin with some artemisia and a blade of wheat, and hang it from a pole, where it would remain until it rotted away.

Some men kept their white buffalo skin all their lives, like a talisman.

The young hunter had not reached that point yet. He was hovering around the animal, not believing what he saw. His reputation as a man was made. In spite of his youth, from now on, he would be able to look down on any warrior who had killed many enemies at war, but could not boast a white buffalo among his trophies. And if, by any chance, a discussion should start about their respective feats, all the young hunter had to do was mention his white buffalo for the old warrior to hang his head down and cover his face in shame.

Back at the camp, the great medicine of the white buffalo soon started working its magic. Many young women were hanging around the hero of the day who took the most beautiful one back to his tepee. There were plenty of other suitors for the other girls. In the evening, the young men of the village adorned themselves with feathers and strutted about the tepees telling of their love conquests. The more beautiful their feathers were, the spicier their stories and the better their chances of finding a mate for the night.

–Larocque, would you like me to introduce you to a beautiful young lady? asked Charbonneau to his companion, who blushed as he declined the offer.

The two men found a place to sleep in Birohka's tepee. He was one of Caltahcota's sons. About ten people had found shelter there. The ground was covered with buffalo skins and a fire was burning in the middle. Soon, everyone could feel the warmth spreading around the tent. Meat was served late into the night.

–You should always hunt with us, Chief of the Small Village, said Birohka sometime in the course of the evening.

–I know, replied Charbonneau with a smile.

Larocque frowned; he didn't understand the exchange between the two men. Charbonneau had to translate for him.

–He says that I bring them good luck.

–Because of the white buffalo?

–Yes, it's the second one since I have been hunting with them.

–Who killed the other one?

–I did.

Charbonneau was not an especially good shot, but luck wise, he was unbeatable. During his first hunt with Caltahcota and his men from the small village of Metaharta, he had come face to face with a white buffalo. Leaving the herd behind, the animal had charged his horse with his horns leveled straight at it. After having gored his mount, heaven knows what the huge beast had in store for him.

Without even taking the time to aim, Charbonneau had fired at the buffalo. The bullet hit it between the eyes, stopping it short just a few feet away from the trader and his frightened horse.

–*Bonne sainte Anne!* Charbonneau had cried out, stunned yet filled with wonder.

A crowd had soon gathered around the French-Canadian, who was just getting over his fright.

–It's a female! one of the Indians had exclaimed. His voice conveyed great excitement.

The Hidatsas all stared at Charbonneau. They had already heard of his sexual exploits from the Mandans. And now, he had killed a white buffalo the very first time he hunted with them.

Caltahcota came up to Charbonneau and, pointing to the dead animal, had declared:

–Of all the riches that a man can possess, the skin of a white buffalo is the most valued. In order to get it, I'm prepared to offer you nine horses, a rifle, many cooking pots and a variety of small objects that you can choose yourself in my lodge.

Charbonneau had started to think. In those days, the free trader had not yet settled in Metaharta. He still went back and forth between the trading posts of the Assiniboine River and Upper Missouri. At the end of his contract with Alexander Henry Junior, he had gone into business for himself, as he had always wanted to do. He bought merchandise on credit from the Northwest Company and exchanged it with the Mandans and the Hidatsas for pelts. On every trip, he made a little profit. And every time he went to Upper Missouri, he fell more in love with the local women, who had firm, beautiful bodies.

Charbonneau dreamt of settling for good among the Mandans or the Hidatsas, as Jusseaume and old Ménard had done, but he wanted to remain free. He did not wish to marry the daughter of a dignitary in order to be able to continue trading, as the other traders did. He didn't want to owe anything to anybody.

Charbonneau had finally answered Caltahcota:

–Allow me to live in your village without any ties and I will give you this white skin.

Caltahcota had answered:

–I will order my men to treat you with all the respect due to a chief.

And that's how Charbonneau received his second nickname in Upper Missouri: Chief of the Small Village.

Chapter Five

The Holiday Season

Toussaint Charbonneau felt a surge of anger when he saw that the river was covered with a slick sheet of ice. "Maudite sainte Anne!" he uttered, immediately regretting his swearing. What was the point of turning the patron saint of voyageurs against him?

It was infuriating nonetheless. Charbonneau had hoped to get back to Fort Mandan on a carpet of soft snow, but the storm that had been expected overnight had never materialized. The fake sun he had seen the day before had betrayed him. The air was perfectly still on the plain and, under a leaden sky, the Missouri ahead looked like a mirror.

Out of the corner of his eye, he saw a wolf coming at him. He took aim and fired. He missed but the bang of his firearm made the animal bolt toward the pack that kept a good distance.

Charbonneau grumbled as he reloaded his rifle. He had almost used up all his powder supplies.

"I should have borrowed a sled!" he said out loud, cursing his lack of foresight.

At daybreak, he had left François-Antoine Larocque in the care of his friends the Hidatsas. On his favorite mare, he had covered twenty miles across the prairie, followed by his two other horses, loaded with skins, meat, fat and guts. He was sweating under his coat and wool bonnet. The ground was almost thawing.

Lured by the scent of fresh meat, the wolves had started their slow chase right after the hunter had left. They were hoping for a free meal and they were going to get it.

Charbonneau's horses were not shod. With their heavy loads, they would not be able to cross the river; their hoofs would slip on the ice; in no time at all, the poor animals would fall flat on their backs and would not be able to get up again.

Charbonneau had no choice; he would have to leave behind a good part of the fruits of the hunt. Even if Fort Mandan was close by, he could not afford to wait for help. He just didn't have enough ammunition to hold the wolves at bay. He had to act, and act fast.

He got off his horse, quickly untied the parcels of meat and threw them as far as he could in the direction of the wolves, which were getting dangerously close.

Beside the buffalo skins, Charbonneau only kept what he needed to prepare some *boudin blanc*. If he had not miscalculated, Christmas was the day after next.

"At least I'll be able to treat my squaws to a decent meal," he said to himself.

He crossed the frozen river, inching forward, holding the reins of his horses, which were numb with fear. It took him more than an hour to cover the short distance –about a quarter of a mile –to the other bank. He resisted looking back to see the wolves devouring the meat that he had hoped to offer the Americans to be in their good graces.

He arrived at Fort Mandan by nightfall. Much to his surprise, several Mandans were still there, lined up in front of one of the cabins. The women waited with baskets full of corn. The men held tomahawks, rifles, knives and pots that seemed in bad shape.

–Charbonneau, come over here! shouted Georges Drouillard, who was standing at the entrance of the cabin.

Charbonneau handed the reins of his horses to a young Mandan and followed Drouillard inside.

The Americans had turned the room into a forge. In the middle, a soldier was hammering metal over the fire, trying to straighten the tip of a rifle. The owner of the weapon, a Mandan from Mitutanka, stared in fascination. He had never seen a blacksmith in action.

During Charbonneau's absence, Private John Shields, who had previously been a blacksmith, had offered to repair the Mandans' metal objects in exchange for corn. Lewis and Clark, who were concerned about the expedition's rapidly decreasing food supplies, had enthusiastically endorsed the idea. Shields had immediately gotten down to work with the assistance of Privates William Bratton and Alexander Smith. Every day, they drew ever–growing crowds of Indians.

In a corner of the room, Charbonneau saw Captain Clark in the company of three Mandans dressed as women. *Berdaches*[14], he thought, looking at the transvestites.

–The Captain would like to know if these creatures have husbands, said Drouillard to Charbonneau. He was waiting for your return to ask you, because Jusseaume is not here. That imbecile has gone to Mitutanka to get his wife. The woman has returned to her father's house. She is jealous of your squaws, you know.

–I know, said Charbonneau.

The trader bowed before the tallest of the *berdaches*. The man's jet-black hair was done in two long braids; he wore a tunic made of skins that hugged his waist tightly. He was decked out with a necklace of glass beads and many earrings. He held a magnificent buffalo skin on which he had painted one of his visions. The *berdache* was an artist, a prophet and a shaman.

–I don't know the other two, but this one's name is Grande-Cotillon[15], said Charbonneau, pointing to the *berdache*. He shares the bed of Little Brave's son.

Captain Clark frowned on hearing Drouillard's translation.

–They sleep together? he asked indignantly. Don't these people know shame?

Charbonneau hesitated for a moment before answering. Ever since he had been living with the Indians, he had come to respect the *berdaches*. His own appetite leaning only toward women, it would never have crossed his mind to take one of these transvestites for a wife, but he knew that the Great Plains Indians ascribed great powers to them. They were men, and sometimes women, who, following a dream or a vision, had decided to live their lives as members of the opposite sex. The Indians believed that they had two spirits, the spirit of men and that of women, a privilege inherited from the Woman-From-Above. The *berdaches* possessed the gift for seeing all of life's dimensions, even the most secret and mysterious.

Charbonneau suspected that Captain Clark would not understand such beliefs. "No American can see the world through the eyes of an Indian," said the French-Canadian to himself.

He finally answered Clark through Drouillard:

–These *berdaches* don't bring shame on anyone. Each one of them does the work of three or four women. There are no better workers in the entire country.

Clark's face twisted with disgust. From Charbonneau's answer, he concluded that these *berdaches* were reduced to a kind of slavery as punishment for their sexual perversion. Convinced that he had settled the matter, he glanced at his watch and ordered Private Shields to close up shop and the Indians to leave Fort Mandan for the day.

–And don't come tomorrow, he informed them through Charbonneau. We will celebrate one of our great feasts.

As they went out, Charbonneau took Grande-Cotillon aside.

–What do you want in exchange for the buffalo skin?

The *berdache* smiled broadly.

–I would like the One Whose Man-Part Is Never Limp to give me a taste of his medicine by spending the night with me.

Charbonneau blushed for the first time in his life.

–Never! he exclaimed.

Grande-Cotillon roared with laughter.

–Whites are all the same! They're afraid of their fantasies.

–Not at all! interrupted Charbonneau. I only ever fantasized about women. You ought to know, aren't you supposed to guess everything?

–That's right, I do guess everything. You want to give the skin to one of your women on your great feast day.

–That's true.

–I'll give it to you in exchange for a promise.

–A promise?

–Promise me that you'll never repeat what earned you that red scar on your buttock.

Charbonneau's face went as white as a sheet.

–How do you know what happened at Fort Hope?

–It's my secret, said the *berdache*. You promise never to do it again?

Charbonneau lowered his head.

–I promise.

Toussaint Charbonneau had changed a lot since he had first come to Upper Missouri.

At sunrise, the American soldiers and the French-Canadian *engagés* gathered at the foot of the pole in the yard of Fort Mandan. Sergeant Ordway hoisted the United States flag and ordered his troop to get ready to salute Christmas Day, 1804. Most of the men raised their rifles, while others loaded three cannons.

–On my command, fire! shouted Sergeant Ordway.

The men obeyed; a volley of shots pierced the morning silence, making the birds fly away from the poplar branches where they perched. On the Sergeant's order, they fired two more times before exchanging wishes in a variety of languages and accents.

–Merry Christmas! *Joyeux Noël!* they exclaimed, shaking hands and slapping one another on the back.

At that moment, Captain Clark arrived before his men. He smiled as he witnessed this demonstration of solidarity that augured well for the rest of the expedition. Despite the early hour, he decided to add to the joy by inviting all his men inside the fort for a glass of brandy.

–To Captain Clark! called out Sergeant Ordway when everybody's glass was full.

–To Captain Clark! repeated all the others.

After one gulp, Georges Drouillard came forth and raised his glass in turn:

–To our journey!

–To our journey! they all joined in.

And they drank down the rest of the burning alcohol, quite determined to celebrate cheerfully their first American Christmas in Upper Missouri.

In the interpreters' room, Toussaint Charbonneau had been awakened by the gunshots. He didn't feel like going out to take part in the festivities. He lay warm and comfortable between his two women who had opened their eyes at the same time as he.

–*Joyeux Noël*! he said, staring at the ceiling.

For a moment, he thought of his mother whom he had not seen since he was eighteen-years-old. Was she still alive?

–*Joyeux Noël*! said Otter Woman, slipping a hand under the covers.

Toussaint's penis rose in all its splendor. Pleased to see how effective her caresses were, Otter Woman sat up and, without further ado, mounted the legendary organ, moving her groin with dexterity. Bird Woman snuggled up to them and Otter Woman gently fondled her between the thighs.

A smile lit up the face of the pregnant woman who closed her eyes, stroking her round belly.

–Merry Christmas, she whispered.

Otter Woman took her time. They were alone in the room. Two days earlier, the Jusseaume woman had left with her two children, slamming the door behind. She had had enough of the humiliation inflicted on her by the Americans who persisted in treating Charbonneau's slaves as dignitaries. She had returned to her father's house where her husband had joined her to try and convince her to come back to Fort Mandan.

With his hands behind his neck, Charbonneau was letting Otter Woman have her way with him. He had learned not to resist: when it came to the threesome's love making, she liked to take the initiative. On that morning, the Shoshoni woman's rhythm was more languorous than fiery. Toussaint closed his eyes. His thoughts turned from his hard penis to the *boudin blanc* that he was going to make when he got up. His mouth watered as he lay there moaning.

He felt Otter Woman's body quiver many times, and Sacagawea's too.

–Merry Christmas, he repeated in a languid voice.

After an hour, the two women were fully satisfied and fell asleep again, leaving Charbonneau unfulfilled. The man freed himself from the embrace of Otter Woman and got out of bed, caressing his erect organ. Standing in the middle of the room, he scratched his head with his free hand, wondering what he should do: wake up Otter Woman and take her from behind or take his pleasure into his own hands. He decided to let her sleep.

Once he had relieved himself, he got dressed, lit a fire and started preparing the Christmas meal: pea soup, corn bread, *boudin blanc.* The menu he had made up himself was the kind that appealed to the Shoshoni women. When they woke up, they ate heartily, sitting on buffalo skins in front of the fire. Their third Christmas was getting off to a good start.

While enjoying Charbonneau's rich cooking, typical of the voyageurs, the two women questioned him about his religion. In the middle of the meal, Sacagawea asked him incredulously:

–Do you mean to say that the man whose birth you celebrate today had neither wife nor children?

–Not that I know of, replied Charbonneau, cleaning his plate with a piece of bread he gulped down greedily.

Otter Woman commented in a sarcastic tone:

–Let's see, now. Your Lord of life walked on water, raised the dead, but couldn't find a woman to sleep with him. How can you compare him to the first chief of the Mandans?

Charbonneau shrugged his shoulders. At the beginning of the meal, he had told them the legend of the first Mandan chief in order to explain to the Shoshonis the mystery of the Immaculate Conception, a belief in his country.

By way of introduction, he had said:

–Now, hear me: the first Mandan chief's mother became pregnant without having relations with a man, just like the mother of Jesus, our Lord of life.

–How is that possible? the two Shoshoni women had asked as one.

–Let me speak, and you'll find out in a moment, had answered Charbonneau.

The French-Canadian spoke Hidatsa to communicate with the women. For this reason, he tended to lose his natural volubility, but not his passion as a storyteller.

Resuming his tale of the first Mandan chief, which he had heard not long after his arrival in Upper Missouri, Charbonneau had continued:

–One day, the First Man was on the bank of the Missouri and he saw a dead female buffalo adrift on the water. The wolves had carved out a hole in its side.

–There must have been enough left to make a good soup, Otter Woman had commented, unable to refrain from interrupting Charbonneau.

–Exactly, he had replied, in a tone that betrayed a slight annoyance. At the same moment, on the opposite bank, a woman also saw the animal floating in the river. She called her daughter and said to her: "Hurry up! Take off your clothes and bring that female back to dry land!" On hearing the mother cry out, the First Man immediately dove into the water and helped the daughter bring back the dead animal.

–Did the First Man keep some meat for himself? Sacagawea had asked, curious to know how the precious spoils had been divided.

–No! Charbonneau had said in a gruff voice. The First Man merely cut a piece of meat and had the girl eat it. She became pregnant on the spot!

The Shoshoni women had looked at each other in amazement. Taking advantage of their silence, Charbonneau had continued his story:

–The girl was ashamed, for she was still a virgin, pregnant though she was. She had to confess to her mother, who shared in her shame.

–What happened to the child, Sacagawea had asked, anxious to know the rest of the story.

–I'm coming to that! had replied Charbonneau growing increasingly impatient. The girl gave birth to a boy who grew at an astonishingly rapid rate. Very soon, he was a sturdy young man and became the first chief of his people. He was a great leader of men, like the son of the Virgin Mary.

The Shoshoni women had accepted straightaway the mystery of the Immaculate Conception, but they still had trouble grasping the true nature of Jesus. What kind of a man was he? He seemed to possess every power, except that of attracting women to his bed and procreating. On the other hand, the first Mandan chief had left countless descendants.

After thinking about it for a minute, Otter Woman had let drop:

–Your Lord of life must have been a *berdache.*

Charbonneau had remained silent for a few seconds, then had said quite seriously:

–I have never heard that Jesus dressed as a woman.

On their first Christmas, the Shoshoni women had found it difficult to understand another tradition from Toussaint Charbonneau's country, the exchange of presents.

In Upper Missouri, men did not wait for a special day of the year to give presents. It was a daily business, a constant challenge for those who wished to distinguish themselves. The rule was simple: in order to gain respect, a man had to offer many gifts. This explained why many of the most eminent chiefs were often the poorest. Someone could enter their home and ask for a buffalo skin, a nice outfit, a horse. To keep their influence, the chiefs had to give up whatever objects of value they owned. In return, they had the right to enshrine their reputation for posterity by painting on their clothes their acts of generosity. This way, they secured a place for themselves in the village of their ancestors, where the righteous went after their passage on earth. There, they lived as before, only better. Food, women, game, everything was plentiful in the paradise of the Upper Missouri Indians.

After having acquired the Shoshoni women, Charbonneau had waited for their first Christmas together before offering them a present. He had given them a beaver trap each.

–Merry Christmas! he had wished his women in the privacy of his lodge in Metaharta.

The two women had gazed at their present with a look of disappointment. They were both wondering the same thing. How could Charbonneau think that he was pleasing them by giving them hunting equipment that would merely increase their chores?

–Fortunately, he only celebrates Christmas Day once a year, had whispered Otter Woman to her companion in their Shoshoni language.

–As for me, Sacagawea had declared, I would rather not receive any presents.

–Eh, you two! Speak in a language I can understand, Charbonneau had bellowed.

For their second Christmas, also celebrated in Metaharta, the Shoshoni women had each received a new dress and a blanket from the Hudson Bay Company. It had made Charbonneau feel really generous. The fact is that, thanks to his women, he had experienced his best trading year since his arrival in Upper Missouri. They worked hard and well, getting the pelts ready, making moccasins and occasionally catching a beaver or two. The trader wanted to show them his gratitude.

They had been pleasantly surprised. In all their lives, no one had ever spoiled them like that. They had to face facts: Toussaint Charbonneau was not like other men. He often treated them kindly. For instance, he enjoyed preparing delicious meals for them, which contrasted with the cruel Le Borgne, their first master, who gave them nothing but scraps, if that. In fact, they didn't know any other Indian women who were treated better than they were by their man. They were fully aware of the brutality of some husbands of the Great Northern Plains. When they lived with the Hidatsas, they would sometime come across women hanging from trees. These wretched wives preferred taking their own lives to going on being beaten by their husbands.

–Your generosity makes you grow in our esteem, the Shoshoni women had both declared.

They regretted not having anything to give Charbonneau and they meant to do it the following Christmas. In the meantime, the Americans had arrived in Upper Missouri, Toussaint Charbonneau had undertaken to travel with them as far as the Pacific and Sacagawea, who was supposed to go along, was now pregnant.

Christmas 1804 was especially important for them. It was possibly the last one that Charbonneau and Sacagawea would celebrate together with Otter Woman. Who could foresee how this journey would end? The uncertainty added a solemn touch to the day's festivities.

After the meal, Charbonneau served coffee –a luxury in the Great Northern Plains–and began distributing the gifts. He gave Otter Woman the buffalo robe painted by Grande-Cotillon. The decoration represented one of the *berdache*'s visions. It depicted a man and a woman going toward each other. In the second half of the drawing, the man and the woman embraced. In the last part, they disappeared under a blanket.

–I saw this scene in a dream, Grande-Cotillon had told Charbonneau. One of your Shoshoni wives will find her brother.

–Which one? had asked Charbonneau.

–I cannot say, had replied the *berdache*.

"The future might clear up the mystery," thought Charbonneau. In the meantime, the buffalo robe would keep Otter Woman warm and attract men's attention. The French-Canadian trader had no objection to her taking lovers while he was traveling to the Pacific.

Charbonneau gave Sacagawea a wampum, a belt made out of beads cut from shells. The trader had received the precious ornament from François-Antoine Larocque in exchange for his services as interpreter to the Hidatsas. According to Larocque, the wampum had been made by Crees living on the shores of the Hudson Bay.

The Shoshoni women admired their presents, which would set them apart from all other women of the Great Plains.

–May your Lord of life watch over you, said Sacagawea gratefully.

Ill at ease, the trader remained silent as he got up.

–Wait, exclaimed Otter Woman. We have a gift for you.

She went to a corner of the room and came back with a brand new blue hooded coat bought from Charles McKenzie, an employee of the Northwest Company.

–*Joyeux Noël!* she said holding it out to Charbonneau.

–*Joyeux Noël!* repeated Sacagawea.

Charbonneau blushed. This was the first time he had received a Christmas present since his arrival in Upper Missouri. He said nothing, at a loss for words to express his emotion.

–Let's go out, he finally said, putting on his new coat.

The two wives bundled up and followed Charbonneau. Outside, the festivities were going full swing. In the middle of the fort, Cruzatte was playing the fiddle, surrounded by American soldiers and the French-Canadian *engagés* who were singing and dancing. They all had a happy Christmas, celebrating this great day until nine o'clock "in peace and tranquility," in Sergeant Ordway's own words as transcribed in his journal.

After having ushered in the New Year of 1805 with a two-gun salute and a round of musket fire, a troop of sixteen men left Fort Mandan. Under low and heavy skies, they walked along the Missouri, headed for Mitutanka, the first Mandan village. Since Christmas Eve, a warm wind had been blowing across the Great Northern Plains, where there was no snow left, and the men, amazed by the mild weather, were making remarks to that effect.

–It's spring in the middle of winter! exclaimed François Rivet.

They were going to put on a dance show at the express request of the chiefs of Mitutanka. The Mandans had heard of the Christmas festivities at the fort and they were curious to know what kind of merrymaking the White visitors enjoyed. And so Captain Clark had authorized a cultural delegation to go to the Mandan village. Pierre Cruzatte and his fiddle went along, of course, and so did Toussaint Charbonneau who would act as interpreter for the detachment. The French-Canadian trader meant to take part in the show himself. Before settling in Upper Missouri, he had been a champion jigger, or so he liked to claim.

Charbonneau walked part of the way with Cruzatte, a thin, nervous little man, who had the misfortune of being blind in one eye and shortsighted in the other.

–Say, Cruzatte, do you know the *Gigue de la rivière Rouge*[16]? asked Charbonneau to his traveling companion.

The fiddler hesitated for a moment. The same jig could bear different names, depending on whether it was played in the Valley of the St. Lawrence, west of Lake Superior or in the Mississippi Valley.

–Are you talking about the *Gigue de l'aveugle*[17]? he finally said, alluding to the most popular dance of French Louisiana.

–Why don't you play a bit of the tune? answered Charbonneau.

Cruzatte placed the violin in the hollow of his shoulder and settled the question with a few fast and precise bow-strokes.

–That's it! cried Charbonneau, recognizing the tune. When the Americans have finished dancing to your music, play that jig for me. I'll show them how they dance back home.

–I hope you can keep up with me.

–Don't you worry about me. When I used to spend my winters on the Assiniboine River, there wasn't a single Canadian who could hold his own against me.

The fiddler half-smiled. He was quite determined to make Charbonneau and all the other jiggers sweat trying to keep up with the furious rhythm of his music.

Pierre Cruzatte was typical of the men who inhabited the new American Frontier. He was born in St. Louis in the days when that town was nothing more than a modest trading post. His father had settled there after having tried in vain to make his fortune in New Orleans, where he had landed upon his arrival in America. A native of France, Cruzatte senior had been hired by the merchant Auguste Chouteau, one of the founders of St. Louis, whose ambition was to take over the fur market in Upper Louisiana. For years, he had piloted his employer's boats up and down the Mississippi, plying the river between St. Louis and New Orleans. On many occasions, he had fought back pirates who wanted to relieve him of his cargo of beaver skins and other merchandise.

He had also sailed on the Missouri, into the Prairie as far as the Platte River, in Omaha country, where he had met the woman who would become the mother of his only child and his wife before God in a marriage celebrated in St. Louis by a parish priest from Mascouche, Canada.

Pierre Cruzatte had barely known his father, who stopped in St. Louis only to leave it faster. He had learned the Omaha language on his mother's knee, and French on the waterfront of his native town where all sorts of nationalities would meet: French, Spanish, French-Canadian, Osage, Omaha, etc. African slaves could also be found there, many of whom had arrived in the company of French-Canadians. These slaves took advantage of their new situation in Upper Louisiana where, in accordance with the law in force in St. Louis, they were paid for work they did in the evenings and on weekends. Many of them had thus managed to make enough money to buy back their freedom.

At that time, St. Louis was governed by the Spanish, whose rule extended over all of Louisiana west of the Mississippi. In 1762, the French king Louis XV had secretly handed over that vast territory to his cousin, the king of Spain. He had hoped that it would be eventually returned to France, which is what happened in 1800, three years before the sale of Louisiana to the United States.

In spite of these transfers, French had remained the language of St. Louis, and French-Canadians continued to emigrate there, drawn not only by the fur trade, but also by the chance to live under a rule other than England's, a power held in contempt, whose flag now flew over their country. Leaving from Lachine in canoes, they all followed the same route, sailing west to the Great Lakes, then going down the Ohio River and the Mississippi as far as the Missouri.

These voyageurs were far from enjoying as good a reputation as the French-Canadians from the North Country, *le Pays d'en Haut*. Alexander Henry junior, Toussaint Charbonneau's former boss at the Northwest Company, had had dealings with some of them and had found nothing good to say about them, describing them as insolent vagabonds, unruly and greedy. Still, they had contributed to the founding and the populating of several villages on the banks of the Mississippi and the Missouri, such as St. Charles, Ste. Genevieve and Fleurissant, where they had imported the culture from the St. Lawrence Valley.

Cruzatte had grown up among these colorful men. As a child, he had haunted the docks of St. Louis, where travelers gathered, looking for work or in search of entertainment. He listened to their tall tales, their songs and the rigadoons of the fiddlers who, during the summer months, had men dancing on the banks of the Mississippi until late at night.

When he was twelve, Cruzatte made the acquaintance of Luc Beaulieu, nicknamed Ti-Zoune, a fiddler from Maskinongé, who became fond of him. In his spare time, Beaulieu had taught him the violin. He had noticed that, though his pupil did not have good sight, he had a good ear. Within one summer, the child had achieved dazzling progress, learning most of the tunes that got the French-Canadians to dance a jig, including *La Bastringue*[18], *La Danse du barbier*[19], *Jolie blonde*[20], *Brandy,* and of course, the most popular jig of the St. Lawrence Valley, *La Grande gigue simple*[21], which was known as *Gigue de la rivière Rouge* west of Lake Superior and *Gigue de l'aveugle* in the Mississippi Valley.

The following spring, Ti-Zoune had said to his protégé :

–Tomorrow, I'm going trading on the James River. I'm leaving you my violin until I come back. Take good care of it, my boy!

–Don't worry, Mr. Beaulieu! young Cruzatte assured him, clutching the instrument to his chest.

Ti-Zoune had never returned from his expedition to the land of the Sioux, where the Indians were already hostile to the trappers and merchants from St. Louis. Cruzatte thus became the permanent guardian of his old friend's violin. He never parted with it and took it everywhere, even on the Platte River, where his mother lived and where he went several times aboard one of the boats belonging to the Chouteau family, with whom he had taken a job, like his father.

And so the sound of Ti-Zoune's fiddle had rung out in the starry nights of the western plains, spreading French-Canadian music beyond the American Frontier.

When they arrived close to Mitutanka, the sixteen men of the delegation walked across the Missouri, taking care not to step in the puddles that covered the ice. They stopped outside the village fence and signaled their arrival by firing shots in the air and giving a foretaste of the musical accompaniment to the dance show. In the midst of a joyful din, Pierre Cruzatte started playing his fiddle, John Potts his tambourine and John Shields his horn.

The troop from Fort Mandan was soon surrounded by the children of Mitutanka who ran all over the place shouting at the top of their lungs. The musicians made their way with great difficulty to the center of the village, where stood the ark of the First Man, a wooden cylinder about five feet high that constituted the altar around which the Mandans celebrated their most important ceremonies.

Mitutanka, the smallest of the Mandan villages, had about forty large and comfortable huts, built out of wood and mud. Some travelers compared these circular dwellings to molehills or beaver hutches. One by one, the adults came out of the huts and formed a circle around the visitors. The men wore ornate buffalo blankets and necklaces of bear claws. Several of them had smeared their faces with vermilion, and held fans of eagle feathers. They were much better turned-out than the women whose tunics of deerskin were sparsely decorated with a few porcupine quills.

In order to see the show better, and also to be seen, some young warriors with colorful clothes climbed on the roofs of the huts that lined the central square. None of them, however, dared to find a spot on the medicine hut, in front of which rose a pole topped by the effigy of the evil spirit, Ochkih-Hadda.

The most important chief of Mitutanka, Big White, took one step toward the visitors and, after paying the customary compliments, said:

–Some of our people heard the music that came from your fortress on your medicine day. They told us that you danced from sunrise to sunset. We didn't believe them because, ever since we have known White men, we have never seen them dancing. Our people swore that they were telling the truth, but we want to see with our own eyes. Show us how the White men dance.

Charbonneau translated Big White's words in French. Georges Drouillard, the hunter, conveyed them in English to the Americans.

As the officer in charge of the troop, Sergeant John Ordway answered Big White:

–Your people have spoken the truth. It is a fact that we dance on our major feast days. And today, we celebrate the day that marks the beginning of our new year. Therefore, we shall perform for you two dances that are special to the occasion and, in between, an acrobatic act that will amaze you.

Charbonneau translated Sergeant Ordway's message and he added a detail of his own initiative:

–Mandan friends, I myself will have the pleasure of showing you the steps of the Red River dance and of challenging anyone to keep up with me!

The Mandans, who knew the Red River, were very interested by Charbonneau's announcement. The men from Fort Mandan had planned the show together before their arrival in Mitutanka. They took their mission very seriously and considered themselves to be the ambassadors of their culture to the Indians.

After another gun salute that terrified the children, the Americans started the show with a country dance, which the French-Canadians called the *contredanse*; it is performed in two lines, a line of women facing one of men. Some of the men had balked at the idea of playing the women's part, but they had been quickly persuaded to get over their reluctance. After all, they were in no danger of being ridiculed by the Mandans, since the Indians had no idea that this dance required the presence of the fair sex.

Cruzatte accompanied the *contredanse* with a tune that all the fiddlers of the States knew well, *Fisher's Hornpipe,* which he had learned from Private George Gibson. Born in Pennsylvania and raised in Kentucky, Gibson had also brought his violin with him. From the start of the expedition of the Corps of Discovery, he had been teaching Cruzatte many American tunes that had not yet reached St. Louis. However, he had not been able to join the delegation to Mitutanka, having come down with pleurisy on Christmas Eve.

At the sound of the violin, each "couple" executed a series of dance figures in turn, switching places with the couple beside them. The series was repeated until all the couples were back in their initial places. Cruzatte played the tune six times, that is, as many times as there were couples on the dance floor.

Although the dancers tried their best, Charbonneau was not impressed. He watched the dance from the sideline while awaiting his turn. As far as he was concerned, the men of Fort Mandan danced as if they had a ball and chain at their ankles and weights on their arms. They moved clumsily, in a self-conscious manner. As a White man, he was ashamed. He remembered the jigs he used to dance when he spent the winter in the Assiniboine River Department. Now, that was dancing!

The Mandans, for their part, looked surprised, not knowing what to make of the strange figures executed by the dancers. They just couldn't see the point of the Whites' pantomime. For them, dancing wasn't only an abstract form of entertainment, but also a concrete way of becoming one with the world. They danced before the hunt, before going to war, before the harvest, miming their past and future feats. They danced to call for rain, to propitiate the spirits and honor the sun, where their Lord of life resided. The White man's dance didn't resemble anything they knew, nor did it evoke anything to their minds.

At the end of the *contredanse*, the inhabitants of Mitutanka sat in an uncomfortable silence. Some did look admiringly in the direction of Cruzatte who played an instrument unknown to them, but most remained skeptical.

Thinking they had given a convincing illustration of the White man's talent for dancing, the Americans withdrew to make room for François Rivet, referred to as the Old Man, who was to perform during the second half of the show with help from Cruzatte, Drouillard and Charbonneau.

Rivet was a short, sturdy and lively man. Born in Montreal, he had a passion for travel; he was not yet twenty when he had gone off to seek adventure on the road to Louisiana. He had been a hunter and trapper for a long time on the Prairie, discovering the West, its boundless sky, the charms and perils of Indian country. As an *engagé* in Lewis and Clark's expedition, he was supposed to go back to St. Louis when the thaw came, letting others reap the glory of reaching the Pacific. Meanwhile, the fellow had no intention of going unnoticed among the Mandans.

Despite his forty-seven years –he was the oldest at Fort Mandan –Rivet was as strong as a horse and as nimble as a monkey. In the early months of the expedition, he had impressed his travel companions by dancing on his hands, his head down and his feet up in the air. That's what he proudly called *La danse à Rivet*, a dance only he was capable of doing in North America; he was about to give an energetic demonstration to the Mandans. They had no clue of what he had in store for them.

Cruzatte led into his favorite tune enthusiastically with a few bowstrokes. It was *La Bastringue,* the first rigadoon he had learned from Ti-Zoune Beaulieu on the docks of St. Louis. Drouillard and Charbonneau stood beside him and started singing the words of what could be rightfully considered the national anthem of French-Canadians:

Mademoiselle, voulez-vous danser
La bastringue, la bastringue?
Mademoiselle, voulez-vous danser?
La bastringue va commencer.[22]

At this point, Rivet began his upside down dance on his hands, to the amazement of the Mandans, who had never seen anything of the kind. The music of the violin filled the air, Drouillard and Charbonneau kept on singing:

Oui, Monsieur, je veux bien danser
La bastringue, la bastringue
Oui, Monsieur, je veux bien danser
C'est pour vous accompagner.[23]

The Mandans closed in around the dancer and his accompanists. His face all flushed, Rivet continued his acrobatic feat, whirling round on one hand, then the other, moving his feet in the air to keep up with the rhythm of the music.

The Mandans were astounded and soon began to dance themselves around Rivet who kept on twirling on his hands. Trying to follow the dancer's movements, they jumped on one leg, then the other, while waving their arms. Not to be outdone, Drouillard and Charbonneau made a quick twirl as they finished the last two verses of their song:

Oh! Monsieur, je sais bien danser
La bastringue, la bastringue
Oh! Monsieur, je sais bien danser
Je suis prête à recommencer![24]

Rivet's hair was drenched with sweat; he was showing signs of fatigue, like the character in the song:

Mademoiselle, je n'peux plus danser
La bastringue, la bastringue
Mademoiselle, je n'peux plus danser
Je vous prie de m'excuser.[25]

At these words, Rivet dropped to the ground, exhausted but beaming.

"How could the show go on after such a success?" wondered Toussaint Charbonneau when he saw the excitement created by Rivet's dance. Each Mandan asked for the privilege of receiving in his hut the man they now called the One Who Dances on His Head.

Charbonneau felt a pang of jealousy. It had been agreed that the show would end with *La Gigue de la rivière Rouge*. During this third and last act, the French-Canadian interpreter would show the Mandans and the Americans the steps and the sequence of movements of this not-so-simple dance and, later, challenge anyone to dance longer than him, while keeping up with the music.

He also wanted to challenge Pierre Cruzatte. Charbonneau was convinced that the fiddler's arm would tire faster than his legs; after all, he was a champion jigger. But Rivet was now getting all the attention from the Mandans. Some of the men went so far as to offer their wives to the hero of the day as an incentive for him to go to their huts. The fellow from Montreal was ready to accommodate everyone; the one from Boucherville felt hopeless. "*Maudite sainte Anne!*" exclaimed Charbonneau to himself. "Why don't you do something?"

His wish was immediately granted. Indeed, at that precise moment, Captain Clark arrived at Mitutanka, accompanied by York, his servant, and René Jusseaume, the French-Canadian interpreter, who had come back to Fort Mandan the day before after having given up trying to persuade his wife to follow him.

The arrival of the three men in the central square of Mitutanka distracted the Mandans' attention. Their eyes went from the red-haired Captain, in his dress uniform, to York, whose ebony skin and giant's build never ceased to amaze them.

On that New Year's Day, Captain Clark had decided to join his men in Mitutanka, out of both curiosity and courtesy. He wanted to see for himself how the cultural event was unfolding. He also wished to give the Mandan chiefs assurances of his respect since, according to the rumors reported to him by Jusseaume, some of them had not appreciated being turned away from Fort Mandan on Christmas Day.

Seeing the Indians gathered round Rivet, Clark understood that the French-Canadian had just given a spirited performance of his famous dance.

–Is the show over? he asked.

–No Sir, answered Sergeant Ordway, there is one dance left.

–Please proceed, said the Captain.

Sergeant Ordway nearly made a change in the program. He thought of asking the Americans to repeat their country dance, just to please the Captain, but after a moment's hesitation, he decided to stick to the original plan, fearing that the Mandans might be offended at having to watch a performance they had already seen. The champion jigger thanked St. Anne in his heart. He would get the chance to stand out, not only before the Mandans, but also before Captain Clark, which might turn out to be useful.

Charbonneau stepped forward to the middle of the square and spoke to the Mandans and the Americans in his mother's tongue.

–Ladies and gentlemen, he announced in a pompous tone, I'll show you the steps and sequence of movements of the *Gigue de la rivière Rouge*, the Canadians' favorite dance.

In an aside, he added for the benefit of Jusseaume:

–Translate that in English and in Mandan!

Jusseaume would have liked to send Charbonneau packing; because of his Shoshonis, he was separated –temporarily, he hoped –from his Mandan woman. However, he had no choice but to comply with his competitor's request. If he wanted to get paid for his services by the Americans, he had to translate the words of that God-awful man.

When he had done so in both languages, Charbonneau made a sign to Cruzatte, who started to play the *Gigue de la rivière Rouge* very slowly. At the sound of the violin, the jigger executed a sequence of steps in slow motion, starting with the right foot, then repeating the same sequence with the left foot. Each of the rhythmic sequences was performed on the toes, the heel or the whole foot.

Cruzatte sped up the pace and Charbonneau, while continuing to dance, challenged the audience:

–Now you've seen the steps and sequences of the dance. Is there someone among you who can dance longer than I? I bet you can't, but you can always try!

Jusseaume translated Charbonneau's words. Laughter burst forth among the Mandans, but none was willing to volunteer. Since no one was moving, Rivet stepped toward the dancer to take up his challenge. He knew this particular jig very well and was eager to bring Charbonneau down a peg or two, but he froze in his tracks when he heard the voice of Captain Clark.

–York! called out the American in a commanding tone. Show Mr. Charbonneau what you can do. I'm sure you can stand up to him. Go.

York had never danced a jig in his life. That was no problem; he went up to Charbonneau without hesitation and stood in front of him. He had no intention of missing this opportunity to show off. He remembered the exquisite favors that his athletic prowess had earned him with the Arikaras, and he had spotted around him Indian women as pretty as Sacagawea.

York chased these romantic thoughts from his mind and concentrated on the jig that Charbonneau was dancing. After a few faltering steps, he was able to complete a sequence of movements, then a second, then a third. The duel began. Cruzatte started playing twice as fast, forcing the dancers to speed up their rhythm. Charbonneau had the faintest of smiles on his lips, as he was confident of getting the better of his opponent. He had seen plenty of novices, all spruce at the beginning of the jig, collapse with weariness after only fifteen minutes.

The Mandans were not all convinced of the superiority of the French-Canadian dancer.

–Great medicine, they said, admiring York's lively movements.

Not being able to resist their passion for gambling, some of them bet on York's victory.

–I bet a horse that the Black giant will dance longer than the little White man, shouted Big White.

–You'll owe me a horse, retorted Three Feathers, one of the dignitaries of the village. You ought to know that the little White man never gets tired. His legs never rest, no more than his organ does.

Nearly all the men in the village ended up placing a bet. On the roofs of the huts, the young warriors stood up to cheer their favorite dancer. Judging from the shouts coming from all sides, Charbonneau and York shared equally the crowd's support.

Cruzatte's bow stroked the strings of his violin faster and faster, making the notes bounce all over the village.

Half an hour later, Charbonneau's smile had faded. York didn't seem to have any trouble following the fiddler's rhythm, which could not have been any faster. With his knees slightly bent and his feet barely leaving the ground, the slave moved from one sequence to the next with a minimum of effort. The Mandans were surprised that such a tall and sturdy man could be so nimble.

Three-quarters of an hour into the dance, Charbonneau was losing confidence. He could feel the sweat streaming down his brow, his legs getting heavier and his breath shorter. He was fuming on the inside against Captain Clark who had involved his Black slave in the White man's dance.

All of a sudden, one of the strings of Cruzatte's violin snapped. Everything stopped, the music and the jig, to the Mandans' great disappointment in the face of the worst possible outcome: no winner, no loser!

The fiddler had done it on purpose, because he didn't have the strength to go on playing. Rather than admitting his fatigue, he had sabotaged his own violin, knowing that he could later simply replace the broken string.

Only Charbonneau suspected the subterfuge.

–I knew you couldn't keep up with me, he said to Cruzatte as he walked past him.

–What are you talking about? asked Cruzatte, trying to look innocent. I could have gone on playing for an hour.

–Liar!

–Instead of insulting me, you should thank your good St. Anne. If the string hadn't snapped, you would have died. Admit it, the Negro would have beaten you!

–Never!

The quarrel between the two men continued in Big White's hut, where the artistic delegation had been invited for a meal and gift exchange. Most of the men from Fort Mandan left Mitutanka at the end of the day. The others, including François Rivet, spent the night, enjoying the full Indian hospitality. Forced to follow his master, York was bitterly disappointed.

Chapter Six

Clark's Map

In early 1805, Upper Missouri became the scene of a remarkable rapprochement between the members of the Corps of Discovery and the Mandans. Lost in the vast plain, explorers and natives alike were able to sate the same passion for discovery, meetings and exchanges. Outside, the temperature dropped by several degrees and snow covered the ground once more, but at Fort Mandan and in the neighboring villages, human relations warmed up considerably.

After the artistic success obtained in Mitutanka, a delegation from Fort Mandan, headed by Captain Lewis, went to the second Mandan village to put on another dance show. Black Cat, the greatest chief of Ruptare, had let them know that his people too wanted to see the One Who Dances on His Head.

As on the previous night, some soldiers and *engagés* finished the day in the company of young Mandan women. In this brand new year, the visitors intensified their contacts with the local women, taking advantage of a sexual freedom that would have been unthinkable east of the Mississippi or of the Great Lakes. Some of the men contracted venereal diseases, but only complained about it later.

Despite this rapprochement, some of the American visitors reserved the right to pass judgment on the customs of the Mandans. And so, young Sergeant Patrick Gass wrote in his journal: "It may be generally observed that chastity is not very highly esteemed by these people." One of the American soldiers, he noted, had spent the night with Big White's daughter, in the village of Mitutanka, in exchange for an old tobacco box. He saw in this an example of the "severe and loathsome effects of certain French principles."

Of course, the "French principles" had nothing to do with the behavior of Mandan women; they lived in a matriarchal society where their decisional role was predominant. During the winter of 1804-1805, they offered the explorers the kind of hospitality that was typical of the Great Northern Plains. Through sex, they succeeded in strengthening the ties that bound their villages to the inhabitants of Fort Mandan, where they found an unexpected market to sell off their surplus corn. In exchange for their sexual favors, they also managed to obtain from the soldiers and *engagés* all sorts of articles that they considered very valuable: paint, glass beads, fabric, hardware, etc.

On January 5, the Mandans of Mitutanka went as far in their hospitality as to invite François Rivet to take part in a buffalo dance, the ceremony that had earned Toussaint Charbonneau his most famous nickname. Rivet was strong and agile, but he could not match Charbonneau's feats. He was offered four Mandan women, but could only satisfy three of them, to his great shame. He tried to apologize to the husband of the unfulfilled one, but the man wouldn't hear of it. Instead, it was he who insisted on asking Rivet to forgive him and his wife.

–I beg of you, do not despise us, said the Mandan as he wrapped a buffalo skin around Rivet's shoulders so that he wouldn't catch cold.

When he returned to Fort Mandan the next day, Rivet gave an account of his evening to the men of the expedition, leaving out no details. True to his responsibilities as an ethnologist, Captain William Clark took a keen interest in the story. With the help of Georges Drouillard, who gave a lively translation of Rivet's account, he wrote down in his journal a detailed description of the buffalo dance, rightly noting that the ceremony was meant to attract the animals on the eve of the hunt. However, he was mistaken about the role of the wise old men in the ritual. Clark wrote that the old men probably established "this very curious custom" so that they could enjoy the favors of young women. He didn't understand that the Mandans believed in the transmission of power and experience through sex. He might have asked Charbonneau for information, since the French-Canadian had become an expert on this aspect of Indian spirituality.

In the middle of January, on a very cold morning, an incident took place, which stemmed from a misunderstanding of quite another nature. Captain Clark was in his room, compiling a map of the region between Fort Mandan and the Rockies. The day before, a Hidatsa warrior had provided him with precious information on the watercourses that flowed through that territory still unknown to the members of the Corps of Discovery. Around ten o'clock, a soldier banged loudly on his door.

Clark interrupted his work and opened the door.

–A Mandan is threatening to kill his wife! shouted the soldier, making frantic gestures.

–Where is he? asked the Captain.

–In the interpreters' room.

Clark put on his coat and ran behind the soldier. He got there just in time. In the interpreters' room, the Mandan was brandishing a knife in front of a terrified woman who tried desperately to hide behind Otter Woman. From a corner of the room, Sacagawea watched the whole scene with dread in her eyes, protecting her big belly with her arms.

–Take aim at him, ordered Captain Clark to the soldier.

When he saw the rifle pointed at him, the Mandan lowered his knife but his eyes continued to flash with anger at his wife.

–Keep an eye on him, I'll be right back, said the Captain to the soldier.

Clark flew out of the room and went to fetch René Jusseaume who, together with a group of soldiers, was busy playing backgammon. The Captain dragged off the interpreter to the scene of the domestic quarrel, where the protagonists had not budged.

Clark had recognized the Mandan woman, a black-eyed beauty. Two days earlier, she had taken refuge in the interpreters' room to seek comfort and protection from Charbonneau's women. She had obviously been beaten and she bore the marks of knife cuts in three places. Her husband had clearly come to the fort to finish her off.

–What did your wife do? asked Captain Clark to the Indian.

Jusseaume translated the question.

–The bitch has slept with one of your men without my permission! answered the Mandan.

–What man?

–The one who wears a raccoon skin on his head.

Clark understood the man was talking about John Ordway. He sent for the sergeant.

As he stepped through the doorway, Ordway saw the Mandan woman and her husband. In a single leap, he intervened between them and was about to pull out a knife from his belt when Captain Clark raised his voice:

–Put your knife away and give this man something to calm him down. He claims that you slept with his wife. Is it true?

–I couldn't help it! the Sergeant replied sharply. She dragged me off to an abandoned hut. Her husband caught us in the act. I didn't know she was married.

–It doesn't matter. Give the man a present.

The Sergeant rummaged through his tobacco pouch, pulled out a plug and handed it to the husband with a grumble. The gift seemed to soothe him.

Clark took advantage of the lull to attempt a reconciliation.

–None of my men will ever disrupt your marriage again, he said to the husband. Go home and try to live in peace with your wife.

At that very moment, a Mandan chief, drawn by the commotion, came into the interpreters' room. Clark informed him of the situation. The chief rebuked the guilty husband and made him promise never to beat his wife again.

Clark doubted that the intervention had been effective. In his journal, he concluded the account of the incident on a fatalistic note: "They both went off apparently dissatisfied."

York's medicine was no longer working. Despite the tea and stewed fruit that Captain Clark's servant brought regularly to Sacagawea, she kept complaining of stomach cramps. Her feeling of sickness was made worse by the diet she was compelled to follow. Since the Christmas meal, she ate practically nothing but corn, as did most of the inhabitants of Fort Mandan.

In the ninth month of her pregnancy, the young Shoshoni woman would have given her nicest dress for a bit of white sausage. Unfortunately, at the end of January, game animals were becoming extremely rare in the surroundings of the fort. Deer and moose were hiding in a wooded area about thirty miles downstream from the villages. Some Mandan hunters had tried to seek them out, but had returned empty-handed, with faces burned by the extreme cold, feet frozen and frostbitten toes. Captain Lewis had to perform a few amputations to prevent gangrene.

As for the buffalo, they had simply disappeared and could not be found, in spite of the passionate dances designed to attract them in the vicinity of the villages.

Always attentive towards her companion, Otter Woman tried to relieve her discomfort by massaging her abdomen, something she could do for hours. It didn't stop Sacagawea from moaning. She felt as if a malicious spirit were taking pleasure in gnawing at her guts. When would she be delivered?

Toussaint Charbonneau was wondering the same thing. Oddly enough, when he heard his pregnant woman complain, he also felt a pain in his belly. He wished he could do something to soothe her pain, but he felt helpless and that made him furious.

One morning, Otter Woman gave Toussaint an opportunity to make himself useful by suggesting he leave immediately for Metaharta. According to the information she had received, a band of Assiniboines had just arrived there.

–They will surely have some pemmican, she said to Charbonneau.

Sacagawea raised her head from the bed where she was lying and said in a weak voice:

–I would eat some pemmican.

–I'm off, decided Charbonneau on the spot.

The trader knew the restorative powers of pemmican, a food made from buffalo meat, dried and pounded, which the Assiniboines used as exchange merchandise. He gathered together in the middle of the room the pelts he had accumulated since the beginning of the winter. He piled up twelve wolf skins, twenty-eight fox skins, two otter skins and three buffalo skins. No beaver skins! Before meeting the Assiniboines, he would sell part of his stock to François-Antoine Larocque, the Northwest Company clerk, who was still in Metaharta.

Around ten o'clock in the morning, the trader took leave of his women and harnessed his horse to a *travois* on which he tied his bundles of fur. He left Fort Mandan under a bright sunshine. The weather had gotten considerably milder; wide strips of earth were emerging from the melting snow. Crows and magpies were flying again over the prairie in search of food. And on the banks of the Missouri, several men were attempting to free the boats of the expedition from the ice.

Charbonneau stopped a moment to observe them. He knew the captains were especially eager to save their keelboat, which, in the spring, would carry back to St. Louis all the samples collected and the documents written since the beginning of the expedition.

He had also learned for whom the precious cargo was intended: Thomas Jefferson, the man whose aristocratic profile was engraved on the silver medal that had been given to his old friend Caltahcota the previous fall. Captain Clark had explained everything a few days earlier in the presence of Larocque, who was passing through Fort Mandan.

The Captain had even offered to send him to Washington to meet the President of the United States.

–When we come back from the Pacific, we shall invite the chiefs of the Big Bellies to meet our President. If you wish, you can go with them to Washington and act as their interpreter.

Flushed with envy, Larocque had translated the Captain's words, adding something of his own devising:

–How I wish I were in your place! You'll be able to meet the author of the Declaration of Independence!

Charbonneau had remained stony-faced. He wasn't sure anymore that he wanted to accompany the expedition as far as the Pacific. From what he had gathered, the captains intended to assign him to the same tasks as regular soldiers. During the entire duration of the journey, he would thus have to row, mount guard and carry loads on his back, like the lowest of the *engagés*.

In his capacity as interpreter, Charbonneau considered that he deserved much better treatment. At any rate, he didn't know a single man from the North, a single free trader, nor a single former clerk of the Northwest Company who would have agreed to be treated like a *mangeur de lard*. These Americans really thought they had the right to do anything they wanted.

– Damn!

The shout came from the group of men working on the riverbank. Jean-Baptiste Lajeunesse had just fallen backwards into the water, causing the men to burst out laughing.

Lajeunesse and the others were breaking their backs for nothing, trying to pull the boats ashore. About eight inches below the surface, the boats were still trapped in thick ice.

"The sudden breaking up of the ice could smash the boats to smithereens," thought Charbonneau as he started on his way again.

He arrived at Metaharta around three in the afternoon and found Larocque in the lodge he had rented from White Wolf. The Northwest Company clerk was drawing up in his journal the statement of his first commercial mission to Upper Missouri. In the first week of February, he would set out again for the trading post on the Assiniboine River with a perfectly satisfactory profit, notwithstanding the theft of two horses at the hands of the Assiniboines.

He got up when he saw Charbonneau coming into the hut. He greeted his fellow countryman cheerfully:

–To what do I owe the honor of welcoming in my humble abode the person who will meet the President of the United States?

–I have some pelts for you, the trader answered curtly, putting down his bundles of fur.

–And I have some questions for you, retorted Larocque. Take off your coat.

Before getting to the questions, Larocque examined the pelts. He agreed to give Charbonneau a cotton shirt, a pair of corduroy pants and a tobacco plug in exchange for seven wolf skins, one otter skin and eighteen fox skins.

–Don't you want to sell me the other pelts? asked Larocque.

–I'll exchange the rest with the Assiniboines, replied Charbonneau. I need some pemmican for my pregnant squaw.

–Don't worry about it, I have some myself, said Larocque.

Delighted, he added:

–That's settled, then. You'll spend the night here. This way, you'll be able to get back to your wife tomorrow. In fact, I would be grateful if you brought back to Fort Mandan the three horses I have left. Captain Clark has promised to keep them for me until spring. Damned Assiniboines, they have already stolen two horses from me!

–How will you return to Fort Assiniboine? asked Charbonneau.

–On snowshoes, answered Larocque.

Charbonneau didn't quite know whether he should admire Larocque's courage or deplore his folly. In the winter, going from Upper Missouri to the Assiniboine River often proved fatal. On the wind-swept plain, the three-week journey was a race against the wind, wolves and thieves.

Toussaint gladly accepted to spend the night in Metaharta. Larocque served him a meal of pemmican flavored with wild berries. The very first bite, which reminded Charbonneau of his winters on the Red River, told him that Sacagawea would get better. Pemmican was a rich and tasty food. There was nothing like it to restore one's strength in the winter.

After the meal, Larocque offered him a cup of coffee. Charbonneau wondered at such a treat; surely Larocque's generosity had an ulterior motive. He was not mistaken; the young clerk wanted to question him on the preparations for Captains Lewis and Clark's expedition. Larocque was particularly curious about the visit to Fort Mandan by Seeing Snake, a Hidatsa war chief.

Larocque had gotten wind of this meeting a few days earlier. According to his source, Seeing Snake had arrived at the fort with a buffalo skin on which he had drawn a map of the territory between the Knife River and the Rockies. Charbonneau had acted as interpreter for him. Captain Clark had shown a keen interest in the information provided by the chief of the Big Bellies.

And now, Larocque wanted Charbonneau to share that information with him.

–Would you draw for me what you saw on that map? he asked his fellow countryman, handing him his quill and a sheet of paper.

Charbonneau didn't budge.

–That information doesn't belong to me, he said.

–I only want to know one thing, insisted Larocque. Where does the Yellow Stone River flow into the Missouri?

Charbonneau half-smiled. He remembered the plan Larocque had set out before Le Borgne.

–You still intend to ascend the Yellow Stone River? asked Charbonneau, looking Larocque straight in the eye.

–Yes, I want to be an explorer, just like my uncle Laurent Leroux, the first White man to explore the Yellow Knives River, near Great Slave Lake.

–Not a word to the captains, said Charbonneau.

–Not a word to the captains, promised Larocque.

From memory, Charbonneau drew the map that he had seen in the captains' room. He didn't have Clark's expert hand, but he remembered well the tributaries of the Missouri as far as the Yellow Stone River.

–Thank you very much, said Larocque as he examined the map.

Larocque had not given up all hope of accompanying the Americans to the Pacific. In fact, he planned to return to Fort Mandan in a few days to ask the captains one last time. Should he meet with another refusal, he would at least have at his disposal a map that would allow him to find on his own the mouth of the mythical river where six-foot long beavers lived.

–Don't mention it, answered Charbonneau. At any rate, you can't miss it. Old Ménard told me: the stones of the river are really yellow.

The next day, Charbonneau returned to Fort Mandan. He entered the enclosure around two in the afternoon. Before rejoining his women, he made his way to the captains' room to deliver a letter from Larocque. As he went in, he saw that the room had been transformed into an infirmary.

In one corner, Captain Lewis was amputating the toes of a young Mandan whose foot was frostbitten. In another corner, Captain Clark was bleeding Drouillard, who was suffering from pleurisy. The captains were administering treatments prescribed by Benjamin Rush, the eminent doctor from Philadelphia, whose advice President Jefferson had sought before the departure of the American expedition.

Charbonneau looked away. Drouillard bore his procedure stoically; the Mandan boy screamed with pain.

Charbonneau took advantage of a lull to hand over the letter to the Captain. In it, Larocque advised him of the arrival of his horses and of his visit to Fort Mandan in the near future, in order to have the broken glass of his compass and its defective needle repaired.

His mission accomplished, Charbonneau turned on his heels and walked away from what seemed to him a chamber of torture. As he crossed the yard, he thought of Sacagawea and of the baby she was about to bring into the world. He wished for the delivery to take place without the intervention of Captain Lewis, who had promised his assistance in case of complications.

He had only just arrived to the interpreters' room when he heard René Jusseaume's irate voice.

–Charbonneau, will you get your squaw to pipe down! She won't stop moaning!

Lying on the bed, Jusseaume was smoking his pipe. He was the only member of his family in the room; his wife and two children were still living with her father.

–If it bothers you, you can go outside, replied Charbonneau, casting a nasty look at Jusseaume.

–Don't mind him! called out Otter Woman from the section of the room that she occupied with Charbonneau and Sacagawea.

On the bed, she was giving another massage to her companion whose abdomen was as round as a ball. Charbonneau walked toward his wives, his arms loaded with all the goods he had acquired from Larocque. He sat down on the edge of the bed and opened one of the parcels that contained the pemmican. He gave a piece to Sacagawea whose face bore the signs of hunger, fatigue and pain.

–There are berries in it, whispered the young Shoshoni woman as she chewed the food.

Charbonneau nodded.

She had a second helping. After swallowing a third one, she smiled faintly, the first time in many days.

–Don't make her eat too much, intervened Otter Woman, snatching from his hands the fourth piece that Charbonneau was about to give the pregnant woman.

Otter Woman ate it herself and got another piece from the parcel. The meat literally melted in her mouth.

On the other side of the room, Jusseaume could feel himself getting hungrier and hungrier. He regretted having addressed Charbonneau sharply. He asked in a more pleasant tone:

–Say, Charbonneau, you wouldn't have an extra piece for a starving Canadian? I'll repay you some day.

Charbonneau was going to send him about his business, but he decided to take him at his word. He got up, threw a package of pemmican on his competitor's bed and declared defiantly:

–I can't wait to see how you'll repay me.

–Don't worry, I'm a man of my word.

–How many days do you think it will take you to cross over the Rockies?

François-Antoine Larocque's question was left in midair for a long time in the captains' room. He had been dying to ask it ever since he had arrived at Fort Mandan for his last visit of the winter.

Meriwether Lewis and William Clark exchanged a quick glance and shrugged their shoulders. They didn't know what to think or say on the question, one that was nevertheless of the utmost importance for their expedition. In St. Louis, the French-Canadian voyageurs had told many a story about the Rockies. To hear them talk, these mountains were inaccessible to man, their rock faces so high and so steep that only a kind of goat, unknown in the civilized world, could possibly climb them. Of course, the voyageurs could not guarantee the truthfulness of these accounts for the simple reason that none of them had ever ventured as far west.

But the captains could not entirely ignore what the French-Canadians said, even if they had a tendency to exaggerate. In Upper Missouri, many Mandans and Hidatsas spoke of the Shining Mountains, which is what they called the Rockies, with equal respect and awe.

-Why Shining? had asked Captain Lewis to Seeing Snake, the Hidatsa war chief who had shown up at Fort Mandan with a map drawn on a buffalo skin.

–Because of the reflection of the sun on the white snow that caps the mountain peaks in both winter and summer, had answered Seeing Snake.

The Captains had been shaken by such a revelation. How high could these mountains be with their everlasting snow? Lewis and Clark were both born in Virginia and they only knew one mountain range, the Appalachians, which could easily be crossed through the Cumberland Gap, in Kentucky.

But how many days must one allow to go over the Rockies?

The two captains had already asked Larocque's question to Seeing Snake. His answer had amazed them:

–Four days.

–Four days!

–Yes, four days. The Flatheads and the Snakes know a path that goes between the highest mountains.

Even Toussaint Charbonneau, who translated the conversation, couldn't get over it. He had wondered if Seeing Snake, known for his craftiness, wasn't deceiving the Americans for reasons that escaped him.

Lewis finally answered Larocque's question.

–According to one of the chiefs of the Big Bellies, it's a four-day trek from the source of the Missouri to the source of the river that flows to the Pacific, the Columbia.

Larocque couldn't believe his ears either. His surprise only grew when he saw Captain Clark unrolling the map he had drawn from the information provided by Seeing Snake and the voyageurs, White and Indian, whom he had met since the beginning of the winter.

The map gave a detailed description of the territory situated between Fort Mandan and the Rockies. It indicated the source and the course of the Yellow Stone River; it showed the location of the Great Falls and the Three Forks on the Missouri, and also of most of the Indian nations of the West, Assiniboines, Crees, Black Feet, Sarsis, Crows, Comanches, Cheyenne, Kiowas, Shoshonis, Flatheads.

To think that Larocque had prompted Charbonneau to betray his employers' trust by asking him to reproduce the map from memory. And now, Captain Clark was granting him the privilege of seeing the original document, a map worthy of the best cartographers of the day. Any explorer would have given his right arm to obtain it.

Leaning over the map, Captain Clark pointed to the spot where he had drawn the Rockies.

–The Snakes and the Flatheads are often found in this region. Every year, they cross over the Shining Mountains –that's what the Indians call the Rockies –to go and fish in a very wide, slow-flowing river. We believe that it is a branch of the Columbia that will lead us to the Pacific.

Larocque was speechless. The captains treated him as if he were a member of the Corps of Discovery; they hid nothing from him, nor did they refuse him anything. On the corner of the table, Lewis had been working for hours at repairing his damaged compass. He had taken it apart, cleaned it and put it back together again. He had found a new needle pointing north and he only had to replace the broken glass. He had interrupted his work once to allow Clark to unroll his famous map in front of Larocque.

Noticing the Americans' kindness toward him, Larocque was feeling hopeful again.

–Will you have the time to explore the Yellow Stone? asked the young French-Canadian innocently, while examining the course of the river and making a mental note of it.

The Yellow Stone and the Missouri seemed to have the same source, in the Rocky Mountains, but each flowed in a separate direction: one headed straight east, the other dipped south before starting on a long ascent toward the north-east. The two rivers eventually joined up again about a hundred miles upstream from the Hidatsa villages.

–We might explore the Yellow Stone River on our way back, said Captain Lewis.

Larocque exclaimed:

–I can well see myself leading some of your men on such an adventure! Provided, of course, that you allow me to join your expedition.

With his hands joined in prayer, Larocque looked at the Captains imploringly.

–My dear Larocque, replied Captain Lewis with a smile, we like you, but you cannot accompany us. Didn't we tell you already?

A pitiful look came on the young man's face as he sighed.

–Yes, you did, he admitted, but those Shining Mountains are tempting indeed!

Clark and Lewis smiled again and nodded approvingly.

Chapter Seven

Charbonneau's Contract

Her head tilted back, her legs spread apart, Sacagawea clutched with both hands the buffalo skin that covered the big bed. She pushed with every muscle in her back and abdomen to deliver the sacred being.

–Haaa! she moaned in a hoarse voice.

But her efforts were in vain once more. No sooner did the head show than it would disappear again, pushed back by the distended tissues, close to tearing. The contractions had been coming for hours without enabling the baby's head to push through.

The young woman was too tired to maintain the crouching posture that Indian women took to give birth and had lain down on the bed. She had never suffered this much. Excruciating cramps would grip her whenever the labor started again and make her scream with terror. And yet, between each painful push, as she caught her breath and regained some strength, she managed to smile at Otter Woman who held her hand and encouraged her in a reassuring voice:

–You'll have a beautiful boy. Don't forget what your mother told you.

Sacagawea nodded in agreement. Her big day had come at last; she would be a mother, the noblest role for a Shoshoni woman.

The two women were alone in the interpreters' room. As soon as the contractions had started, Charbonneau and Jusseaume had fled so as not to bring bad luck to the child. Childbirth was not men's business on the Great Northern Plains. But this one was going to be different.

The father spent part of the day on the bank of the Missouri watching the comings and goings between the fort of the Americans and the other bank.

Captain Clark and a dozen men were coming back from a hunting trip, transporting on sleds the meat of the game they had killed. More than a ton! Not being shoed, the horses had been unable to cross the frozen river with their loads, just like Charbonneau's horses before Christmas.

On this eleventh day of February 1805, the weather was fine and cold; the wind was blowing from the north-west. "A good day to be born," thought Charbonneau as he lit his pipe.

At about noon, he saw Georges Drouillard walking toward him; he had taken part in the hunting expedition, having completely recovered from his pleurisy. Captain Clark had bled him, purged him and made him sweat. Finally, he had applied grease on his chest. The treatment had proven effective.

Drouillard handed Charbonneau a package in which he had put the entrails, fat and meat of a buffalo, everything that was needed to make some succulent *boudin blanc*. That winter, the half-breed had had the opportunity to taste for himself the famous recipe of the French-Canadian.

–It's for your wife, said Drouillard. I found out that she is in labor. It will help her regain her strength.

Charbonneau took the package.

–You're a true friend, he said, and then added:

–Looks like the hunt was good.

–Not bad, Drouillard answered him.

Eight days earlier, Clark and his men had gone hunting downstream from the villages. They had walked thirty miles on the ice and across wooded areas where they sank in the snow up to their knees. They had killed forty deer, three buffalo and sixteen moose, which they had stored in a small enclosure built to protect the meat from voracious wolves at night.

–I killed the three buffalo on top of about a dozen deer and moose, explained Drouillard.

This came as no surprise to Charbonneau. He knew of no better hunter than Drouillard. He certainly understood why Drouillard received twenty-five dollars a month, the best salary of all the members of the expedition, with the exception of Captains Lewis and Clark who, according to rumor, made forty dollars a month. As for the soldiers, they had to make do with five dollars a month.

Toussaint Charbonneau hoped to get as much as Drouillard, if not more, for he was convinced that he held the key to the expedition's success. Without the horses from the Shoshonis, which his wife had promised to secure, the Americans would not be able to cross over the Rockies, whatever Seeing Snake said.

Charbonneau offered his companion some tobacco; he lit his pipe. Drouillard had flair: he wore a red bandana, and his black hair hung down to his shoulders, framing a bony face in which sparkled fiery eyes. He dressed like a frontier man: fringed jacket, deerskin leggings, embroidered moccasins.

Drouillard was born in Sandwich, on the other side of Fort Detroit. His father, a French-Canadian from the St. Lawrence Valley, earned his living as a trapper, guide and interpreter. One day, he had disappeared without a trace. His mother, a Shawnee, settled with him south of St. Louis, on the banks of the Mississippi, with her own people. And so he had grown up among the Plains Indians, French-Canadian voyageurs, French and Spanish merchants, British and American soldiers, assimilating the languages and customs of all of them.

On November 11, 1803, Drouillard was at Fort Massac, on the Ohio River, when he had met Captain Lewis. The American was going down the river toward St. Louis aboard the keelboat that had just been built in Pittsburgh. All along the river, Lewis hired men for his expedition across the American continent, publishing job offers in the local papers. At Fort Massac, he had been persuaded by the administrator of the trading post, the American William Swan, to enlist the services of Drouillard as interpreter.

–He will be very useful to you, Swan had said. Not only does he speak Shawnee, which is close to Oto, but he also knows the sign language that all the Great Plains nations understand. He is also an excellent hunter.

Drouillard had shown himself to be a tough negotiator. On top of his monthly salary, he had gotten a thirty-dollar bonus out of Captain Lewis upon signing his contract. He had also managed to maintain his civilian status within the military expedition.

Fifteen months later, on the banks of the Missouri, Charbonneau said to him:

–My son will be a half-breed, just like you.

–How do you know it will be a boy?

–A dream my wife had.

The hunter nodded; he also believed in the significance of dreams.

At the end of January, a day after feasting on the wild berries pemmican, Sacagawea had announced to Charbonneau that he would have a son. Upon waking, she had told him:

–I had a dream.

She was lying in bed between Charbonneau and Otter Woman.

–Tell me your dream, had said Charbonneau.

On her left, Otter Woman was also listening attentively.

In her dream, Sacagawea had a big belly, but winter was over. Under the warm summer sun, she was strolling in a green, peaceful prairie. As she walked in the tall grass, she admired the beauty of nature and was one with all of creation, offering up a prayer to the butterfly who fluttered about her. She stroked her round belly, thanking the sacred being who had chosen her to come into this world, thereby sanctifying her life as a Shoshoni.

Her mother appeared out of the blue, floating above the grass. She didn't really recognize her features, but she was sure of her identity. It was really her mother, the woman who had raised her at the foot of the Rockies and whom she had not seen since Le Borgne's warriors had abducted her.

Her mother asked in a soft voice:

–Have you finished embroidering your child's moccasins?

–Yes, the daughter answered, Otter Woman has helped me.

–Have you used beads for the soles?

–Yes, Toussaint Charbonneau got me some.

The mother smiled; she seemed pleased with the answer.

–That's good. Now listen to me. You'll have a son. He will be as important as a chief, but he won't be one. He will travel to foreign lands and call on princes. But before that can happen, he must survive. It all depends on you. You must be strong.

And with these words, the mother disappeared.

Sacagawea had woken up with a smile on her lips. For the first time in days, she had not felt cramps in her stomach. Was it because of the pemmican or the dream?

–I'll have a son, she had said proudly to Charbonneau and Otter Woman. My mother told me so in my dream as she floated above the tall grass.

–I'm happy for you! Otter Woman had exclaimed.

–We shall name him Jean-Baptiste, Toussaint had declared. It's my father's name.

Charbonneau and Otter Woman had no reason to doubt the meaning of Sacagawea's story. In the Great Northern Plains, dreams were considered prophetic. However, Sacagawea had kept to herself the rest of the vision about her unborn child visiting countries she did not know.

When would this boy finally be born? Late in the afternoon, Captain Lewis walked resolutely to the interpreters' room, anxious to get an answer. He knew that Sacagawea's labor had started at the first light of dawn. It was nine hours later, and Lewis still had no news. He was beginning to worry.

When they saw the Captain approaching, Charbonneau and Jusseaume, who were smoking their pipes in the yard, tried to stand in his way.

–You can't go into the room; it's bad luck! said Charbonneau, blocking his path.

Lewis stopped, looked scornfully at him, then turned to Jusseaume and asked in English:

–What is he saying?

–He says that you can't go into the room. Men are not supposed to be present at childbirth. It brings bad luck.

Lewis ordered Charbonneau to step aside and knocked on the door. There was no answer. He knocked again. Still no answer.

Suddenly, the shriek of a woman in agony rang out. Lewis didn't wait one more second. He opened the door and went in. He found Sacagawea lying on a buffalo skin; in the half-light, he made out the young face bathed in sweat and tears. The Shoshoni girl was sobbing after yet another futile effort.

Otter Woman was kneeling before her companion; she turned to the Captain; he looked at her inquiringly. She shrugged her shoulders as a sign of helplessness. Then she pointed to the herbs she had used in the hope of hastening the delivery. It had obviously been without success.

Lewis made a gesture to indicate that he would be back. Outside, Charbonneau and Jusseaume were still smoking in the yard.

–What's going on? asked Charbonneau.

–It's a difficult birth, very painful, replied Lewis. It's to be expected with a first delivery.

Lewis started toward the captains' room. Jusseaume gestured to stop him and spoke from his experience as a father:

–In that case, the mother must swallow a piece of a snake's rattle. To speed up the delivery, there is nothing better.

–I happen to have some, said Lewis running to his room.

A few moments later, he came back with a black leather case. Leaving Charbonneau and Jusseaume outside, he returned to Sacagawea's bedside. She seemed completely worn out. In Captain Lewis, she saw her last hope, the White man's medicine that would put an end to her suffering.

The Captain pulled out of his case two fragments of the tail of a rattlesnake, which he crushed to tiny pieces in a spoon. He added a little water and gently made Sacagawea swallow the medicine. She closed her eyes.

Lewis left the room soon after and glanced at his watch without thinking. It was four o'clock in the afternoon. A few minutes later, Sacagawea gave birth to a beautiful child.

Did the rattlesnake fragments really bring on the delivery? That night, before going to bed, Meriwether Lewis asked himself that question. He wrote in his journal: "Whether this medicine was truly the cause or not I shall not undertake to determine, but I was informed that she had not taken it more than ten minutes before she had brought forth."

In the evening, Sacagawea treated herself to some of the delicious white sausage cooked by Charbonneau. Otter Woman also ate, chuckling with pleasure, all the while looking languorously at Toussaint who had come to sit next to his women. He was in a highly emotional state, feeling a mixture of happiness, pride and apprehension. His world had just been turned upside down. That little animal, snuggled up to the young Indian woman looking so drawn, was his son, Jean-Baptiste. Early on, Toussaint had severed all family ties, and later had been careful not to create new ones. These two women, and now, this child...

–This is good, said Otter Woman, curling up in Charbonneau's arms.

A flight of ducks, the first of the season, soared over the Missouri River, which was swollen by the rise in the water level resulting from the spring thaw and the breaking up of the ice. A strong current was sweeping along chunks of ice that knocked together with a noise of shattered glass. In a few days, swans and wild geese would fly over Upper Missouri on their way to the Great North.

"Winter is over," thought Toussaint Charbonneau. With his head high and his chest thrown out, he was walking along the river, a few steps ahead of his women and son who was one-month-old. Jean-Baptiste was comfortably settled in a baby-carrier lavishly decorated with porcupine quills.

The riverbank was bustling with activity. In front of Fort Mandan, some men were busy repairing the hull of the keelboat, which was slightly damaged. The day before, using a winch and a rope made of moose skin, they had finally succeeded in freeing the boat from the ice. Just a few hours later, the ice had started breaking.

A little further on the bank, another group of men were carving pirogues out of poplar trunks with their axes. The Corps of Discovery would attempt to reach the Pacific on such small boats, most of which were built by the French-Canadians who were experts in the craft.

As an experienced waterman, Pierre Cruzatte had been put in charge of the repairs; as planned, the keelboat would return to St. Louis without him, but loaded with a scientific and literary treasure. When he saw Charbonneau walking by with his family, Cruzatte cried out:

–How is the new father doing?

–Couldn't be better, replied Charbonneau, waving to the fiddler. And that goes for the mother and little one as well.

Many Mandans from Mitutanka and Ruptare had come to Fort Mandan to see the preparations for the journey. They were particularly interested in the building of the canoes, a type of transportation with which they were not familiar. To cross the river in the summer, they used small skiffs that consisted of a frame of willow branches covered with the skin of an adult male buffalo. The tail of the animal was used as towrope. The rest of the time, they traveled on foot or horseback.

Some Mandans were admiring a group of young braves involved in a most dangerous exercise. Charbonneau and his wives joined the spectators. These extremely agile young men were jumping from one block of ice to the other in order to catch the dead buffalo floating downstream. They used long poles to push the bodies ashore. Sometimes, they stepped on chunks of ice that were no more than four square feet. Each spring, some braves drowned while practicing this activity. They were carried off by the current with the animal carcasses that gave off a putrid smell.

The Mandans nevertheless considered it well worth the risk. With the rotten buffalo meat, they cooked a greenish soup they loved. One day, Charbonneau, having finally overcome his disgust, tasted some and had to admit that the soup was indeed delicious.

On the horizon, a cloud of smoke filled the sky. The Hidatsas had set fire to the prairie near the Knife River. This way, they hastened the new growth of grass so as to feed their horses and encourage the buffalo to return.

Charbonneau was about to resume his walk when he saw René Jusseaume running towards him. Not even pausing to catch his breath, the interpreter had cried out excitedly:

–Le Borgne has just arrived at the fort! The captains sent me to get you. Come on!

Charbonneau's face lit up.

–Did he bring the madwoman's daughter?

–Yes, replied Jusseaume. She is such a beauty!

Charbonneau headed back to the fort, taking his family and Jusseaume with him. This visit by Le Borgne delighted him; it would allow him to do a little self-promotion. On the eve of negotiating his contract with the Americans, the French-Canadian was looking for opportunities to make himself useful. This visit was exactly what he needed.

He found Le Borgne and his entourage in the interior court of the fort. Seeing their old master made Sacagawea and Otter Woman sick to their stomachs; they turned on their heels and took refuge in the interpreters' room. If he had recognized his former slaves, the Hidatsa chief didn't let on. He greeted Charbonneau with a nod.

Le Borgne was as imposing as ever. He wore a huge headdress of crow's feathers; in one hand, he held a long spear decorated with scalps, and a war shield in the other. The rest of his attire did not fail to amaze his American hosts: the greatest of the Hidatsa chiefs had on a long red frock coat, part of the uniform of British army officers.

Captain Lewis had a burst of anger on seeing Le Borgne in such a costume. Since the arrival of the Americans in Upper Missouri, the Hidatsa chief had refused to either visit or receive them. And, lo and behold, on the eve of the expedition's departure, he showed up at Fort Mandan, partially dressed like a damned Englishman!

Lewis managed to control himself. Before leaving, he was eager to set out his "Great Indian Plan" to the Hidatsa chief. He believed that he had convinced the Mandans and the Arikaras to make peace with each other and to trade with American merchants, but this nice plan was worthless without the collaboration of Le Borgne whose influence extended from the Arikara villages to the foot of the Rockies.

Captains Lewis and Clark received the Hidatsa chief with as much pomp as possible. They had two cannon shots fired in his honor and showed him around all the interesting sights of the fort, including the forge where Privates John Shields and William Bratton barely managed to keep up with demand. In front of the door, several Mandans were lining up with baskets of corn at their feet.

–What are those people doing in the fire? asked Le Borgne, pointing to the blacksmiths.

–They are making tomahawks, answered Charbonneau in Hidatsa.

–How much is a tomahawk?

–Seven baskets of corn for one tomahawk.

A snarl made the Hidatsa chief's monstrous face look even uglier; he fixed the gaze of his one eye on the captains.

Ill at ease, Lewis and Clark led the chief back to the center of the yard where Sergeant John Ordway had gathered some presents. The captains offered the Cyclops an American flag, a medal bearing the effigy of President Thomas Jefferson, a shirt, bracelets and other jewelry.

Le Borgne picked up one of the bracelets and tied it around the wrist of the one woman in his entourage. It was the madwoman's daughter, the Hidatsa girl whom the cruel chief had taken from one of his warriors. The captains came to the same conclusion as Charbonneau and Larocque: this young woman was indeed gorgeous; she had long, silky hair, a face like an angel and a perfect figure. She was an Indian queen, what all voyageurs dreamt about.

After the presentation of the gifts, Captain Lewis tried to set out his famous plan to the great warrior chief.

–We would like to discuss with you the advantages of peace among the Indian nations and of commerce with the Americans, declared President Jefferson's envoy to the Great Northern Plains.

Charbonneau translated the Captain's words, but Le Borgne acted as if he hadn't heard anything. He said to the captains:

–Some young men of my nation, no doubt a little naive, have told me that there is among you a man who is all black. Is it true?

The captains were surprised by the question, but they hastened to satisfy Le Borgne's curiosity, thinking that they had found a way to impress him at last.

–Go and fetch York, ordered Clark to Sergeant Ordway.

A few moments later, Ordway came back with York. Le Borgne could not hide his amazement. He closely examined Clark's servant, spat on his finger and rubbed the black skin to try and wash out what he believed to be paint. York winced.

–Take your hat off, ordered Clark.

York obeyed.

–Touch his hair, and you'll see that it's not a White man painted black, said Clark.

Le Borgne touched York's short, frizzy hair.

–You're right, he declared to Clark through Charbonneau. This man is all black.

Seeing that his visitor had been duly impressed, Lewis tried once more to talk diplomacy.

–As I was saying, the advantages of peace and commerce are many...

Charbonneau translated the introduction, but Le Borgne did not allow Lewis to continue. He had suddenly regained all his arrogance.

–You're two-faced, he said. While you speak of peace to the Hidatsas, your men are making tomahawks in the fire for the Mandans.

Charbonneau went pale. Le Borgne continued, making a face at the captains, which he meant as a smile:

–Strangers, don't waste your time in idle discussions, but rather make the most of my hospitality. I have come with the greatest beauty of my nation. I'm offering her to you for the evening.

Charbonneau was beginning to sweat. He thought it his duty to translate every single one of the chief's words. When he heard himself called "two-faced," Captain Lewis had to hold back his anger once more. He made an effort to conclude the meeting without insulting Le Borgne. In the end, however, he could not contain himself.

–We are truly touched by your hospitality, he said, but we must decline your offer. It's a question of dignity for us, you wouldn't understand. As far as our proposal is concerned, perhaps you will feel better disposed toward us when we come back from the Pacific. Mr. Charbonneau, whom you see here, would be ready to accompany you to the capital of the United States so that you can see for yourself how unquestionably great our country is.

He turned to the French-Canadian and added:

–Isn't that so, Mr. Charbonneau?

The interpreter nodded his assent. With Jusseaume's help, he translated Lewis' last words, barely hiding his disappointment. Le Borgne would never agree to go to Washington and bow before the President of the American people. Charbonneau had wished to make himself useful. All he had probably succeeded in doing was to set Lewis against him by translating the chief's insults.

–What? You're back already? called out Charbonneau when he saw the young clerk from the Northwest Company.

–Yes, I've arrived this afternoon with new merchandise, replied François-Antoine Larocque with a smile. I've left Mr. McKenzie and the others in Ruptare.

They shook hands heartily. Charbonneau was quite fond of this young man who was so anxious to become an explorer. And Larocque in turn respected Charbonneau, the only White man who lived among the Big Bellies, Le Borgne's friend, husband to two women and lover to many more.

Charbonneau greeted the captains, then, turning to Larocque, he asked for the latest news:

–How is our good old master on the Assiniboine River? As big a thief as ever?

–Mr. Chaboillez is doing very well, answered the clerk. He always treats me kindly and generously. As a matter of fact, he just officially entrusted me with the mission of exploring the Yellow Stone River on behalf of the Northwest Company.

–When are you leaving? asked Charbonneau.

–In June, replied Larocque, beaming with excitement.

–You'll discover the source of the Yellow Stone before the Americans.

–I certainly hope so!

Captains Lewis and Clark left the two French-Canadians alone for a while in order to resume their work, interrupted a few hours earlier by Larocque's arrival.

They had a lot to do in these last days at Fort Mandan: finish writing a document entitled *Estimate of the Eastern Indians*, a descriptive study of the nations they had met, since the beginning of the exploration, from St. Louis to Fort Mandan; classify the plants, skins, skeletons and various objects collected among the Indians –painted buffalo skins, peace pipes, bows, arrows, quivers, pots, etc.; put everything in crates, chests and even cages. Indeed, the keelboat would carry back some live animals.

Charbonneau pulled up a chair and lit his pipe. Larocque relit his. They soon disappeared behind curls of blue smoke.

–There is big news from Montreal, started the young clerk as he puffed on his pipe.

Montreal. It had been a long time since Charbonneau had heard the name of the city where he had worked for six years before starting on the road to the West. Montreal... That was almost twenty years ago.

–Is that so? said Charbonneau, pretending to be interested.

–Yes, and he added solemnly: Simon McTavish is dead.

–Simon who?

–Come now! Simon McTavish, the head of the Northwest Company! Now that the old vulture is gone, Alexander Mackenzie will finally be able to take his rightful place at the head of the company. I'm telling you, this marks the beginning of a new period of exploration.

Charbonneau shrugged his shoulders. He didn't share at all Larocque's interest for the power struggles within the Northwest Company. He lived his life as he pleased, miles away from the St. Gabriel street building that housed the offices of the financiers of the fur empire. His only concern was his next journey to the West.

–Well, I'll be damned! exclaimed Charbonneau admiringly after Larocque had finished telling him about his trek on snowshoes from Upper Missouri to the Assiniboine River.

His admiration was mixed with joy. The young man's presence was just what he needed because the trader was looking for an interpreter to negotiate his contract with the Americans. He had hoped to find Drouillard or Labiche in the captains' room, but Larocque would serve his purpose even better, for the Americans seemed to hold him in high esteem.

Seeing Clark writing at his table, Charbonneau thought it both useful and pertinent to tell him a good story about Le Borgne. With his anecdote, he hoped to win the Captain to his side before starting the negotiations. Since the beginning of the winter, Charbonneau had learned to know and appreciate the red-haired American, whom he found less haughty and distant than Captain Lewis. In the past few months, the trader had passed on to Clark an important part of his knowledge on the practices and customs of the Big Bellies. And he was about to add to it with another story.

Before starting, he winked at Larocque, who had willingly accepted to act as his interpreter.

–Captain Clark, said Larocque, Mr. Charbonneau would like to tell you a story. It's about Le Borgne.

Clark put down his quill and smiled. He liked Charbonneau's stories. He had saved some for posterity by transcribing them almost word for word in his journal.

–I'm listening he said, crossing his arms.

The storyteller began, using the present for the past.

–Some time ago, one of Le Borgne's wives decides to leave him and follow her lover. Almost immediately, the lover abandons her and she is forced to return to her father's house. As soon as he learns about it, Le Borgne rushes to his father-in-law's.

Charbonneau paused to relight his pipe and give Larocque the time to translate the beginning of the story. When the interpreter had finished, he continued.

–Le Borgne sits by the fire and starts smoking with his father-in-law. He completely ignores his wife, who is sitting in a corner.

Meanwhile, the village elders arrive to try and calm the chief. Le Borgne quietly goes on smoking as if nothing were wrong. When the time comes to leave, he grabs his wife by the hair, drags her to the door, and with one swing of his tomahawk kills her under her father's eyes.

As he spoke, Charbonneau sliced through the air with his arm.

Captain Lewis had also stopped working to listen to Charbonneau's story. His face twisted with horror as he heard the English translation of the woman's death. However, Charbonneau had not finished.

–After having killed his wife, Le Borgne turns to those who are present and says: "If one of her relatives wants to avenge her death, he will always find me at home." The poor woman's fate did not arouse a desire for revenge in any member of her family.

–That man is a monster! exclaimed Lewis, his face contorted with disgust.

–Not always, replied Charbonneau.

–What do you mean? inquired Clark.

Charbonneau winked again at Larocque, then asked Clark:

–With your permission, I would like to tell you another story.

Clark nodded his assent, as did Lewis, who stopped to listen.

–This takes place shortly after the incident I have just related. Another one of Le Borgne's wives flees with a young man. But the lovebird can't afford to support her in the style she wishes. The woman decides to go back to the village and beg for her husband's forgiveness. The chief sends for her lover. The poor man arrives in the village, certain that he will die. Le Borgne, however, has a surprise in store for the lovers. He asks them if they are still in love. They reply that only poverty has forced them to part. Instead of getting angry, the chief gives the woman to the man she loves, together with three horses.

–Maybe he was seeking to be forgiven for his cruelty toward the other wife, commented Captain Clark.

–Maybe, said Charbonneau.

–How about a glass of brandy, gentlemen, interrupted Clark, who had been somewhat shaken by Charbonneau's stories.

–With pleasure! said Charbonneau.

He did not drink as a rule, but he accepted the brandy the American Captain offered him. On the other hand, Lewis, who liked alcohol, was only too glad to join in. The trader gulped down a big swig; the drink went to his head and dispelled any remaining doubts about his negotiating strategy: he would show himself firm and uncompromising. The captains could not refuse his demands, since the success of the expedition depended on him. At any rate, Clark would surely side with him.

Through Larocque, he made it known to the captains that he wished to settle the matter of his contract. They acquiesced to his request.

–I am willing to accompany you with my wife as far as the Pacific, but I have certain conditions.

Captain Lewis raised an eyebrow.

–What conditions?

–First of all, I want the same salary as Drouillard. Second, I will not work, whatever your situation may be, nor mount guard. Those are tasks for *mangeurs de lard*. I also want to be able to leave whenever I wish, with as many supplies as I can carry.

When he heard Larocque's translation, Captain Lewis was astonished by Charbonneau's nerve.

–Who do you think you are? he cried out. There's no question of us accepting your conditions! Now, you listen to me: you'll get the same salary as Drouillard, twenty-five dollars a month, and you will work, and mount guard as any other member of the expedition. You'll be paid at the end of the trip; should you leave us in the middle of the expedition, you can forget about your money. As for the supplies, the answer is no.

Charbonneau wasn't at all surprised by Lewis' reaction. He had suspected that the Captain would protest. He laid down his trump card looking Clark straight in the eye.

–If you refuse to treat me as a free man, I will simply stay here with my wife, but I can assure you that you won't be able to get any horses without her. Old Ménard lost everything trying to cross over the Rockies. Don't think for a minute that the Indians over there have something better in store for you.

Larocque translated Charbonneau's ultimatum. A heavy silence fell on the captains' room. Lewis and Clark exchanged glances. Clark was shaken by Charbonneau's warning. He had to admit that the presence of his wife was crucial to the success of the expedition, and not only on account of the horses from her tribe. With her baby on her back, Sacagawea was also a powerful symbol of peace so dear to the Americans.

Clark saw Lewis' gaze hardening. He understood that his colleague would never accept Charbonneau's conditions. A military man, born in Virginia, close to the President of the United States, could not give in to the whims of a French-Canadian who lived in sin among the Indians of the West. A fine representative of the Catholic religion indeed, this Charbonneau!

Clark turned to the interpreter:

–Your demands are inadmissible. If you do not accept our conditions, we shall leave without you and your wife.

Larocque was furious with Charbonneau. He intervened, speaking directly to his countryman:

–You are making a serious mistake, Sir. You're not dealing with ordinary trappers back home. Captains Lewis and Clark are heading an expedition sponsored by the President of the United States. You have the chance to participate in an adventure about which books will be written; you will be part of the legend of the West.

Charbonneau wasn't listening. Nothing would make him back down.

–I'm a free man, not a *mangeur de lard*, he repeated.

Pointing to the door, Captain Lewis said to Charbonneau:

–In that case, we'll ask you to gather your belongings and leave the fort immediately with your squaws.

Charbonneau left without a word. He was in a foul mood and, when he got to his quarters, he kicked the door and stormed into the room.

Sitting on a buffalo skin, Sacagawea was breast-feeding her baby by the fire. Next to her, Otter Woman was sewing moccasins for the journey she would not go on herself, to her great regret.

–Pack our stuff, we're leaving! shouted Charbonneau. And don't forget the tepee!

Dumbfounded, the two women looked at each other. They didn't make a move: Charbonneau's face was flushed with rage and alcohol; his anger filled them with fear. He started pacing the room back and forth, hitting the palm of his hand with his fist repeatedly.

In the hope that the same hand would not come down on her, Otter Woman asked a question in her sweetest voice.

–Why are we leaving?

–Because I say so, Charbonneau uttered curtly, stopping right in front of her.

He eyed her scornfully and his fist came crashing down once more in the palm of his hand. Gathering her wits about her, Sacagawea spoke up just in time to avoid a confrontation.

–Did the Americans treat you disrespectfully?

The French-Canadian looked at her; he saw his son greedily sucking at his mother's breast. The little one was already sturdy; on his head, he had a tuft of black hair. The scene had a calming effect on the father.

–The Americans don't know what they're doing, he said, sitting at the foot of the bed; all of a sudden, he looked demoralized. They think they can cross over the Rockies without us.

An alarm went off in Sacagawea's head. Her dream! In a worried tone, she asked Charbonneau:

–Does this mean that we won't be going to the great salted lake?

–We are staying here, answered Charbonneau.

Then, standing up, he added:

–All right, that's enough, start packing!

With a heavy heart, Sacagawea got up and settled Jean-Baptiste on her back. She packed with the help of Otter Woman, all the while refusing to believe that one of her most cherished dreams was falling apart, the dream of treading upon her native soil once more. Her other dream had come true already when the sacred being had sprung from her loins, laughing and full of life.

While the women packed the family's belongings, Toussaint Charbonneau smoked his pipe and brooded.

The women pitched the tepee only three hundred feet from Fort Mandan, under a poplar tree whose resinous buds were beginning to spread their sweet scent. Sacagawea was glad that they had not gone too far from the Americans. When everything was ready, Charbonneau went inside and lay down on a buffalo skin. Despite the cool night air, he stayed away from the fire and his women.

He was mostly annoyed at himself for having accepted the drink the Captain had offered him. He remembered Jean-Baptiste Perrault, his first boss in the fur trade. Hadn't he told him to beware of alcohol? He should have remained sober and used cunning instead of behaving like a cocky fool. Now, he was without a job, and with a severe headache to boot!

He gazed at the skins of the tepee; they had been tanned, treated and assembled by his women. The buffalo robes were sewn together with cords and pulled tight over nine big poles. The Shoshoni women had done a good job. He could easily have traveled with this light tent and have been very comfortable during the entire expedition with the Americans.

–Damn! he grumbled, still angry with himself.

He was also sorry to have to part with Clark, by far the most pleasant of the Americans. The Captain had been the first to congratulate him when Jean-Baptiste was born. At any time of the day, he would drop in to see how child, mother and father were doing. Charbonneau thought of Clark as a friend, but he could not go back and reduce his conditions without losing face.

–Maudite sainte Anne!

Sacagawea got up and placed the child on her back; after exchanging a few words with Otter Woman in Shoshoni, she went out. The full moon shone over the silent plain and its silver light shimmered on the river. The young woman walked around Fort Mandan, breathing in the smells of spring. What could she do? How could she convince Charbonneau to change his mind? As she reflected on these questions, she was overcome by dizziness, as if the ground suddenly gave way beneath her.

She was so looking forward to leaving with the expedition! To see the Three Forks, where she had learned to swim like a fish with her sisters... To breath once more the air of the plateaus filled with the scent of artemisias... To be reunited, at the foot of the Shining Mountains, with members of her family. Which ones, she wondered... Only the Great Spirit knew how many had escaped the cruelty of Le Borgne and his warriors.

"I shall lie," Sacagawea said to herself as she passed before the two soldiers on guard duty at the fort's entrance. "Yes, I shall invent a dream."

Determined to act, she went back to the tepee. With her back to the fire, Otter Woman was riding Charbonneau who held her by the waist with both hands. She drained him of all his aggressiveness, which took most of the night.

At daybreak, Sacagawea got up and sat down cross-legged next to Charbonneau. She waited for him to wake up as she breast-fed her baby.

She peered into his face, thinking of the decision she had made the night before. Was she really about to lie to him? This White man who slept before her was endowed with great medicine, no one doubted it in Upper Missouri. He attracted the buffalo to the plain, including the white-coated females. He made love to Indian women without ever getting tired. Sacagawea wanted to believe that his reputation would spread far and wide, throughout time and space, as far as that of her son.

Charbonneau opened his eyes. He saw Sacagawea sitting in front of him, their child in her arms. The young Shoshoni woman stared at him with her big black eyes.

–I had a dream, she said.

–Another one? remarked Charbonneau in a fuzzy voice.

He rolled over on his side, turning his back to Sacagawea as if he had no interest in the matter. He thus found himself facing Otter Woman, who looked hard at him, amazed that he paid no attention to something as important as a dream. He closed his eyes and rolled over on his back again with a sigh.

–Tell me...

–You will see the great salted lake, started Sacagawea, putting on an inspired look. Thanks to the expedition of the Americans, people will still know your name in seven generations. I saw that in my dream. Your son will also be part of the legend. When he grows up, he will visit foreign lands and meet chiefs who wear silver crowns. We must leave with the Americans; it's our destiny.

Charbonneau remained silent. He was not naive; he suspected that Sacagawea would use every means to persuade him to leave with the expedition. When she had learned that she would take part in it, she had started to sing songs from her native country. She had kept on singing even during the most difficult times of her pregnancy. There was something suspicious about her "dream."

But Sacagawea was not the first to tell him about his "legend." The day before, in the captains' room, Larocque had spoken the same word. He had told him that, if he accompanied the captains, he would be part of the legend of the West. Wasn't the young man mistaking his own dreams of glory for what he believed to be the destiny of his fellow countryman?

After a moment, Charbonneau opened his eyes again. His head was burning and he winced as he finally said:

–It's not in my destiny to be treated like a *mangeur de lard* by the Americans.

Sacagawea lowered her eyes, but kept hoping.

The month of March was drawing to a close. Preparations for the journey were practically finished; all the boats were ready, the keelboat as well as eight canoes and two pirogues. Captains Lewis and Clark were only waiting for the river to be totally free of ice to give the signal for departure.

Spirits were high among the members of the expedition. Every evening, in the fort's yard, Pierre Cruzatte took out his fiddle and had the men dancing to his tunes. They didn't need alcohol to have a good time. They had enjoyed the last five months among the Mandans, a friendly nation, but they couldn't wait to start off again.

Their health, however, was not as good as their morale. A short time before the departure, several men had to be treated for venereal diseases. Captain Lewis gave them mercury, a very effective remedy against syphilis.

The tepee still stood under the poplar tree. Toussaint Charbonneau just couldn't bring himself to break camp. He would hang around the fort, watching the soldiers at work, talking to the engagés, weighing the pros and cons of the expedition.

At night, under the tent, he would hear the sound of the fiddle and the shouts coming from the fort. Having spent the winter with the members of the expedition, he shared in their excitement as the day of their departure drew near. He would undoubtedly keep his honor intact by staying in Upper Missouri, but he would miss something by not leaving with them, of that he was sure. He would waste the opportunity to go where no man of his race had gone before and to be a credit to the reputation of French-Canadian voyageurs.

When he woke up, on the next to last day of March, he observed Sacagawea and Jean-Baptiste. What if she were telling the truth and he were to become a legendary hero by joining Lewis and Clark on their journey west? To see the Shining Mountains, the expanse of salted water stretching out endlessly in the distance... The Great Plains and the forests of the North held no more secrets for him. What if his wife were telling the truth about her dream?

That morning, he went out early and positioned himself at the entrance of Fort Mandan. Since the evening of the negotiations, he had not set foot inside the fort, nor spoken to the captains.

After a while, Georges Drouillard appeared; he was on his way to inspect his beaver traps.

–Drouillard! Listen, could you do me a favor?

–You've changed your mind! exclaimed Drouillard, without waiting for him to finish speaking. I knew it. You're leaving with us!

–Yes, I'd like to, replied Charbonneau.

And he added, looking Drouillard straight in the eye:

–Go and tell the captains that I was naive, that I spoke like an idiot. I will come along with my wife... on their conditions.

–Wait here!

The hunter set off like a shot and quickly came back triumphantly.

–They agreed! he announced. Captain Clark wants to know if you can bring your tepee. They will reimburse you for it at the end of the trip.

–If I can sleep with my wife and child in my tepee, it’s o.k. with me, answered Charbonneau.

–But of course! and Drouillard burst out laughing. You and your wife can sleep in your tepee!

Part Two

To the Pacific

Chapter Eight

The Great Journey

On April 7, 1805, the men spent most of the day loading the keelboat. On the bank of the Missouri, not far from Fort Mandan, there were enough goods to fill a museum of Natural History: twenty-five crates and cages for the zoological stock, fifteen packed with sixty-seven samples of soil, minerals, salts, and as many boxes or barrels filled with plant specimens. In addition, there were two stuffed antelopes, a male and a female, and their bones; three ground squirrels, a male badger and a female, a white weasel, the skeleton of a prairie wolf, that of a white and gray hare, two moose antlers, those of a black-tailed stag together with its tail, and an assortment of skins. Seven boxes contained articles made by the Indians, such as clothes, like a magnificent buffalo robe on which was painted a famous battle that had pitted the Sioux and the Arikaras against the Mandans and the Hidatsas. Three cages housed the living specimens: a prairie hen, a swift fox and four magpies whose existence in North America was still unknown to science.

All that constituted the treasure collected by Lewis and Clark since they had left St. Louis, eleven months before. Even more precious, the documents relating to the expedition, including astronomical and meteorological charts, maps and Clark's journal, completed the load. The red-haired Captain was deeply embarrassed at the thought that the President of the United States would read his journal. Lewis was a much better writer, but he had spent the winter compiling most of the records on the Indians, leaving his friend to keep a daily journal. In a letter that came with the documents, Lewis warned the President: "You will also receive herewith enclosed a part of Capt. Clark's private journal, the other part you will find inclosed in a separate tin box. This journal is in it's original state, and of course incorrect, but it will serve to give you the daily detales of our progress, and transactions. Capt. Clark does not wish this journal exposed in it's present state, but has no objection, that one or more copies of it be made by some confidential person under your direction" and submitted "to the perusal of heads of departments, or such others as you may think proper."

The captains had entrusted to Richard Warfington the responsibility of taking the keelboat and its crew to St. Louis. Warfington had to ensure that the cargo reached President Jefferson promptly.

The pilot of the boat was Joseph Gravelines, an excellent sailor and interpreter whom they had met the preceding October among the Arikaras. He would go down the Missouri as far as St. Louis, making stops in the Arikara villages to take on board some chiefs of these neighbors of the Mandans. Later, as had been agreed with Captain Lewis, he would accompany the chiefs to Washington and there would translate for them to the American president.

–We want the Arikara chiefs to become agents for American policies in the Great Plains, Lewis had reminded Gravelines.

Six American soldiers and a French-Canadian *engagé,* Jean-Baptiste Deschamps, completed the crew. Deschamps was anxious to rejoin his wife in St. Charles, at the mouth of the Missouri. Étienne Malboeuf and Charles Hébert, respectively from Lac-au-Sable, in the Charlevoix region, and Ste. Genevieve, in the Mississippi valley, would follow the keelboat in a canoe.

At four o'clock in the afternoon, Meriwether Lewis gave the signal for departure. As they lowered their paddles into the water, Malboeuf and Hébert started to sing as one voice that could be heard on both banks of the river where Mandans and Hidatsas had gathered:

V'là l'bon vent, v'là l'joli vent
V'là l'bon vent ma mie m'appelle
V'là l'bon vent, v'là l'joli vent
V'là l'bon vent ma mie m'attend.[26]

The keelboat could still be seen when William Clark started in the opposite direction with the members of the Corps of Discovery, split up into six small canoes and two large pirogues filled to capacity with supplies. From the banks, the local people waved to the explorers.

Aboard one of the pirogues, Toussaint Charbonneau and Sacagawea looked back many times at the figure of Otter Woman gradually disappearing in the distance. Charbonneau wondered whether the Shoshoni woman would still be there on his return from the Pacific. The day before, he had asked her to take care of his horses while he was gone, and of his hut in Metaharta, the small Hidatsa village on the Knife River. But it was physically impossible for him to prevent her from leaving, unless he sold her or loaned her to a chief or a warrior, which he couldn't bring himself to do. One thing was certain, he would miss her liveliness, especially her sexual drive. He had never met, in all of Indian country, a woman with such a one-track mind. And God only knows that this was not a country of prudes!

With her eyes riveted on the shore, Sacagawea could not hold back her tears. In the days just before their departure, she had begged Charbonneau to try and persuade the captains to make room for Otter Woman in the expedition. Charbonneau had rebuffed her curtly:

–If the captains had wanted another Shoshoni woman, they would have said so. Count yourself lucky to have been chosen!

Sacagawea was losing a sister, her constant companion since Le Borgne had abducted them, four years before. And for the first time, she found herself alone with Charbonneau, without her close friend, the one who could curb the trader's zeal and soothe his anger even better than she. What would become of her relationship to the French-Canadian without her fellow Shoshoni?

Otter Woman was too sad to divulge her plans to either Charbonneau or Sacagawea. If she decided to stay in Metaharta, she could, not only look after Charbonneau's interests, but also do some trading of her own; that appealed to her since the fur trade business and beaver trapping held no secrets for her.

On the other hand, she could take a horse and quietly go back to her native country. In that case, she would have to hide from Charbonneau. He had warned her:

–If you follow us and I see you on one of my horses, I'll take it away from you. You'll have to continue on foot; we'll see how you cope with bears.

Charbonneau could not tolerate Otter Woman asserting her independence in front of the members of the expedition.

The woman's silhouette vanished on the horizon. The other French-Canadians in the expedition also started singing the same song as their fellow countrymen traveling to St. Louis. Charbonneau turned his back on Fort Mandan and joined in:

Derrière chez nous, y a-t-un étang
Derrière chez nous, y a-t-un étang
Trois beaux canards s'en vont baignant

V'là le bon vent, v'là l'joli vent...[27]

On his mother's back, Jean-Baptiste Charbonneau started wiggling and laughing when he heard the tune punctuated by the splash of the paddles hitting the water.

The expedition included thirty-seven members: two captains, four sergeants, twenty-five privates, among whom were Pierre Cruzatte, Francis Labiche and Baptiste Lepage; five civilians –Charbonneau, Sacagawea, their son, Georges Drouillard and York –and a Newfoundland named Seaman.

Captain Clark had boarded one of the big pirogues with the civilians and one soldier. With his head held high, he watched the Indians assembled on both banks of the river. He was two thousand miles from St. Louis, the city that marked the boundary of the world of Whites, and more than two thousand miles from the Pacific, where the continent ended. He was about to enter a vast territory where no American had gone before. He would have to cross over the Rockies, brave the elements and wild animals, deal with unknown, possibly warlike, nations. As all other Americans in the expedition, he felt great pride in having the opportunity to take up such a challenge.

He wished to share that feeling with those who traveled with him in the pirogue; Drouillard, a skilled boatman, was at the helm, and he had hoisted one of the sails to take advantage of a good rear wind.

–I hope you'll never forget this day, said Clark to his companions, a French-Canadian, a Shoshoni woman, three half-breeds and a slave with African roots.

His voice was vibrant with emotion as he added:

–Never before has the White man taken this route. Never has a civilized nation been involved in such an exploration.

When he heard the translation of the Captain's words, Charbonneau nearly choked. He had told Clark about old Ménard, who had traveled along the same route to go to the Rockies where the Crows had stolen his fur bundles and his horses. Had the American already forgotten?

Charbonneau had an urge to jog his memory, and also to mention the name of the La Vérendrye brothers who had reached the Rockies region more than half a century before old Ménard. François-Antoine Larocque had often spoken of this family of explorers from Three-Rivers, who had been commissioned by France to reach the Western sea. Didn't it count for the Americans?

He finally decided to nod as if he agreed with Captain Clark's assertion. He didn't even deem it useful to talk of his own hunting expeditions west of the Knife River.

From the riverbank, Meriwether Lewis observed the departure of the canoes and pirogues; he was also overcome with intense emotion as he saw the men paddle in perfect rhythm on the waters of the Missouri. He couldn't have wished for keener spirits or greater harmony on their part. Since the end of the winter, not a mutter of discontent had been heard. He hardly recognized the band of undisciplined soldiers he had recruited along the Ohio and the Mississippi.

With only his dog, Lewis intended to cover on foot the distance from Fort Mandan to the first encampment of the expedition, which would be set up across Ruptare, the biggest Hidatsa village. Having spent days and days writing his *Estimate of Eastern Indians,* Lewis felt the need to exercise. He also wanted to be alone.

He had a melancholic disposition, but this was one of the happiest days of his life. Since his teenage years, he had always dreamt of making this journey to the ends of the continent. As fate would have it, he had become private secretary to a president with a passion for the West, and later, commanding officer of the Corps of Discovery whose mission was to explore that mythical territory. In a few months, he was sure of it, he would reach the Pacific at last, the ocean that led to the riches of Asia. If all went well, he could even be back at Fort Mandan before winter.

He followed the progress of the flotilla from afar, walking along the north bank of the Missouri. Seaman dove into the river a few times, chasing after a muskrat, each time unsuccessfully. At sunset, Lewis arrived in Mitutanka where he decided to stop and pay a courtesy call to Black Cat, the most important chief of this Mandan village. The chief was not home and so, after a brief stop, the Captain set off again.

Two miles further, he saw a cone-shaped light in the distance. It was Charbonneau's tepee, or rather Sacagawea's: the light from the fire inside filtered through the worn skins of the structure and a bluish smoke rose from the top of the cone.

The men of the expedition slept under the stars around a big fire that threw out sparks. The night was cold and windy, but a blast of hot air hit Lewis as he walked into the tepee. It felt good to be there after a long day's walk.

Two hours earlier, Sacagawea had pitched the tent and prepared the beds, which consisted of buffalo skins and blankets. Charbonneau and Drouillard had gathered wood for the fire and York had cooked a meal of corn and meat.

The captains' beds were on either side of the entrance; York slept on Clark's left, Drouillard on Lewis' right; Charbonneau, Sacagawea and Jean-Baptiste occupied the rear of the tepee.

–Good evening you all, Lewis called out as he entered.

–Good evening, Captain, the occupants answered as one; they were already lying on the buffalo skins, digesting their meal and commenting on the events of the day.

Lewis turned down the plate of food that York offered him. He wasn't hungry and he wanted to write. He pulled out of his bag his journal in which he hadn't written a single line since February. He sat on his skin and took no further notice of the people around him. He wished to express on paper what he had experienced on that special day, the extraordinary feeling of standing on the threshold of a new world and belonging to the brotherhood of discoverers.

He dipped his quill in the ink well and wrote: "Our vessels consisted of six small canoes, and two large perogues. This little fleet altho' not quite as respectable as those of Columbus and Capt. Cook were still viewed by us as much pleasure as those deservedly famed adventurers ever beheld theirs; and I dare say with quite as much anxiety for their safety and preservation. We were now about to penetrate a country at least two thousand miles in width, on which the foot of the civilized man had never trodden; the good or evil it had in store for us was for experiment yet to determine, and these little vessels contained every article by which we were expected to subsist or defend ourselves..."

Lying on his side, his head resting on a hand, Charbonneau followed with his eyes the quill that ran over the page. He would never be able to read what the Captain was writing, but he thought he could guess the general meaning. The La Vérendryes had indeed gone as far as the foot of the Rockies, but they had lacked the means to cross over the mountains and reach the Western sea. They had failed to take with them sufficient men, weapons and supplies. And above all, they had not been able to rely on interpreter-guides, like himself and Sacagawea, who held the key to this world unknown to Whites. Larocque was right: books would be written about this journey to the Pacific, and Charbonneau's name would appear among those of other explorers of the West.

Exhausted and dazed by the heat, they all fell asleep at last. They offered an unusual picture, a human circle of striking diversity: Lewis and Clark, two Virginia aristocrats, one of whom had been close to the President of the United States, were sleeping under the same tepee as York, a Black slave, Drouillard, a frontier man, half French-Canadian, half Shawnee; Charbonneau, a voyageur born on the banks of the St. Lawrence River; Sacagawea, a sixteen-year-old Shoshoni bought by a White man, and little Jean-Baptiste, half Shoshoni and half French-Canadian.

Sacagawea walked along the Missouri with her baby on her back; she broke into a song of rejoicing. All around her, nature was bursting into colors, scents and sounds. The poplars and maple trees were budding; the willows were covered with catkin, the elder trees and the dogwood with blossoms. Magpies chattered from branch to branch and wild geese in the hundreds gorged themselves on the new grass. As far as the eye could see, the greening prairie was strewn with flowers that gave off heady perfumes.

Sacagawea exulted:

–Oh, Sun! Oh, Lord of life! Glory to you!

The sacred star was reaching the height of its course across the boundless sky. It was the warmest day of this early spring. With the palm of her hand, Sacagawea wiped the sweat from her bronzed forehead and lifted her fingers to her lips to lick the salty taste. A smile lit up her face. The great sea that the Whites called the Pacific must have the same taste.

The Shoshoni woman had been walking along the south bank of the Missouri since sunrise. She followed in the footsteps of Clark, Charbonneau and York. On that morning, the Captain had announced his intention to walk as far as evening camp. Lewis, who had enjoyed numerous walks since he had left Fort Mandan, had offered to replace him in the white pirogue, since there had to be a captain on board at all times. Clark had invited Charbonneau and his little family to accompany him.

This very pleasant walk aroused Sacagawea's senses. From the shore, she could see the men in their canoes. Most of the paddlers had taken off their shirts, baring their skin as white as the milk that flowed from her breasts. The young woman wondered what such a white skin would taste like. The men she had known, including Charbonneau, all had a dark complexion.

Past a bend in the river, the walkers met a group of Hidatsa hunters who were building an enclosure on the riverbank. Clark and Charbonneau stopped to have a smoke with the Indians, while York stayed back. Sacagawea breast-fed Jean-Baptiste in the shade of a poplar tree.

Among the hunters, Charbonneau recognized Caltahcota, the old chief of Metaharta.

–We're waiting for the deer to return, declared the chief after having agreed to puff on a pipe.

He explained that the animals crossed the river at that very spot each spring. They left from the Black Mountains, in the foothills of the Shining Mountains, and spread out all over the prairies north of Missouri, as far as the Saskatchewan River.

–Next fall, the deer will go back the same way, added Caltahcota whose naked, still muscular chest was covered with reddish brown stripes and horizontal yellow lines.

Using signs and some English words he had learned in the last few months, Charbonneau tried to translate the Hidatsa chief's explanations to Captain Clark.

Caltahcota continued the conversation by congratulating Charbonneau on the birth of his son, but reproaches quickly followed his compliments. In early November, the chief had been the first to tell the French-Canadian trader of the arrival of the Americans in Upper Missouri. He had asked him to be his eyes and ears among the intruders. He would never have suspected that Charbonneau would go into service with them to help them reach the great salted lake!

–I thought you were our friend, Chief of the Small Village, said Caltahcota, using one of Charbonneau's nicknames. I fear that this crossing to which you lend your support will mark for us the beginning of the end. Other Whites will follow in your steps; our lives will never be the same.

Charbonneau defended his loyalty in a tone that was meant to be reassuring.

–I'm the friend of the Big Bellies today and I will be tomorrow. When I return, if you wish, you can visit the great chief of the Whites, who lives where the sun rises. I will accompany you. You'll be able to defend your nation's interests.

–We'll see, said Caltahcota, looking skeptical.

They parted after this exchange, which Charbonneau did not attempt to translate for Clark. Caltahcota was probably right; life would never be the same for the Big Bellies.

They walked for another two miles before getting to a stream about thirty feet wide. They removed their boots and moccasins and crossed it. On the other side, they ran into three former *engagés* of the expedition, François Rivet, Jean-Baptiste Lajeunesse and Paul Primeau. Leaning on their upside down canoe with their faces to the sun, they were smoking a pipe.

–What do you know! It's our friend Charbonneau! called out Rivet, also known as the One Who Dances on His Head, and he got up to shake hands with his fellow countryman.

Lajeunesse and Primeau also shook hands with Charbonneau and Captain Clark. As they were no longer needed by the expedition, the three voyageurs had decided to head up the Missouri as far as the Yellowstone river to check out for themselves the rumor that the region teemed with beaver.

–How many skins up to now, Charbonneau inquired curiously.

–Fifteen in three days! exclaimed Rivet; and with only two traps and one rifle!

Charbonneau whistled to express his admiration. Rivet went on enthusiastically:

–If we could convince the Indians around here to work on beaver, we would make a fortune! I've never seen such beautiful skins! You don't have to take our word for it. Look!

He pulled out some skins from under the canoe and proudly showed them off to Charbonneau and Clark. Then he added:

–Not only are the beavers magnificent, but they come out in broad daylight! That proves they're not hunted here.

In the spring of 1805, Rivet and his men would be the first Whites since old Ménard to get to the Yellowstone River to hunt beaver. Following in the expedition's footsteps, the trappers knew they would be protected from any violence from the Assiniboines and other nations of the region.

Late that afternoon, Captain Lewis chose a beautiful spot for the night's encampment, a place where the south bank of the Missouri jutted out into the water. It was planted with willow trees; across it, water rushed down a cliff upstream from a graceful curve in the river. He called it Little Basin.

Sacagawea set up the tepee and prepared the beds with York's help. When everything was ready, she went to gather plants for the evening meal in the fading light of day. Scraping the ground with a pointy stick, she dug up about thirty white, oval-shaped tubers. In the glowing light of the setting sun, she washed the roots in the river. When she got back to the camp, she gave them to Charbonneau, who was delighted:

–White potatoes! I'll make a soup!

Much appreciated by the Indians as well as by the French-Canadian traders, the tuberous root of the *Psoralea esculenta*, which they also called prairie apple, was known to Americans as the prairie turnip. After tasting the soup, Captain Lewis declared that the root reminded him of the Jerusalem artichoke.

That evening, both captains and civilians also ate deer steak and beaver tail, which in Lewis's words, Toussaint had turned into a "crunchy treat." The deer and the beaver had been killed by Drouillard earlier that day.

Toussaint Charbonneau was at the helm of the white pirogue, the thirty-foot flagship of the expedition. Although he was inexperienced as a boatman and afraid of the water, he had insisted on steering the narrow, flat boat, as if he wanted to brave fate. Captain Lewis, who was on board, together with Sacagawea, Jean-Baptiste Charbonneau, George Drouillard and three other men, had not objected.

After a few hours at the helm, Charbonneau had managed to convince himself of his aptitude for sailing. The pirogue was doing a good speed, pushed along by the wind that swelled its two sails. Pleased with his performance, the voyageur thought it appropriate to sing a song for the occasion. In a strong voice, he started:

V'là l'bon vent, v'là l'joli vent
V'là l'bon vent ma mie m'appelle
V'là l'bon vent, v'là l'joli vent
V'là l'bon vent ma mie m'attend.[28]

Drouillard soon joined in:

Derrière chez nous...

Suddenly, Sacagawea cried out excitedly, interrupting the song.

–Toussaint, look! and she pointed to a white-tailed and white-headed eagle gliding in the blue sky, scanning the plain and the shore for fresh carcasses.

The budding boatman and the other passengers followed the big bird of prey with their eyes.

–The bald eagle is the emblem of our country, said Captain Lewis, speaking to the Shoshoni woman for the first time. We admire it for its longevity, great strength and majesty.

Drouillard translated his words in French. Charbonneau conveyed them in Hidatsa to his wife who seemed surprised. The eagle was the most important bird among Indians too. It symbolized war, power and spiritual elevation.

With one hand on the tiller, the other up to shade his eyes from the dazzling sun, Charbonneau wondered what the emblem of his native country was. The beaver? It had to be the beaver. After all, whenever the French-Canadian voyageurs spotted one of these rodents, they became as excited as Sacagawea upon seeing the eagle. However, he did not know what the beaver symbolized, nor did he have the time to reflect further on the question. The passengers' attention was drawn to a pile of buffalo carcasses on the riverbank. The animals had drowned while trying to cross the river on the ice at the end of winter; following the sudden rise in the water level, they had been washed ashore, where the "white bear" would gorge itself on them.

White bear is what the Indians of the West called the grizzly. The night before, near the mouth of the Little Missouri, one of the tributaries of the river, Drouillard had found the tracks of a grizzly around another pile of carcasses by the water. In the white pirogue, he described what he had discovered.

–They were huge, he said, spreading his hands in an attempt to demonstrate the phenomenal length of the tracks. I saw many, and they were freshly made!

Lewis stared wide-eyed.

–Gentlemen, I guess we'll soon meet the grizzlies.

The Captain, as most members of the expedition, was both curious and nervous at the thought of coming across grizzly bears, the biggest flesh-eating mammals in North America. Among the passengers, only Charbonneau and Sacagawea had already seen these bears whose ferociousness was legendary. And what the French-Canadian had to say about them was rather worrying, all the more so as he did not hesitate to mix myth with fact.

–Unless they're eight or ten, the Indians don't dare attack this animal, he said to his fellow travelers. And even then, they often have to beat a hasty retreat after losing one or two members of their party.

–What weapons do they use to kill this monster? asked Lewis.

–They hunt it with bow and arrows, or else with bad rifles, answered Charbonneau. Unfortunately, unless they hit the grizzly right through the heart, they become its prey. These bears, I'm telling you, charge at men more often than they run from them.

Lewis shuddered. Drouillard smiled while he stroked the rifle that he held between his legs.

–They haven't faced a real hunter yet, he said.

In the middle of the afternoon, the wind gained in strength, whipping up tall waves. A sudden gust hit the pirogue at full force, dangerously tipping it to one side. That's all Charbonneau needed to lose his head.

–What do I do? What do I do? he kept repeating in an anguished voice.

Without waiting for an answer, he executed the worst possible maneuver, so that the boat sailed broadside on to the wind. It came close to capsizing and the crew was saved only by a lull in the wind. Lewis ordered Drouillard to take the helm and strike the sails, which he did immediately. The pirogue was saved.

Captain Lewis realized that he had made a serious mistake in letting Charbonneau steer the white pirogue. It was loaded with everything precious to the expedition: instruments, papers, medicine and most of the gifts for the Indians. It also carried a woman and child, as well as three men who, not knowing how to swim, would probably have drowned if the boat had overturned at more than two hundred yards from the shore.

Charbonneau was as white as a sheet. He had exactly the same thought, but the humiliation he felt at being replaced by Drouillard got the better of his fear. As soon as he got the chance, he would pilot the white pirogue again. He was a stubborn man.

On April 14, 1805, after covering fourteen miles, Lewis and Clark's expedition set up camp on a wooded spot that jutted out into the water, on the north bank of the river. It was near an island; just a bit further, two streams flowed into the river. To show Charbonneau that they did not hold against him the wreck they had narrowly escaped, the captains paid tribute to him by naming the wider of the two streams Charbonneau Creek.

The preceding fall, Charbonneau had camped there for a few days with a group of Hidatsa hunters. It was on his return from this expedition that he had learned about the arrival of the Americans in Upper Missouri. He had never gone further west. This place was his personal frontier.

Clark determined the longitude and latitude of Charbonneau Creek with his sextant and his chronometer. That evening, under the tepee, he noted down the data in his journal.

–I hope the name Charbonneau Creek is to your liking, he said to the French-Canadian.

Drouillard, who was translating Clark's words, was a little jealous of the recognition given to his partner.

Lying on his buffalo skin, Charbonneau merely smiled. He certainly appreciated the Captains' gesture. He would have a stream named after him not far from the Yellowstone River. Other voyageurs after him would meet at Charbonneau Creek. It was his first indelible mark on the West.

For the next few days, Charbonneau followed the expedition on foot with Captain Clark, sometimes accompanied by Sacagawea and Jean-Baptiste. The little one was as sturdy as ever, jumping in his baby-carrier every time a bird or an insect caught his attention.

Clark enjoyed having Charbonneau's family around. He found the father very pleasant, the mother attractive and the baby adorable. He didn't need words to communicate; he felt close to them simply by taking them along with him across the prairie, where spring continued to work its wonders.

The poplar trees were showing their first leaves, whereas the plum trees were already in full bloom. The new shoots drew ever-growing numbers of geese, swans and ducks to the plain. It all made Charbonneau forget about the boating mishap. West of the stream bearing his name, he was entering a new world. From the top of a cliff, he surveyed admiringly huge herds of buffalo, wapitis, deer and antelopes such as he had never seen before. In this uninhabited region, game did not flee before men; on the contrary, they would come closer, curious about the two-legged animals. Occasionally, a buffalo calf, a wapiti or a stag would actually follow Charbonneau and his companions over a considerable distance.

But this garden of Eden was sometimes disrupted by violence. One day, Charbonneau had witnessed the slaughter of a calf by a pack of wolves that had first dispersed the buffalo herd by chasing it. If their young could not keep up with the herd, the females did not defend them; in their flight, they didn't even look back.

Charbonneau had chased away the wolves by firing his rifle and was able to take for himself some of the delicious meat from the calf.

While walking toward the Yellowstone, Charbonneau spotted many grizzly bear tracks, but what fascinated him the most was the abundance and the size of the beavers. The watercourses of the region, the Missouri and all its tributaries, teemed with these animals whose fur had been drawing generations of his countrymen. On the riverbanks, the rodents carried on their ceaseless activity, hacking down poplars and young willows to feast on the bark.

"What a country!" thought Charbonneau, gazing at the devastation wrought by the beavers. "A man from the Northwest Company could become fabulously wealthy by opening a trading post here!" The beavers were not only plentiful, but also bigger and fatter than anywhere else. Even their fur was finer, darker, more luxurious.

One morning, Charbonneau and Drouillard came close to blows over one of these extraordinary animals. Both men had come out of the tepee at the same time to go and check the traps they had set the day before near a burrow. They came upon quite a sight: a four-foot-long beaver, weighing about a hundred pounds, had caught one of its paws in Charbonneau's trap and another in Drouillard's.

–I'm taking the fur! said Charbonneau, who had never seen such a big beaver.

–No, retorted Drouillard, the fur is MINE! The traps belong to me.

–You lent me one! replied Charbonneau indignantly.

–That's just it, they're mine!

–You damned dead dog! shouted Charbonneau, unsheathing his knife.

At that moment, Captain Clark arrived at the scene and intervened between the two men.

–Gentlemen, gentlemen! What's going on?

When he saw the huge beaver, Clark burst out laughing. He heard both sides of the argument, then passed judgment.

–I'm granting the best part of the beaver, that is, the fur, to Georges Drouillard who, let's not forget, owns the two traps. I give the rest to Charbonneau; I'm sure he'll turn it into a good meal.

Charbonneau was furious, but he abided by Clark's decision. In the evening, he boiled the beaver's tail and served it to the captains who absolutely loved this dish that tasted somewhat of cod.

–It's delicious, said Captain Lewis.

Charbonneau shrugged his shoulders. The American had no idea of what a good meal was.

The last days of the trip between Charbonneau Creek and the Yellowstone were difficult. On many occasions, a fierce north-westerly wind brought the expedition to a standstill, navigation by sail or paddle being impossible. Charbonneau had to put an end to his walks on the plain in order to help the men pull the white pirogue with a towrope.

He had serious eye trouble, as did the others, because of the sand that blew about in such thick clouds that at times, the men could not see the other bank. Light and fine, the sand crept into everything: the men breathed, drank and ate it. It had also gotten colder and in the morning, the water formed a layer of ice on the paddles.

In spite of the difficulties, on April 25, 1805, the expedition reached the mouth of the Yellowstone, the famous river that no White man had yet ascended to its source, which, according to the Indians, was located in the Rockies.

They headed up the Yellowstone for a short distance; two miles from its confluence with the Missouri, the captains set up camp. Lewis proceeded with the necessary observations to determine the position of the river. All the members of the Corps of Discovery were in good health and happy to be there: the mere name of Yellowstone conjured up dreams of six-foot-long beavers. At night, around the campfire, they would get excited at the commercial possibilities that the region offered. The captains added to the general cheer by serving some alcohol. Cruzatte played his fiddle and they all spent the evening "with much hilarity, singing & dancing," as Lewis noted down in his journal. In this same journal, the river the French-Canadians called *Roche-Jaune* officially became the Yellowstone.

Contrary to the stories spread by Charbonneau, the grizzly bear does not attack man; it's rather the other way around. On May 5, 1805, the Corps of Discovery was able to ascertain this fact for itself.

The expedition had covered seventeen miles across another beautiful, fertile region, where game was plentiful. In the evening, to everyone's surprise, a grizzly appeared on the shore, not far from the camp. As soon as he spotted the giant bear, William Clark grabbed his rifle and went down toward it with Drouillard, who also carried a rifle. The animal saw the two men out of the corner of its eye, stopped for a moment to have a good look at them, then continued walking on the bank of the Missouri, ignoring their presence. Without a word, Clark and Drouillard took aim at the grizzly and fired. Hit by at least one bullet, the animal roared and swam away from the shore. It managed to cross more than half the river and reach a sandbar where it stopped to catch its breath. It had been hit in a lung.

The Captain and the hunter jumped in a canoe and went to finish off the bear that died about twenty minutes later, its body riddled with ten bullets, five of which had perforated the lungs. And so ended the expedition's first encounter with a grizzly bear.

Lewis, Charbonneau and several other men joined the hunters on the sandbar, where they admired at leisure the great carnivore. Some were so impressed by the terrifying legendary beast that their jaw dropped.

–How much do you think it weighs? asked Lewis, going around the monster bear whose reddish brown hair was much longer and thicker than that of black bears.

–About five hundred pounds, answered Captain Clark, standing proudly next to the animal.

–One hundred more, easily, said Lewis.

The Captain pulled out his instruments and measured the grizzly. The mouth was ten times bigger than the black bear's. From the tip of the nose to the end of the back paws, the beast measured eight feet, seven and a half inches. The neck, the chest, the shoulders, all about the bear was massive and powerful. As he examined the animal's genitals, Lewis thought he noticed another difference from the black bear. He pulled out his notebook and wrote: "Testicules pendant from bely and placed four inches assunder in seperate bags."

On this point, Lewis was strangely mistaken; the testicles of the grizzly are in the same spot as those of the black bear. However, he did not exaggerate at all when it came to the claws of the animal, which were close to five inches long.

Charbonneau felt a shiver run down his back as he imagined one of the giant paws tearing into him. What would he do faced with a grizzly? He was very bad at handling a rifle. All the men in the expedition had the same thought, even the good shots among them. To get the better of such a big animal, you needed many bullets, as Clark and Drouillard had just discovered.

The captains divided up the grizzly among the men; they retrieved as much of the fat as they could, knowing that they could make good use of it later.

Back in the tepee, Charbonneau had trouble falling asleep; he couldn't stop thinking of the grizzly's paws. He tried to imagine aiming at such a beast and killing it, but every time something went wrong: the rifle didn't fire and it was he who became the prey. After a while, Charbonneau decided to put himself in St. Anne's hands. If one day he were to come face to face with a grizzly, the patron saint of voyageurs would surely rescue him. Had she not always done so when he had prayed to her?

Three days later, still traveling on the Missouri, the expedition made a stop at the mouth of a big river on the starboard side. Judging by the volume of water flowing into the Missouri from this tributary, the captains thought that it might provide a passage to the Saskatchewan River to the north. In that case, the Americans could, as President Jefferson wished, challenge the stranglehold that the Canadians had on the fur trade as far as the fiftieth parallel.

Happy with their discovery, Lewis and Clark called it the Milk River, because of its white shade, which recalled the color of tea to which a little milk has been added.

Charbonneau went ashore with Clark and Drouillard to explore the region. The three men climbed to the top of a hill and saw the Milk River disappear on the horizon following a north-west trajectory.

–It must be the river that the Big Bellies call the River That Mocks All Others, said Toussaint Charbonneau

Captain Clark nodded, putting away his binoculars. In a dreamy tone, he commented:

–I'm sure this river is navigable.

–Me too, said Drouillard.

The next day in the afternoon, the expedition arrived at another remarkable river that flowed into the Missouri, on the south side this time. It was about half a mile wide, as wide as the Missouri, but its bed was practically dry. The Captains named it Big Dry River.

That day, the expedition took advantage of favorable winds and covered twenty-four and a half miles, a greater distance than usual. Lewis walked, which gave him the opportunity to shoot a shore bird unknown to him; it was a willet, a species that was not found east of the Mississippi. He also killed a buffalo and he set aside the best cuts for Charbonneau who had promised to make the famous *boudin blanc* that Drouillard was always raving about.

And so, on May 9, 1805, about one month after leaving Fort Mandan, the Corps of Discovery enjoyed a gastronomical interlude that contributed to the legend of the French-Canadian voyageur.

That night, Charbonneau transformed the left bank of the Missouri into a Parisian kitchen, and adapted to the American West a recipe from France, the country of his ancestors. At sunset, when the sky takes on a reddish hue, he set himself up with his ingredients and his knife on a big rock that jutted out into the river, and started to work. Lewis looked on attentively, and so did Seaman, licking his chops.

Aware that he was being watched, Charbonneau emphasized every one of his gestures with dramatic flair. Not that he knew anything about the theater, but he played the part of chef brilliantly. First, he emptied out six feet of intestines taken from the buffalo. To achieve this, he grabbed hold of one end of the gut with his right hand, then, with the thumb and forefinger of his other hand, he lovingly massaged it to the other end so as to press out "what isn't good to eat," as he explained to the American Captain.

When the gut was emptied out and cleaned, Charbonneau proceeded to carve the part of the buffalo he had requisitioned, the shoulder, the best part of the animal according to him; of course, the Prairie Indians preferred above all the raw liver of the animal. "Each to his own," Toussaint used to say to himself. Armed with his hunting knife, he cut the meat into thin slices, then chopped it finely. He mixed it with kidney fat, added salt, pepper and a few spoonfuls of flour.

He set the mixture aside and went to work on the intestines again. He tied a knot at one end before turning them inside out. Then, he started to stuff them, using his fingers skillfully to push the meat mixture inside. "What's good to eat," he explained to Lewis, who noted down in French the words of the cook.

Once he had completely filled the gut, Charbonneau tied the other end. Then he went to "baptize" it in the Missouri, plunging it twice into the water and sprinkling it once more. He boiled the sausage before frying it in bear's fat to brown it. The smell of the fried food attracted all the others who soon formed a circle around Charbonneau, also licking their lips in anticipation.

The chef cut the *boudin* and served the slices steaming and dripping with meat juices and fat. This was better than any feast: the members of the expedition were falling over themselves to get their share. As Lewis wrote, Charbonneau's *boudin blanc* was enough to "esswage the pangs of a keen appetite or such as travelers in the wilderness are seldom at a loss for."

In the white pirogue that was sailing at full speed, Sacagawea gazed smilingly at Jean-Baptiste's cheerful face. He was tanned from the spring sun that shone on the Missouri; at a little more than two months, the baby was radiant with health. The young mother gave thanks to the Lord of life for granting her a child so beautiful, strong and happy.

The flapping of a sail drew the Shoshoni woman from her contemplation. The wind was blowing harder, whipping up great waves. Sacagawea decided to put Jean-Baptiste in a safe place and so she tied him up in the baby-carrier. As usual, he did not protest: on his mother's back, as in her arms, he was in heaven.

When Toussaint Charbonneau noticed that she was looking in his direction, he called out to her:

–Don't forget, when we get to the camp at the end of the day, I want you to go and pick some wild onions.

The young woman nodded her assent; wild onions were plentiful in the region. She then looked away so as not to worry about the fact that Toussaint was at the helm of the boat. It was the first time since he had almost caused a wreck that Charbonneau had convinced Drouillard to let him steer again.

–If you let me, he had promised the hunter, I'll prepare *boudin blanc* for you tonight.

–You'll make the boat capsize! Drouillard had said.

The cook had protested:

–Think of the *boudin blanc* instead of worrying about that. I'll even add wild onions to the sausage stuffing. It'll be sinfully delicious!

Drouillard had cast his eye along the riverbanks. On one side, he saw Lewis walking with his dog; on the other, Clark and his servant, York. For the first time since the beginning of the journey, no captain was aboard the white pirogue.

Unable to resist the temptation of Charbonneau's *boudin blanc*, Drouillard had given up the helm to Charbonneau. In order to ease his conscience, he had nonetheless warned the cook:

–I'm telling you! If you overturn the pirogue, I'm going to kill you!

–Don't waste your ammunition, Charbonneau had answered insolently. If the boat overturns, I'll drown!

He had been at the helm for an hour and all was well. With one hand on the tiller, his pipe stuck in his mouth and his beard flying in the wind, Charbonneau was dreaming of yet another feather in his cap. Not content with being an admired chief and an almost indispensable interpreter, he wanted to become the regular pilot on the white pirogue, thus taking the place of Drouillard, Lewis' right-hand man. His culinary successes had gone to his head.

Charbonneau managed quite well as long as the wind blew from behind, but in the middle of the afternoon, a gust hit the pirogue sideways, and the great helmsman panicked. Instead of sailing before the wind, he turned broadside. The wind blew so hard that it snatched the sheet of the sail from Francis Labiche's hands and knocked the boat on its side.

–*Bonne sainte Anne!* screamed Charbonneau as he saw the water pour into the boat. Help me!

From each bank of the river, Lewis and Clark heard the French-Canadian's screams. When they saw the white pirogue partially overturned, their hearts sank: the crew was in great danger, and so was the expedition. The loss of the contents of the boat would prove disastrous to the Corps of Discovery: without instruments, maps, presents, they wouldn't be able to cross over the Rockies and reach the Pacific.

Lewis and Clark both fired their rifles into the air to attract the crew's attention and signal that they should cut the halyards and strike the sail. But the men did not hear them.

In the middle of the river, Charbonneau kept on imploring:

–*Bonne sainte Anne*, save us!

For a short while, utter confusion prevailed in the pirogue, which was still on its side, taking in water. Two crew members who, like Charbonneau, could not swim, were hanging onto the boat, terror-stricken. Finally, Drouillard, one of the few who had kept his wits about him, succeeded in hoisting the sail and the pirogue straightened up again.

He then pointed his rifle at Charbonneau and shouted in a tone that left no doubt about his determination:

–Charbonneau, take back the helm or I'll kill you!

The water was very choppy; the contents of the boat were scattered on the waves. Threatened with death, Charbonneau grabbed the tiller. Drouillard immediately ordered two men to pour the water out with buckets. Holding on with both hands, Toussaint looked on as the river carried off the precious bundles.

At this moment, in a display of courage, Sacagawea dove into the waters of the Missouri. Struggling against the current, she set about retrieving one by one the objects that were drifting away. Keeping her head above water, she brought back to the boat whatever she caught and went back for more again and again. Still on her back, little Jean-Baptiste clung to his mother's hair, wriggling in the icy water, but without screaming or crying. On the contrary, he seemed to be encouraging his mother in her rescue attempts.

Charbonneau steered the pirogue ashore, still at gunpoint. They had narrowly escaped another disaster. Lewis came running to the spot where the boat was drawing alongside the bank. Without blaming Charbonneau or Drouillard, he and his men pulled out the things that were loaded on the pirogue –medicine, instruments, papers, books, merchandise, supplies – and set them out to dry.

Lewis was glad to see that only the medicine was spoiled. The rest had been salvaged, for the most part thanks to that Indian woman who was now breast-feeding her child by the fire. Among the books she had managed to save were a treatise of Botany, essential to Lewis, and an encyclopedia in four volumes dear to Clark, *A New and Complete Dictionary of the Arts and Sciences.*

That evening, Lewis had to acknowledge that Sacagawea had shown as much courage and resolve as any other member of the expedition during the accident, but he did not tell her. He did, however, give her husband a piece of his mind:

–Charbonneau, you are without a doubt the most timid boatman in the world. I never want to see you at the helm of the white pirogue again.

Visibly pleased, Drouillard translated the Captain's words. When he heard them, Charbonneau lowered his head without saying a word.

Lewis did not hold it against him very long. Around the fire, he offered him and all the others a glass of rum. After such a scare, the captains felt that the men needed a little boost.

Charbonneau had nearly died. Under the tepee, in the dark, he thanked Sacagawea by first caressing her hair. Then, he drew her against him and took her silently from behind.

With her eyes closed, Sacagawea sighed while thinking of her mother's prophecy. Floating in the tall grass, she had said to her: "Your son will be like a chief; he will travel to foreign lands, but first, he must survive. It all depends on you." The Shoshoni woman felt she had done her duty. She had ensured her son's survival, and at the same time, saved Toussaint's neck and the American expedition.

Could anything less be expected from the daughter of a chief?

Chapter Nine

The Rockies

As the expedition advanced toward the upper course of the Missouri, the landscape changed. The ground became stony, uneven and rugged. Instead of poplars and willows, pine trees and cedars grew on the sides and tops of high hills. Grass was scarce, and so was the buffalo. It probably didn't rain often in this region, as evidenced by the many completely dry riverbeds they passed on their way.

One day, however, the expedition went by a lovely river that the Captains named after Sacagawea, to pay tribute to her heroic feat on May 14. Toussaint Charbonneau felt really jealous. His name was only linked to a modest stream.

They were now entering the "Deserts of America," as William Clark noted down in his journal, referring to the region that the Indians of the West called the Bad Lands. It was indeed arid, but it had spectacular views. Unfortunately, the members of the expedition were not able to enjoy them. For days, they fought a fierce westerly wind that blew up sandstorms on the banks. The men had to tow the pirogues using ropes made of skins or hemp.

Charbonneau was assigned to this thankless task. Since his last misadventure as pilot of the white pirogue, he could hardly protest. He scraped his feet on the sharp stones scattered all over the banks of the Missouri, which cut right through his moccasins To avoid further pain, he and the other men went into the water up to their armpits to tow the boat. The ropes broke many times.

They made progress nonetheless. Twenty miles one day, fifteen the next, twenty-seven the day after. Strangely enough, instead of getting warmer with time, the weather was getting colder. At night, water froze in the pots and, in the morning, a layer of ice covered the paddles. It was after much effort and pain that the men succeeded in riding the raging rapids that blocked their way, but they were never heard to complain.

For they were getting inexorably closer to the Rocky Mountains, whose name was on everyone's lips, making them forget the hardships of the journey.

The air was so clear that, when he extended his arm, Charbonneau felt as though he could touch the sky, the river that snaked its way through the cliffs and the row of pines on the horizon. He breathed deeply, filling his lungs. Ah! At last, he could walk freely, without having to pull on the towrope. That morning, Captain Clark had taken pity on him and invited him to walk on land as far as the encampment for the evening. Sacagawea and Jean-Baptiste had stayed behind with Captain Lewis.

York went along with them. The Captain's servant was in a bad mood. The night before, he had left his rifle in the white pirogue. A big buffalo had crossed the river, run straight at the campfires and trampled York's weapon underfoot, thereby bending it. The beast had narrowly missed the tepee, thanks to Seaman, who had caused it to change direction. But the buffalo had done enough damage to the white pirogue to prompt Lewis to write that the boat was "attended by some evil genii."

Captain Clark had not replaced York's rifle. As he walked empty-handed behind his master, the slave felt powerless and unjustly treated. After all, when a White soldier broke his weapon, the Captains provided him with a new one on the spot.

The threesome climbed up several hills. At the top of one of them, Clark came across a ram, a type of hoofed animal unknown to him. He took aim and killed it. When he examined it, he was surprised by the disproportionate size of its head and its scrolled horns in relation to the rest of the body. He called the animal big horn.

In the early afternoon, after an exhausting climb, they reached the top of one of the highest points of the region. From there, they saw the Rockies for the first time.

The jagged, snow-covered peaks stood out against the blue sky. Their eternal snows sparkled in the sun. The Indians were right: the Rockies were indeed the Shining Mountains.

The explorers were lost in wonder as they gazed at this incredible barrier that towered on the horizon. It seemed very close in the crystal-clear air, and yet, it would still take weeks of effort to get there. And even then, their troubles would not be over; they would have to cross over these awesome mountains that reached up to the sky. The men remained silent for a few minutes, as each one pondered his own resolve.

Charbonneau said to himself once more that the horses of the Shoshonis were absolutely essential to the success of the expedition. He thought of the La Vérendrye brothers whose dream of reaching the sea in the West had been shattered against the great barrier. Without the help of the local Indians, the explorers from Three-Rivers had been forced to retrace their steps with a heavy heart. They had nonetheless claimed, in the name of France, the Great Western Plains, which were added to the Louisiana territory.

Toussaint felt a great sense of responsibility; his assistance would prove crucial to the negotiations with the Shoshonis. That way, he would make everyone forget his blunders as pilot of the white pirogue.

Clark kept on admiring the Rockies, feeling great joy. One year after leaving St. Louis, he was finally getting closer to the source of the Missouri, which up until then was looked upon as coming out of nowhere, or at least from the unknown. With his sextant and chronometer, he would soon be able to determine precisely the place from which the Missouri sprang from the ground, thus winning one more victory over ignorance.

And yet, a major obstacle stood in their path. Clark tried to imagine the difficulties that the snowy mountains held in store for the men of the expedition, the additional hardships they would have to endure. It was enough to melt away his pleasure.

–Let's go, he said to his companions.

They went down the hill to get back to the camp for that night, on the south bank of the river. Clark then informed Lewis and the other men of what he had seen earlier, avoiding to dwell on the hard times he anticipated, so as not to spoil the mood of the troop.

Under the tepee, in the dark, York remembered an old slave he had known in Louisville, Kentucky. He had been freed by his master who wanted to show him gratitude at the end of his life. York thought that a slave also deserved to be freed after having helped his master cross over the Rockies.

On the last day of May, the expedition traveled over a distance of about fifteen miles, across an incomparably beautiful region. High walls of stone, almost perpendicular, stood on both sides of the Missouri, as genuine architectural masterpieces. The wind had eroded the off-white cliffs of flaky sandstone. Some held up colonnades topped by huge globes or slabs, others were adorned with cathedral pulpits or organ pipes; still others resembled fairy tale castles, with their turrets and pinnacles.

Pulling on the towrope, Toussaint Charbonneau thought he saw, amidst chapels with pointed steeples, the statue of a naked woman. He stopped many times, as did the others, to point to a grotesque structure.

–Look, a beaver hat! he called out to Sacagawea who followed the men on foot along the bank, with her son on her back.

Just as he said these words, the rope of the white pirogue, the only one made of hemp, broke. The boat swiveled around and nearly hit a rock. Meriwether Lewis witnessed the incident from the shore, and he couldn't help thinking that one day this pirogue would end up at the bottom of the river. But that didn't prevent him from enjoying the romantic landscape. As he advanced, the Captain started believing that the enchanting sights would never end. He was filled with wonder at the niches and recesses in the cliffs where the swallows had built their nests.

Thousands of these birds enlivened the splendid desolation of the great Stone Walls with their chirping.

–Charbonneau, take your rifle and come with us! ordered Captain Lewis; he was surrounded by three hunters, among them Georges Drouillard.

Toussaint was delighted. He had had just about enough of pulling the towrope and was ready for a good hunt, all the more so as hunger had been gnawing at him for quite a while. In fact, since they had reached the Bad Lands, they had been deprived of fresh meat. Charbonneau grabbed his rifle and followed Lewis.

The hunters walked along the bank of the Missouri for most of the day. They saw the landscape change again, the cliffs become more spaced out and lower. At the bottom of a precipice, they found the remains of at least a hundred buffalo. The carcasses gave off a horrible stench.

–It's what you get when you hunt the buffalo the old-fashioned way, said Charbonneau, holding his nose.

Drouillard translated for Lewis.

–What hunt are you talking about? asked the Captain.

With undisguised pleasure, Charbonneau answered his question, embellishing the information he had gotten from Le Borgne:

–There still are Indians who hunt buffalo on foot. Here's how they do it. To begin with, they choose one of the fastest and most agile young men of the tribe; they dress him up in a buffalo skin and head to mislead the animals. In that strange getup, the young man takes up his position at a good distance between a herd and one of the precipices on the river.

Charbonneau allowed enough time for Drouillard to translate, then continued his explanation, while walking away from the putrid pile.

–At the same time, the other young men hide behind the herd and on its sides. When the signal is given, they rise together and charge into the herd screaming. Panic-stricken, the buffalo rush toward the young Indian in disguise, who leads them toward the river. If he is fast enough, the young man will find another hiding place from where he'll be able to watch the buffalo leap into the void. If he's not, he will be trampled underfoot by the animals or carried along with them to the foot of the cliff. The Indians take whatever meat they need in the pile of carcasses.

Lewis remained silent. He pictured himself in the place of the buffalo at the head of the herd, realizing too late that he was heading for the precipice, trying in vain to back off or even stop, but being pushed into the drop by those who followed and did not see the danger. He shuddered in horror.

Charbonneau stuck out his chest. He was proud of his story that described quite accurately a widespread practice in Upper Missouri before the arrival of horses. Unfortunately, his story did not explain how this particular herd had died. It had probably perished while attempting to cross the frozen river and the ice had given way under its weight.

The hunters continued walking. The cliffs were followed by ever-flattening, ever-widening lands. Vegetation grew again everywhere. In the plains near the river, Lewis found wild cherry trees, currant bushes, dog roses and prickly pears in bloom.

Game was more plentiful there than in the desolate region they had just crossed, so that in the course of the day, the hunters killed six wapitis, two buffalo and two deer. They cut up the meat from the animals and carried it to the riverbank, where one of the men mounted guard while waiting for the canoes and pirogues to arrive.

At the end of the day, as they were getting ready to return to camp, the hunters saw before them a huge grizzly bear; it was less than a hundred feet away. Lewis did not hesitate: he took aim and fired. The bullet lodged itself in the bear's shoulder; the animal stood up on its hind legs and roared with rage. It was a terrifying sight.

The grizzly came down on its forepaws and rushed toward Drouillard who stood on Lewis' right. Not wanting to waste his ammunition, the hunter turned around and took to his heels in the hope of finding a tree to climb or a hole in which to crawl.

The grizzly abruptly changed direction and charged at someone else, Toussaint Charbonneau as it happened; it chased him, probably picking up the appetizing scent of cooking on him. Stricken with fear, the French-Canadian fled, firing his rifle into the air.

–Help! he screamed, running at full speed toward the plain.

Hunted down by the biggest carnivore of North America, Charbonneau managed to hide in a thick bush where he prayed to St. Anne with unparalleled fervor.

–*Bonne sainte Anne*, patron of voyageurs, save your Toussaint Charbonneau!

For a good while, the grizzly circled round the bush, trying to lay its paw on the cook. Drouillard came up to the bear surreptitiously and finished it off with a bullet straight in the head.

Charbonneau emerged from the bush as white as a sheet and quaking at the knees.

–It's me, your *bonne sainte Anne*, laughed Drouillard. This one is worth a good serving of *boudin blanc*, isn't it?

Charbonneau didn't answer and just stared at the beast that had almost killed him. He really didn't know whether he should thank Drouillard or St. Anne.

The group of hunters finally reached camp at nightfall. It was set up in a lovely poplar grove, across the mouth of a large river. As it was getting late, Captains Lewis and Clark postponed exploring this unexpected watercourse until the next day. In the meantime, they took advantage of a cloudless night to note down the position of the stars.

This site had already been occupied by Indians. One of the soldiers discovered a pair of moccasins they had left behind. Lewis showed them to Sacagawea to find out whether this type of shoe belonged to her nation.

–These moccasins belong to the Black Feet, who live on this side of the Shining Mountains, she answered through Charbonneau.

Under the tepee that night, Lewis and Clark had trouble falling asleep. How could one explain the presence of the river they had just seen, which no Indian had ever mentioned to them? Which of the two branches was the Missouri?

The next morning, June 3, 1805, the members of the expedition crossed the Missouri and set up a new camp at the confluence of the two large rivers. The expedition faced a dilemma: which of these two branches was the right one? The success of the whole undertaking depended on the answer to that question, described simply as "interesting" by Lewis.

According to the information provided by Seeing Snake and other Hidatsa chiefs, the Missouri did not have any more tributaries north of the River That Mocks All Others, the one the captains had renamed the Milk River. The Great Falls were supposed to be the next landmark on the Missouri, not this mysterious fork.

The captains and the men spent the day studying the two watercourses. The branch on the right, or north, was deeper, but not as wide as the branch on the left, or south. Its waters had the same color as the Missouri, a whitish brown, the same rate of flow, the same foaming.

–The north branch is the Missouri, declared Pierre Cruzatte at the end of the day. I was born on this river; I've been sailing on its waters all my life. I can't be wrong.

–He's right, added Toussaint Charbonneau, who claimed to be somewhat of an expert himself, given that his place of residence was Upper Missouri. This branch is the Missouri River.

Sacagawea did not dare give her opinion. She had never seen this fork in her whole life. The members of the expedition sided with Cruzatte, a man who was appreciated as much for his fiddle as for his integrity and boating experience. They all agreed with him, except Captains Lewis and Clark.

–We believe that the south branch is the Missouri, said Lewis. Its waters are more transparent, they flow over well-polished, round and flat stones. That would indicate that the river comes from a mountainous region.

The men did not change their minds and continued to agree with Cruzatte.

–In that case, we shall continue to examine the question, said Lewis. Tomorrow, Captain Clark and myself will go exploring with two small teams to be sure in our own minds. Each team will head up one of the two branches for a day and a half, more if needed, and will return to camp to make its report.

The men willingly accepted Lewis' decision; he could have imposed his point of view since he was the commanding officer of a military expedition. The captains had chosen instead to use caution. Since they had left Fort Mandan, two months had passed, among the most favorable to exploration. If the expedition took the wrong branch, it ran the risk of wasting the rest of the summer months. Would the men get over their discouragement? Would the mission survive?

For the time being, the men trusted Cruzatte, but Lewis and Clark were not blind: the branch with the limpid waters had to be the Missouri, since its source was in the Rockies. From there, according to Seeing Snake, the expedition could easily reach the source of the Columbia, the river that flowed to the Pacific.

After the evening meal, the captains offered the men a glass of rum to cheer them.

Two teams left on reconnaissance at dawn. Lewis chose Drouillard, Cruzatte, Shields, Windsor and Lepage to go up the north branch; Clark went up the south branch with the Fields brothers, Sergeant Gass, Shannon and York.

Charbonneau had been invited to join Captain Clark's group, but he had declined. He wanted to stay with Sacagawea because she wasn't feeling well.

The other men were happy to stay in camp. Their feet were all bruised from the rocky terrain they had walked on for the last few weeks. Some of them had lost a lot of weight and strength; they could barely stand or walk. That didn't spoil their good mood; the

Rockies were in sight at last. During the day, they kept themselves busy preparing wapiti skins for the making of clothes.

For his part, Charbonneau climbed the heights between the two watercourses in search of willows. With the bark of that tree, he would brew a decoction that worked on pain, fever and itching, symptoms that Sacagawea had complained about.

The day before, when he had returned to the tepee for the night, Charbonneau had found the young Shoshoni bathed in sweat, doubled up with pain, with her hands pressed against her lower abdomen. Jean-Baptiste was sleeping beside her.

–What's wrong? he had asked his woman.

–It hurts, she had simply answered, in a voice choked by sobs.

–Where?

–There.

Sacagawea had pointed to her abdomen. Charbonneau had laid his hand there and the young woman had winced with pain, her black hair matted with sweat on her pallid forehead.

–I'll get some willow bark tomorrow.

His wife had closed her eyes and shaken her head.

–It's on fire, she had whispered.

From the top of the hill, the view was exceptional. The plains stretched in all directions as far as the eye could see; countless herds of buffalo grazed in the thick grass, guarded by their usual shepherds, wolves. Bands of wapitis could also be seen and some antelopes, by themselves or with their little ones. The weather was beautiful; had it not been for Sacagawea's condition, which worried him, Charbonneau would have burst into song.

He remained quiet and pulled out his tobacco pouch: it was nearly empty. He thought of the shortages ahead, he lit his pipe and inhaled the smoke deeply, savoring the pleasure of which he would soon be deprived.

He could see the two branches of the fork vanish into the unknown. It was really impossible to tell which one flowed from the Rockies, the range of snow-clad peaks that went on forever. As he gazed at the landscape that lay before him, he thought of Boucherville, his native village. It was far in the past, another life.

The paddle had taken him to the Great Plains that had become his new country. And now, he risked losing everything by attempting to cross over these Rocky Mountains. What if Sacagawea had deceived him for the sole purpose of seeing her family again?

He started worrying about his wife's health again; with his axe on his shoulder, he resumed his search for willow bark. He had seen Sacagawea get weaker during their crossing of the Bad Lands. In that desert, buffalo and beavers were nothing more than memories. Not to mention *boudin blanc*! As all the other members of the expedition, Sacagawea had had little to eat, which was worse for her since she was breast-feeding. And little Jean-Baptiste had gradually lost his liveliness and his smile.

After gathering enough pieces of bark, Toussaint went back down to the camp where the men were bustling about the fire. He took a small pot, filled it with the clear water from the south branch of the river, then returned to the tepee. Sacagawea wasn't feeling any better.

–I'm thirsty, she said when she saw Charbonneau.

–I'm preparing something for you to drink, he answered, kneeling down next to her.

He put the pot on the fire and dropped the pieces of bark in the water. The herbal tea, he hoped, would quench Sacagawea's thirst and soothe her pain. Jean-Baptiste stretched out his arms to his father who held him and tried in vain to make him laugh. Toussaint said to himself that the baby had to be worried too; he held him tight to reassure him, if at all possible.

Going up the right branch of the river proved difficult. At first, Lewis and his companions made slow progress because of the slippery rocks and pools of mud or, as they moved away from the riverbank, the small cactus whose prickles tore their moccasins. At night, they slept in the rain and once, even under the snow.

But Lewis was able to find out for sure. He was convinced that the right branch was not the Missouri. This imposing watercourse did not have its source in the West, but in the North, probably in the region of Saskatchewan, which teemed with fur animals. On the commercial plane, this river was destined for a great future.

Furthermore, it had a majestic beauty, which Lewis described as "romantic." It is for this reason that he named it after the young woman he hoped to marry, Maria, his sixteen-year-old cousin. In his eyes, Maria Wood was the prettiest of Virginia girls, and he wanted to pay tribute to her by giving her name to one of the most important tributaries of the Missouri.

On the last day of exploration, Lewis saw the Maria River in all its splendor. It had rained again that morning, but the clouds had finally dispersed, letting through the sunshine and blue skies. Undoubtedly, the Maria did not have his cousin's fair complexion, but the Captain in love did not fail to find its many charms, which he described later in his journal in these terms: "It passes through a rich fertile and one of the most beautifully picaresque countries that I ever beheld. Through the wide expanse of which, innumerable herds of living animals are seen, it's borders garnished with one continued garden of roses, while it's lofty and open forests, are the habitation of myriads of the feathered tribes who salute the ear of every traveler with their wild and simple, yet sweet and cheerful melody."

The bark decoction had brought Sacagawea only temporary relief. When Captain Clark came back to camp, her condition had deteriorated. The young mother remained prostrate on her buffalo skin, unable to get up; next to her, Jean-Baptiste was crying, not having been nursed since the night before.

When he walked under the tepee, Clark could not conceal his concern.

–How long has she been like this? he asked Charbonneau through Labiche, who had followed the two men under the tent to act as interpreter.

–Ever since you left to explore the south branch, answered Charbonneau. I made her drink a tea made with willow bark, but it's not effective anymore.

Sacagawea's face was thinner, her complexion waxen; she was huddled up, staring into space. She had sweated profusely for two days, and now her teeth were chattering. The pain, which two days earlier was centered in her lower abdomen, had now spread to her back.

Clark had her breathe some smelling salts to bring her out of her torpor. The next day, to soothe her pain, which seemed to have gotten worse, he gave her some opium. But no remedy cured the Shoshoni woman from the illness that gnawed at her guts.

Lewis being away, Clark didn't know what else to do. He asked heaven for the speedy return of the regular doctor of the expedition; he was worried about the young woman's health, but also about the health of the baby whom he heard crying for the first time. He simply adored the child and affectionately called him "Pomp" or "Pompy." As he had written in his journal, he was his "little dancing boy," the mascot of the expedition.

Little Jean-Baptiste didn't dance anymore, and his mother's health continued to decline.

Lewis' team came back to the camp late afternoon on June 8, 1805, after having spent three nights on the road, that is, two more than had been anticipated. Clark had worried about the delay.

Lewis arrived exhausted, but pleased for having established which direction to take. And so he was rather surprised to see that none of the men who had accompanied him shared his view. Cruzatte, Drouillard and the others continued to think that the north branch was the Missouri. The captains were still the only ones to want to take the other branch.

Lewis discussed it with Clark, and that night, around the fire, he announced his decision: the expedition was going to head up the south branch.

–We have examined our maps, he declared in a lively tone. We have compared the data they provide with the information from the Indians; we have explored both branches over a certain distance, and we have decided that the south branch must be considered as the Missouri itself. That is the right route.

Cruzatte stood up to answer. He said calmly:

–I'm ready to follow you wherever you tell us to go. But I fear the south branch will lead you far away from the Columbia River.

–I'm of the same opinion as Cruzatte, said Charbonneau after he heard the translation.

Many other voices joined in:

–I'm of the same opinion.

Lewis took Clark aside. After a while, he came back before the men.

–Here's what we'll do to settle the question once and for all. One of us, with a few men, will follow the course of the south branch on land as far as the Great Falls or the snowy mountains, whichever comes first. The other Captain will sail right behind in the boats, with the exception of the red pirogue, which we'll leave here with other articles. If we're going the wrong way, we'll soon find out.

Cruzatte took no offence at the captains' decision. He pulled out his fiddle and the performance began. The men spent the rest of the evening singing and dancing in the best of moods. This time, Charbonneau could not resist singing a little song from his native country. But under the tepee, Sacagawea was still in pain.

The next morning, the two captains agreed that bleeding was in order for Sacagawea.

–The bad blood must be drained, said Lewis after his colleague had described the young woman's symptoms.

–Of course, said Clark, I should have thought about it before. I'll take care of it. She will be less afraid with me.

Ever since Hippocrates, in the so-called civilized world, the sick were bled for any reason. However, Charbonneau protested when Clark announced his intention.

–She's already bleeding! he exclaimed.

–Where? asked Clark, who held a bowl in one hand and a small knife in the other.

–In the lower regions, answered Charbonneau, using a euphemism to refer to the woman's genitals.

–She's having her period, you idiot! and Clark shrugged his shoulders.

–No! insisted Charbonneau. You mustn't bleed her! Make her a poultice!

–For now, Captain Lewis has recommended bleeding.

Clark thus brought the matter to a close and knelt down in front of Sacagawea who looked at the Captain's knife with alarm.

Charbonneau did not persist in his opposition. Followed by Labiche, he left the tepee, refusing to witness the operation.

–Charbonneau, don't just stand there! Give us a hand! Cruzatte called out.

The fiddler and other men were busying themselves around a cache they had dug out not far from the camp. Before facing the Great Falls, the captains had decided to store part of the expedition goods to lighten the load on the boats.

Charbonneau was very concerned about his wife; he walked toward the cache in a daze. Around the hole, he saw the merchandise and the supplies the Corps of Discovery would have to do without: gunpowder, salt, flower, salted pork, grizzly skins, beaver traps, rifles, etc. He instinctively estimated the goods to be buried at about a ton.

–Come and join us, Charbonneau, said Cruzatte. Grab a keg and put it in the cache.

Charbonneau obeyed. He got hold of a keg and placed it at the bottom of the cache that had been lined with grass to keep the supplies dry. So as not to get robbed by the Sioux or other tribes, French-Canadian trappers often hid their valuable goods in holes dug in the ground.

Once the cache had been filled, the men pulled the red pirogue on dry land to a small island at the entrance of the Maria. The Corps of Discovery would also do without this boat for the rest of the journey. As it headed up the south branch, the expedition would have to ride some major rapids and extra hands would be needed to tow the canoes and the white pirogue.

Captain Lewis arrived on the island with Clark just as the men were finishing tying the pirogue to some trees in order to protect it from the rising water.

–Build me a fire, he ordered the men as he got out of a canoe with Clark. He put an iron in the fire until it was red-hot and used it to burn his name into the trunks to which the pirogue was tied: “U.S. Capt. M. Lewis.”

As they were about to return to camp, Charbonneau looked at Clark inquiringly. The Captain sent for Cruzatte.

–Tell Charbonneau that his wife is much better. When I left, she was sleeping like a baby.

Dripping with sweat, Sacagawea was moaning at the bottom of the white pirogue, holding her baby tight. She would have liked to lie in the shade at the other end of the boat, but she didn't even have the strength to get up. Under the relentless sun, she felt as if she were melting in the heat.

The day before, Captain Clark had bled her a second time. When she had seen her blood dripping in the bowl, Sacagawea had fainted. Her life was slipping away just as she was about to see her people. Why was the Captain tormenting her? Didn't anybody tell him that she had a great mission to accomplish? Wasn't she supposed to survive so that her son could grow up to visit distant lands and meet crowned heads?

Charbonneau was out of his mind with worry, but there wasn't much he could do for the mother of his son. To make matters worse, he spent the whole day towing the white pirogue with other men. He scraped his feet again on sharp rocks and stumbled on the stones that rolled under his soles. He was completely exhausted, and so were the other members of the expedition. For two days, he had been struggling in the biggest rapids of the Missouri.

Captain Clark followed from the riverbank the laborious progress of the white pirogue and canoes that had to be pushed rather than towed. He envied Captain Lewis who was leading a small team on foot up the south branch. If it was indeed the Missouri, Lewis would have the honor of being the first American to see the Great Falls, the last obstacle on the river, which Seeing Snake had described as the greatest wonder of the world.

In early afternoon, when the sun was beating down, Clark had the white pirogue brought ashore. He noticed immediately that Sacagawea had become extremely weak. With Charbonneau's help, he carried mother and child to the other end of the boat where a small shelter provided some shade. Then, the expedition set off again, going past several islands crawling with rattle snakes.

On that day, the Captain received a letter from Lewis, delivered by Private Joseph Fields. Lewis was proudly writing to announce the discovery of the Great Falls of the Missouri, about twenty miles upstream. He was waiting there with his men, Drouillard, Gibson and Goodrich.

In the evening, they settled in a former Indian camp, at the foot of a low cliff. Captain Clark, for the first time in three days, gave up on the idea of bleeding Sacagawea again, yielding to Charbonneau's pleas; the French-Canadian ascribed his wife's worsening condition to that particular medical practice.

–If you keep on bleeding her, you'll kill her, he had said to the Captain.

Clark thus merely administered medicine to the Shoshoni woman, but to no avail. Under the tepee, she moaned all night. "Her case might be dangerous," wrote Clark in his journal on June 14, 1805.

The next morning, Sacagawea was worse than ever. She was feverish, she vomited and lost a lot of blood vaginally. Charbonneau saw the signs of desperation on her emaciated face. As he bent down to carry her in the boat, he heard her whisper:

–I'm going to die. Save Jean-Baptiste.

When she was laid down in the pirogue, Clark applied a poultice of Peruvian bark to her intimate parts. He also gave her some opium for the pain.

And as the boat floated along the crystal-clear waters of the Missouri, the young Shoshoni sank into a strange dream. Seeming to have shed her weight, she entered a world without pain or hope. A kind of surprised fatalism followed the dejection she had felt that morning; she would die without fulfilling her mother's prophecy and she would abandon her son before even having weaned him.

That night, the pain, the sweats, the moaning and groaning resumed, mingled with Jean-Baptiste's crying. Captain Clark tried to give Sacagawea other medicines, but she rejected them forcefully.

–*Non!* she cried out in French, pushing away the salts and the laudanum.

Charbonneau was desperate. He grabbed an axe and went off in search of a big poplar tree. About a quarter of a mile downstream, he found the tree out of which he would carve a canoe. He started chopping the tree, wielding the axe with rage rather than skill. He had gotten it in his head to return to his village, Metaharta. With luck, Otter Woman would still be there and she would take care of Sacagawea. He had to turn back; that was his only chance to save mother and child.

He couldn't bear any longer to stand by, helplessly watching her suffer. No treatment had been effective, not even the poultices he himself had suggested. To continue on the journey meant certain death.

He kept on chopping, with tears streaming down his cheeks; little Jean-Baptiste would not survive his mother's death. The thought made him even angrier; his axe came down hard, and chips of wood flew all over.

–They won't die! cried out Toussaint, hitting the tree with a vengeance. They won't die!

Drawn by the shouts of the distraught father, Clark and Labiche came up from behind.

–Charbonneau, for the love of God, what are you doing? said Clark.

Toussaint didn't hear the Captain, or Labiche, and just went on chopping furiously. Raising his voice, the Captain repeated his question. This time, Charbonneau heard him. As he turned around, Labiche translated the Captain's words.

–I'm building a canoe, he answered with glazed eyes.

–But why? Clark looked surprised.

–To go back home, with my wife and child.

The Captain became alarmed.

–It's sheer madness! Do you realize that we are nine hundred miles from Fort Mandan?

–I won't go one step further toward the West, protested Charbonneau with a tone of determination. If I must bury my wife and son, it will be at home, on the Great Plains.

The Captain looked at Charbonneau, who had started chopping again, but didn't say a word. He wondered how he could make him see reason. After a while, he said:

–Wait at least until Captain Lewis examines your wife. We will catch up with him tomorrow at the bottom of the Great Falls. Don't forget what he did for her when she was giving birth.

When he heard the translation, Charbonneau dropped his axe and fell to the ground; burying his face in his hands, he started crying softly.

The other two turned away, ill at ease.

Sacagawea's face had become like an old woman's; her pulse was barely detectable and her arms and fingers were twitching. Her life was faltering

–Drouillard, come here! ordered Captain Lewis emerging from the tepee where he had just sounded the chest of Sacagawea.

He hadn't seen her in six days: she was a mere shadow of her former self. He said to the hunter:

–Go to Sulphur Spring and bring back some water. Hurry, it's for Charbonneau's wife.

Drouillard started running, followed by Charbonneau, who couldn't keep still any more. Lewis had found the spring a few days earlier: it fell into the river from the top of a rock; its water, as limpid as could be, contained sulphur and iron. In his youth, he had heard of a sulphur spring in Virginia that was supposed to possess healing properties. The water from the sulphur spring might save Sacagawea.

Lewis went back under the tepee where the young woman was lying on her buffalo skin, with her son sleeping next to her. The Captain applied another poultice on her abdomen and gave her some more opium. He repeated the treatment later in the day. He was very concerned, not just about Sacagawea and Jean-Baptiste, but also about the continuation of the expedition. He had to face facts: without Charbonneau's wife, the Corps of Discovery could not obtain from the Shoshonis the horses needed for the portage between the Missouri and the Columbia. The Indian girl had to be saved, otherwise the mission that Thomas Jefferson had entrusted to him would fail, near the Great Falls of the Missouri, still far from its destination.

Drouillard and Charbonneau came back to the camp with two flasks filled with sulphur water. Lewis gave some to Sacagawea, whose eyes lit up instantly.

–I'm hungry, said Sacagawea when she woke up the next morning.

She smiled and picked up the baby. That was a sure sign she was feeling better. The pain in her abdomen and back had vanished, the bleeding had stopped and her fever was down. Charbonneau thanked St. Anne and served his woman breakfast: freshly-caught trout, which were plentiful at the bottom of the falls. For dinner, he brought her grilled buffalo, well seasoned with salt and pepper.

Captain Lewis had her drinking the sulphur water all day. In the evening, he took her pulse: it was stronger and more regular. He attributed her illness to an obstruction of her menstrual flow, the result of a chill. He felt it was now reasonable to believe in her full recovery.

Two days later, Sacagawea felt so much better that she went in search of "white apples" with Toussaint. She ate them later with fish. In fact, she ate so many that she made herself sick; by the end of the afternoon, she had a fever and a stomach ache again.

When he saw the condition she was in, Lewis reprimanded Charbonneau, through Drouillard.

–You fool! Didn't I tell you what she should eat?

–Yes, but she wanted white apples, answered Charbonneau.

–It was up to you to forbid her to eat them!

The Captain was furious; he turned his back to Charbonneau to look after Sacagawea. He administered a few doses of saltpeter to bring her fever down. Before retiring, he gave her some drops of opium, so that she slept soundly through the night.

When she awakened, Sacagawea was perfectly healthy again. Sucking at her mother's breast, Jean-Baptiste started smiling again.

Chapter Ten

The Great Portage

Charbonneau noticed the roar of the Great Falls in the morning of June 15, that is, a full day before actually seeing the first cascade. As the white pirogue got closer, he heard the sound more distinctly. He expected something grandiose; he was not disappointed. When he came round a bend in the rapids, an awesome sight appeared before him: a curtain of white mist, two hundred yards wide and twenty feet high, towered over the Missouri, perpendicular to its bed. Water from the river rose in a fine drizzle, after having literally disintegrated over the rocks on which it crashed loudly from a height of ninety feet.

Above the foam, Charbonneau saw a rainbow created by the reflection of the sun on the mist. Captain Clark, watching from the riverbank, was just as impressed, but he was brought down to earth when he joined Captain Lewis, who had been waiting for him for two days at the bottom of the falls.

–Do you see that? said Lewis, pointing to the first of the Great Falls. Well, there are four more, spread out over sixteen miles at least.

–Sixteen miles! exclaimed Clark. Seeing Snake told us that a five-mile portage would be enough to get beyond the Great Falls! And he only mentioned two falls!

–It's not his first mistake, commented Lewis bitterly.

The captains looked at each other, both thinking of what the Hidatsa had told them about another portage, between the

Missouri and the Columbia. According to Seeing Snake, you only needed about four days to cross over the Rockies and reach the source of the river that led to the Pacific. He was probably wrong about that too.

Lewis and Clark set up camp in a wooded area near the mouth of a stream they named Portage Creek. For the next five days, they nervously but meticulously prepared for the portage, the most difficult and dangerous part of the expedition since they had left St. Louis.

Since the distance was much too great for men to carry the canoes and the baggage on their backs, the captains ordered six soldiers to build two carts. They carved the wheels out of the trunk of a poplar and made the axles by cutting in sections the mast of the white pirogue.

Lewis and Clark had decided to leave behind the boat that had caused them so much trouble ever since they had left Fort Mandan. Lewis was hoping to replace it, once they got beyond the falls, with an iron boat that the expedition had been carrying in kit form since St. Louis.

The captains asked Cruzatte to dig another cache and hide more goods and supplies. They stored the books, all the specimens of plants and minerals collected from the beginning of the journey, two barrels of salted pork, half a barrel of flour, a keg of powder and a few other articles the expedition would have to do without.

It was agreed that Clark would supervise the portage, which would require many trips between the camp at Portage Creek and the one at White Bear Islands, a site they had spotted a few days earlier, upstream from the falls. Lewis would settle there to complete the assembly of the metal boat: its frame would have to be covered with skins to make it float.

As for Charbonneau, he would remain at the Portage Creek camp with Sacagawea and York. They would cook for the men responsible for carrying the equipment and prepare reserves of dried meat for the rest of the journey.

The hunters had no trouble finding game. The buffalo came in large numbers to drink on the bank across the camp at Portage Creek. They also seemed to like the mineral water of Sulphur Spring that had saved Sacagawea's life.

During his first days in Portage Creek, Charbonneau managed to make his meager supply of tobacco go further by mixing it with the inside bark of the stoloniferous dogwood, a shrub he found in the undergrowth of the surrounding woods, among the blue elders, the bitter cherry and hazel trees.

–Taste this, you can smoke it! said Charbonneau to Clark who marveled at the mixture, well known to French-Canadian voyageurs, who lived in dread of running out of tobacco on their journeys.

After trying it, Clark had to admit that the aroma of the special blend was delicious and its effect, rather intoxicating.

Meanwhile, Sacagawea spent her free time doing a bit of trout fishing, happy to be alive and anxious to see her own people at last.

The first team left Portage Creek early on June 22, 1805, with a cart loaded with the parts of the iron boat as well as the baggage of Captain Lewis and the three men who would help him assemble the intriguing contraption.

Having already scouted the region, Captain Clark led the troop, taking care to avoid the ravines that, in several places, cut across the plain, which was even on the whole, but rose constantly. To find his way, Clark followed the markers he had previously driven into the ground. However, he had to stray from the trail to walk around the many herds of buffalo that roamed all over this region rich in blue grama, a type of grass they loved. Clark never lost sight of the snowy peaks of the Rocky Mountains that sparkled in the distance.

For the men who pulled or pushed the carts, this first portage was no picnic. They had to stop frequently to repair the axles. Finally, they had to replace them with new ones carved out of big willow branches, a job that took them two hours to complete.

But the problem with the carts was nothing compared to those caused by the opuntias and echinocereus, small cactus only a few inches high. Their prickly leaves tore through the leather moccasins, injuring feet already sore from the sharp stones of the Missouri.

The troop was exhausted when, at sundown, it finally reached the camp at White Bear Islands, eighteen miles from its starting point. These islands in the middle of the Missouri, which was eight hundred yards wide at that point, owed their name to the grizzly bears that often came ashore. The day before, Captain Clark had left some meat for the team, but the wolves or the grizzlies had helped themselves to about half the food supplies.

The men went to sleep feeling hungry, but that didn't prevent them from sleeping soundly under the starry skies.

The next morning, Clark and his team returned to Portage Creek early enough to hoist two canoes onto the plain, in preparation for the next portage.

While they were eating, the Captain announced to Charbonneau and York that they would have to leave the kitchen to Sacagawea.

–Tomorrow, we shall leave with the two carts, said Clark to Charbonneau through Labiche. We'll need all our men.

Charbonneau did not protest. Like the other members of the expedition, he was ready to endure the worst hardships to make it through the portage of the Great Falls, cross over the Rockies and reach the Pacific. Deep down, he stood by Lewis and Clark, and Sacagawea's recovery had cured him of any desire to go home.

After their meal, the men repaired their moccasins, fitting them with double soles to protect their feet from the cactus and the sharp-edged footprints left by the buffalo during the last rains. They used buffalo leather, which was stronger than deer's.

Charbonneau, accompanied by Labiche, went to see Clark before retiring for the night. He supported his mission, but that didn't make him blind.

–Sir, said Charbonneau, looking the Captain straight in the eye, I don't want to meddle, but the iron boat will never float. You should tell Captain Lewis; that will save us a lot of time.

Clark smiled and gave him a friendly tap on the back.

–Charbonneau, when we want your opinion, we'll ask for it.

–I'm just trying to help, said Charbonneau as the American turned away.

He shrugged and went back to the tepee where Sacagawea was nursing Jean-Baptiste. The little one, to the great delight of his parents and Captain Clark, had started to dance again.

–I'm leaving tomorrow with the others, said Charbonneau as he lay down next to his woman.

She nodded in agreement. She would be left alone at the camp in Portage Creek with Sergeant Ordway and Private Goodrich, in charge of watching the remaining supplies and merchandise.

Charbonneau pushed the cart with both hands and so he was helpless against the constant onslaught of mosquitoes buzzing around his head. The voracious insects preyed relentlessly on the exposed parts of the body, and their stinging added to the misery of the prickly cactus that lacerated his feet.

Bathed in sweat under the blazing sun, the cook soon started regretting his pots. He muttered to himself, but didn't dare complain out loud. After all, the men who had taken part in the first portage were worse off than he was. Some limped, others, worn down by heat and fatigue, could barely stand.

They stopped often to rest. Each time, the men collapsed on the ground and many fell asleep on the spot. However, as soon as they heard the signal, they set off again without grumbling and in good spirits, though the exhausting nature of their work quickly dampened their positive attitude.

When they arrived at the camp on White Bear Islands at the end of the day, they were surprised to find Lewis busying himself around the fire. He had sent his three companions off to hunt wapitis, whose skins were needed to cover the metal frame of his boat, and now he was preparing a meal for the first time in the entire journey. As the troop traveled further west, distinctions between captains, sergeants, privates and civilians all seemed to disappear. Later, around the fire, Cruzatte played his fiddle and managed to get some of the men to dance.

Charbonneau took part in only one portage. In spite of her good intentions, Sacagawea could not prepare by herself a meal to satisfy more than thirty hungry men; Captain Clark asked the interpreter to put on his apron again. Charbonneau was not altogether displeased: in all his life as a *coureur de bois*, he had never been involved in such a difficult portage. At breakfast the next morning, he perked up the Captain with a cup of black coffee, which he hadn't had since the winter.

In the course of the next few days, the men continued to carry baggage and goods from one camp to the other, braving the rain, the mud, the wind and even the cold, since the temperature often went from one extreme to another. One afternoon, they were caught in a hailstorm in the middle of the plain. A man was knocked down three times by hailstones as big as a fist; those who wore no hat were bleeding from the head. Clark made them drink a glass of rum to help them recover. Some of the men who had not drunk alcohol in a long time got sick. They nonetheless carried on with their grueling task.

The encampment at Willow Run was three quarters of the way between Portage Creek and White Bear Islands. Sometimes the men stopped there when they thought they might not complete the portage before sundown. Since the transportation of the equipment was nearly done, Toussaint and his family moved there on June 29. Taking advantage of the last glow of sunset, Captain Clark decided to go and admire one more time the last of the Great Falls, which roared half a mile upstream from the camp. He took York along and Charbonneau's family. York eventually went off on his own; he had been given a rifle again and permission to go hunting.

Clark and his companions walked along the cliff that overhung the river and revealed a magnificent view of the fall. Charbonneau gazed, lost in wonder again. The water rushed down a fifty-foot rocky drop, as smooth as marble. No artist could have painted a more perfect waterfall.

Soon, the spectators were brought out of their state of rapture by a big cloud that was moving in. Fearing they might be caught in a downpour or a hailstorm, Clark motioned to his companions to follow him. He looked for shelter, but couldn't find any place where his group did not run the risk of being pushed off into the river by fierce winds. Finally, about half a mile from the falls, he discovered a deep ravine protected by overhanging rocks.

He went down with Charbonneau and Sacagawea. When they reached the bottom, they set down their rifles, compass and other articles. The young mother took Jean-Baptiste in her arms to reassure him. The baby, who was muffled up in a buffalo skin, started to babble happily.

It started to rain soon after, lightly at first, then more and more heavily. The water began to flow to the bottom of the ravine where it formed a stream that swelled before their very eyes. It would obviously turn into a torrent of mud and sweep everything in its path. They had to leave this shelter immediately.

Charbonneau grabbed his rifle, took Sacagawea by the arm and started climbing up. Clark helped him by pushing with his right hand the Shoshoni woman who was overcome with fear. With his other hand, he got hold of his rifle and his bullet bag, leaving the rest behind. When he also started climbing, the water was up to his waist. A few minutes later, the level of the water rose to ten feet and the swelling torrent uprooted trees and carried chunks of rock along its tremendous rush to the Missouri.

Whipped by the lashing rain, her hands covered in mud, Sacagawea let go of the buffalo skin in which Jean-Baptiste was wrapped. But she was quick to react and miraculously caught the half-naked baby before he disappeared with his blanket in the flooded ravine.

Captain Clark found York at the edge of the ravine; he had started looking for his master as soon as the storm had begun. The Captain ordered him to run to the camp and bring back something warm to cover up Jean-Baptiste and Sacagawea who were freezing. Fearing a relapse, he gave the young woman some alcohol straight from the flask. He passed it on to Charbonneau before helping himself. They had had a narrow escape.

The next day, Charbonneau and his family reached the camp at White Bear Islands. The portage was completed two days later, after two weeks of superhuman efforts. The men had drawn on their last reserves of energy and endured indescribable suffering; their feat had enhanced their stature in the eyes of their captains and ensured their place in history.

On July 4, 1805, Captain Clark's team finished covering the metal structure of the boat with skins. The only thing left to do was to make sure that the hull was waterproof. One of the soldiers had christened the boat, not without irony, The Experiment.

All the members of the expedition couldn't wait to set off again, to meet the Shoshonis at last, but none more than Captain Lewis. In eighteen days, the Corps of Discovery had only covered eighteen measly miles. And at what cost! Lewis had lost all hope of getting back to Fort Mandan before the end of the year. Nearly three months after leaving its winter quarters, the expedition had not yet reached the Rockies.

Summer was wearing on, but Lewis did not want to leave without the boat of his dreams. In his eyes, *The Experiment* met the needs of the troop perfectly. It was light enough to be carried easily by five men, yet sturdy enough to sail with a load of at least eight thousand pounds, plus the crew.

However, Lewis was the only one displaying such confidence. Like Charbonneau, most of the men doubted it would ever float. But nobody would have dared to oppose Lewis on this matter, not even Clark who was among the skeptics.

Lewis had hoped to find pines near the camp of White Bear Islands. He intended to use the resin from these trees to waterproof the seams of the boat, but there were none in the surroundings.

–We shall use bee's wax mixed with coal dust and buffalo suet, he decided after examining the skins sewn together.

After that, he invited the men to sit down to eat. It might not have been sumptuous, but the meal was much appreciated. Assisted by Sacagawea, Charbonneau served buffalo steaks, salted pork, meatballs and beans. At the end of the meal, they drank some alcohol to celebrate the anniversary of the independence of the United States.

–Enjoy, gentlemen, that's the last of the alcohol, announced Captain Clark, unwittingly putting a damper on the jovial atmosphere of the supper.

Cruzatte for his part didn't let it get him down. He played his fiddle and the men danced until a downpour interrupted the festivities in the middle of the night.

It rained all the time and the air was constantly humid, so that the skins that covered the hull could not dry. Lewis had the boat suspended over a row of little fires to accelerate the process. But the bad weather persisted; two days later, hailstones fell as big as bullets. As if that weren't enough, grizzly bears prowled about the camp at night, which did nothing to boost the men's morale; fortunately, the dog's yelping kept them at a distance. But they still had to contend with mosquitoes, ever more numerous; they seemed to have turned up from all corners of the region to make the most of the presence of these thirty bodies. Night and day, their stings and constant buzzing made life a living hell.

On July 8, the sun came out at last and the air warmed up; Lewis was able to dry the boat. He had two coats of "tar" applied to the skins. The next morning, all the members of the expedition gathered on the bank of the Missouri, just across White Bear Islands, for the christening of the boat.

It floated on the water like a cork. Lewis was reassured; he ordered the men to fit it with seats and oars, then to load all the boats and get ready to leave. The work was making good progress when a strong wind rose unexpectedly; it blew so fiercely that the waves crashed into the canoes. They had to be unloaded, but part of the baggage was already wet before it could be put under cover on the shore.

The wind remained violent until late in the evening, forcing the expedition to postpone its departure. Lewis noticed that the coat of waterproofing was coming off *The Experiment*, so that the seams were letting in water. It was beyond repair. He had to resign himself to the failure of the project that had been so close to his heart.

–Sink the boat, he ordered his men, looking vexed.

Charbonneau turned to look at Captain Clark, but the latter lowered his eyes.

It was decided that *The Experiment* would be replaced by two pirogues. The next day, Captain Clark, Charbonneau and a few other men crossed to the other side of the river in search of the trees they needed. They found some poplars of the right size eight miles upstream from the camp.

They broke twelve axe handles in their attempt to cut down two trees and hollow out the trunks; Sergeant Pryor dislocated his shoulder, so hard did he wield his axe. The men worked day in, day out, and finished the pirogues in six days, launched them and returned to camp. Although they were heavy, the two boats clove through the water as light bark canoes. Delight followed the frustration of the previous days; the men shouted merrily.

–It's better than a boat made of skins, said Charbonneau mockingly.

When he heard the translation, Clark replied:

–Charbonneau, instead of talking nonsense, why don't you sing something.

Five days after leaving the camp at White Bear Islands, Toussaint Charbonneau found himself singing a song that he hadn't dared strike up when he had first seen the Rockies:

M'en revenant de la jolie Rochelle
M'en revenant de la jolie Rochelle
J'ai rencontré trois jolies demoiselles...

Pretty soon, Cruzatte, François Labiche, Georges Drouillard and Baptiste Lepage joined him as they paddled.

C'est l'aviron qui nous mène, qui nous mène
C'est l'aviron qui nous mène en haut...

Charbonneau sang at the top of his lungs without paying attention to the words; he was obsessed with the idea that each time he lowered his paddle in the water and pulled, it took him deeper into the Rockies. He would never have believed that the river could actually carve its way through the mountains. And he would never have believed that a canoe could travel so far into the highlands of the West.

After singing his heart out, Charbonneau turned to Sacagawea, who sat behind him in the canoe, with Jean-Baptiste in her lap.

–Have you ever come here before?

–No, answered the young Shoshoni woman, who did not recognize any of the familiar places of her youth.

For about an hour, the boats of the expedition had been advancing between amazing cliffs that rose vertically on each side of the Missouri up to twelve hundred feet. In some of the narrower passages, they seemed to meet at the top, although they were at least a hundred yards apart at the base, where the deep waters of the river flowed.

At the bottom of the canyon, the temperature was stifling. And to think that, just before coming to what Captain Lewis called the "Gates of the Rocky Mountains," they had seen snow on the lofty peaks of the surrounding mountains. What a contrast! Charbonneau and many of the others had removed their shirts as they paddled strenuously against a current ever stronger and often crossed by rapids.

–Keep your eyes open, he said to his Shoshoni woman for the tenth time that day.

–You can set your mind at ease and paddle, answered Sacagawea who was fully alert.

For a few days now, they had been crossing what she knew to be Shoshoni country. Captain Clark, who preceded the expedition on land with York, had spotted campsites that resembled those of her people. In one of them, the American had noticed that the pines had been stripped of their bark.

–The Shoshonis remove the bark to get the resin, Sacagawea had explained through Charbonneau and Drouillard. They also use the soft part of the wood as food.

She knew then that she would see the Three Forks again, the place where the Hidatsas had abducted her five years earlier. She wondered if she would she still feel at home in this part of the country.

The darkest night soon fell on the river. The rocks took on a sinister look; in some places, they appeared as monsters ready to pounce on the members of the expedition. They traveled four more miles, trying to avoid the barely visible reefs, before they came to a stretch of dry land big enough to set up camp. They found a spot, planted with pine trees, on the left bank of the river. A strong breeze was blowing between the rocky walls; for the first time in days, the members of the expedition did not need their mosquito nets to sleep.

–Do you recognize anything? asked Charbonneau, turning to his woman.

This time, Sacagawea didn't even bother answering. Since the beginning of this scorching day, by far the hottest the expedition had known, she had scanned the banks, the islands, the mountains, searching for a familiar sign, but found nothing she could identify with certainty.

Of course, she did recognize the birds flying in the sky, falcons, great mountain woodpeckers, crows, snipes and others, as well as the animals she caught a glimpse of on the banks, but nothing in the scenery awakened any memories in her. Otters were frolicking in the water, and that reminded her of Otter Woman, who had perhaps followed them on horseback, many miles back.

–You've never been here? insisted Charbonneau.

His incessant questions expressed a general uneasiness shared by most of the troop; July was drawing to a close and they still hadn't come across a single Shoshoni. In fact, since they had left Fort Mandan, they hadn't seen a single Indian, with the exception of Caltahcota and his band of hunters in early April.

What if the Corps of Discovery were to miss the Shoshonis? It certainly was possible. The members of that nation did not live permanently in the region; they were nomads and they did not come down the east side of the Rockies until the end of the summer, on their way to the Prairie where they hunted the buffalo. All they had to do was go by a week too soon or a week too late to miss them.

And what if the expedition did not find horses to complete its journey over the Rockies? This question preyed on everyone's mind. In the middle of the afternoon, Sacagawea suddenly cried out:

–Toussaint! Look!

Charbonneau quickly turned around. Sacagawea was pointing, on their right, to a brook whose chalky waters flowed into the Missouri. She looked triumphant.

–You recognize the brook? asked the interpreter.

–Yes! she exclaimed enthusiastically. This is where we used to come to get white paint! We'll soon reach the Three Forks!

The Three Forks! Charbonneau hurried to tell the news to Captain Lewis and the other men. They were all delighted. The Three Forks marked the end of the Missouri. At last, the expedition was getting closer to the source of the river.

One more question was on the Captain's mind.

–Are there any falls from here to the Three Forks, he asked Sacagawea.

–No.

–Are you sure?

–Yes.

Despite her reassurances, Lewis remained skeptical. He had trouble believing that a river could flow over such a long distance in the middle of mountains without being impeded by waterfalls or impassable rapids.

Late in the evening, they reached the encampment set up by Clark. All day long, up hill and down dale, the Captain had continued searching for the Shoshonis, but his efforts had been futile and he was in pretty bad shape. He had done so much walking on cactus that his feet had become running sores.

–If you wish, I'll take over from you tomorrow, said Lewis when he saw the state his companion was in.

–Absolutely not, I'll keep on walking, replied Clark in a tone that couldn't bear to be contradicted.

He ordered Frazier and the Fields brothers to be ready to accompany him the next morning. Since Sacagawea's discovery, Charbonneau's mind had been eased, and he asked permission to join the walkers.

–I want to go with you. I'll find the Shoshonis!

Captain Clark looked at Charbonneau; he was about to refuse him permission, but he changed his mind, thinking that perhaps the presence of the French-Canadian would end his streak of bad luck.

Clark and his four companions followed an Indian trail all day, walking at the bottom of a valley hemmed in by high mountains; on their sides grew a few scattered pines and cedars.

Under a blazing sun, they advanced in silence, except to report the presence of a stag, a wapiti or a bear. When it was time to eat, they roasted the ribs of a deer shot by Charbonneau. Toward the end of the afternoon, Clark killed a wapiti; Frazier and the Fields brothers hung it from a tree near the river, so that when the men came along in their canoes, they would pick it up.

Charbonneau walked at the back of the line. Suddenly, at the top of a cliff, he spotted some rams, a dozen females with their lambs. Seemingly defying the laws of gravity, the animals skipped from rock to rock with ease; yet, the slightest stumble would have hurled them to the bottom of the precipice, five hundred feet below.

–Living up there, these animals have nothing to fear from men, bears or wolves, he declared out loud, forgetting that his companions did not understand French.

However, they seemed just as excited by the sight as he was. A little further on, they saw a wild horse drinking from a brook, but it ran off long before the walkers got near.

They had covered twenty-three miles when Clark set up camp in the valley, not far from where they had seen a large number of wapitis take flight. That night, by the light of the fire, Charbonneau noticed the extreme weariness on the Captain's face and his feverish eyes. The American was literally making himself ill over his search for the Shoshonis.

Charbonneau was just as obsessed with finding them. He wanted to be of assistance in getting horses for the expedition, to help Clark as the Captain had helped him, in late June, in front of the fourth drop of the Great Falls. But something else motivated him. He was anxious to be first in meeting the Shoshonis, thereby honoring what he believed to be an ancient tradition: in the West, the first White men to see Indians were always French-Canadian. The Spanish, of course, had been in the South West for two centuries already, but that didn't count in Charbonneau's eyes because they conducted their operations near home base, not thousands of miles away like the voyageurs who left from Montreal. Perhaps because of the landscape itself, so relentlessly grandiose that it was overwhelming, the Chief of the Little Village felt more deeply the historic significance of the expedition. He would become part of the legend, as predicted by his wife's dream.

The next day, the sun, the mosquitoes and the cactus continued to inflict pain on the explorers. They still didn't see a ghost of a Shoshoni; at most, they detected some horses' footprints going back four or five days. Charbonneau was exhausted and he sprained his ankle at the end of the day; the scream of pain he let out echoed across the mountains. It is thus on one leg that he finally arrived at the Three Forks, at the end of the Missouri. The three rivers of equal width that joined together wound their way lazily through a big valley. According to Seeing Snake's information, the branch further to the west led to the true source of the Missouri.

The French-Canadian trader forgot all about the pain in his ankle when he saw that the region was teeming with beaver; the hunt was even more promising there than at the Yellowstone. And even if nobody could understand him, Charbonneau cried out in French:

–We must build a trading post at the Three Forks! It's beaver heaven!

Clark and the three soldiers understood very well why he was so excited; they also recognized the commercial potential of the site. They set up camp there and waited for the canoes to arrive.

In the evening, around the fire, Sacagawea told the members of the expedition what had happened to her in that very spot five years earlier. Her story had to go through Charbonneau and Drouillard before it was conveyed to the Americans. The Shoshoni woman was eager for them to hear it.

–We used to come and camp here, she began. Every summer, we would stop here for a few days before heading down to the plains to hunt the buffalo. Five summers ago, the Hidatsas surprised us while we were swimming. We tried to flee by crossing the river in shallow waters, but the Hidatsas caught up with us and attacked. They killed four of our men and as many women. They also took the lives of many of our boys in order to take the women prisoner. I was captured with three other girls by Chief Le Borgne whom you know.

Out of modesty, Sacagawea didn't let her feelings show as she told this painful episode of her life, which led Lewis to think that the cruelty of the Hidatsas had not had much of an impact on her, and that she was not moved by the fact she was now back in her homeland.

Before retiring, Lewis wrote down in his journal: "Tho' I cannot discover that she shows any immotion of sorrow in recollecting this event, or of joy in being again restored to her native country; if she has enough to eat and a few trinkets to wear, I believe she would be content anywhere."

How wrong he was! Just a few feet away, the young woman could not fall asleep, excited at the thought of seeing her family, but also frightened at the prospect. Might not these five years, nearly six, spent among other tribes and Whites, have changed her as a person? She did not have the answer within, or at least could not find it yet.

The captains decided to trust Seeing Snake and continue the journey along the branch that was furthest west, which they named Jefferson in honor of their President and sponsor. They called the other two branches of the fork Madison and Gallatin. Captain Clark had no strength left and his feet were covered with abscesses; he finally had to resign himself to continuing the journey by canoe. And so, on August 1st, Lewis left in search of the Shoshonis with Sergeant Gass, Drouillard and Charbonneau who, despite his fatigue and sore ankle, insisted on walking. They crossed deep valleys, scorched by the sun. No shade anywhere, not a puff of wind and, all around, mountain slopes with sparse vegetation. Five days later, Charbonneau couldn't stand it anymore and had to quit too. Losing hope of ever finding the Shoshonis, he joined Clark in the canoe.

–Where are those damned Snakes? he asked Sacagawea, who traveled in the same canoe with Jean-Baptiste.

This was one of those rare occasions on which the French-Canadian used the name that his fellow countrymen had given the Shoshonis. His tone became intense, more aggressive, as if he held it against his woman that her people could not be found. Exasperated, Sacagawea didn't answer.

It got increasingly difficult to paddle. The men had to tow the canoes through the rapids and over countless beaver dams. Though they were exhausted, they forged ahead, propelled by an unshakeable will.

A few days later, Sacagawea recognized, on a high plain on her left, a hill the Shoshonis called Beaver Head, because it looked like the great rodent.

–We'll find the Shoshonis around here, I'm sure of it, she said, hoping she was right.

During the following days, Captain Lewis noticed that the surrounding mountains did not seem as high, and yet they were also covered in snow. He concluded that the expedition had never stopped gaining altitude since it had entered the range of the

Rockies; indeed, they had been climbing imperceptibly along the embedded valleys that rose gradually.

He was amazed again that the Missouri and its tributaries remained navigable so far into the mountains. If the Columbia and its own affluents were similar, the crossing of the continent by its watercourses, President Jefferson's dream, would turn out to be possible and safe. Of course, he was ahead of the rest of the expedition by several days, and he did not accurately gauge how difficult it was for the canoes to ride the numerous rapids.

On August 12, Lewis and his three traveling companions reached a source that they identified as the Missouri's. Springing from the ground at the foot of a low mountain, it ran down a gentle slope over half a mile and into the Jefferson, which in turn flowed into the Missouri.

Lewis, Drouillard, Shields and McNeal knelt before the brook and quenched their thirst in the clear and ice-cold water. This was the moment they had been waiting for! Drouillard stood up again and straddled the trickle; then stretching out his arms, he cried out:

–Lord of life, I thank you for letting me live long enough to straddle the mighty Missouri.

Lewis was also overcome with emotion. Technically, he was mistaken about the real source of the Missouri, but symbolically, he was indeed the first American to head up that river as far as the Rockies, to the place from which it sprang.

His joy was short-lived. As he surveyed the arid and desolate region, he could not help wondering where on earth the Shoshonis were.

Chapter Eleven

The Homecoming

The men had to tow the canoes through another series of rapids. Their limbs were stiff from fatigue and the cold water, but their hardships were far from over.

About three miles upstream, Sacagawea was walking along the river, followed by Charbonneau and Clark. She kept her eyes wide open in the hope of seeing a sign that would indicate the presence of her people, or that Lewis and his men had passed that way. They had not been seen in six days. Where could they be? Had they found the Shoshonis? Had they reached the continental divide, that mythical place in the Rockies where the waters flowing to the Atlantic, the Gulf of Mexico and the Arctic are parted from those flowing to the Pacific?

These questions preoccupied Sacagawea, just as they worried the other members of the expedition. But she had other things on her mind that concerned only her. Should she stay with Jean-Baptiste in her native country where she had dreamt of returning during her long captivity? Was she really willing to leave her son's father? Could she do it? Should she?

She instinctively touched her left cheek. She remembered Charbonneau's slap. Three days earlier, during the evening meal, the French-Canadian had hit her for the very first time. She had seen him slap Otter Woman who used to defend herself tooth and nail. But she herself had never felt his burning hand across her face.

She had aroused his anger by dropping into the fire a fish she was grilling. Toussaint had reached into the flames to try and retrieve it, but had only succeeded in burning his fingers.

–Idiot! he had cried out, slapping the young woman in the face. We're starving and you throw good food into the fire!

–I dropped it, she replied, burying her face in her hands.

Jean-Baptiste had looked at his father with surprise. Not far from the scene, Captain Clark had also witnessed Charbonneau's gesture and had dashed over to the fire where the interpreter's family was.

–Charbonneau! If I ever see you hit that woman again, you'll have to deal with me! he said in English.

All the men had gone hunting or fishing; there was no one about to translate. Charbonneau had nevertheless understood the Captain's disapproval very well; he felt humiliated and had left to join the other fishermen on the riverbank. On the way, he had remembered his promise to Grande-Cotillon, the Mandan *berdache,* on Christmas Eve. He had just broken that promise and this realization added to his sense of shame.

Secretly grateful, Sacagawea was aware of how much her life had changed. In 1800, she had been abducted by a monster, Le Borgne, who had held her prisoner and mistreated her for two years before selling her to an uncouth fellow, Charbonneau, who, in spite of everything, had made her feel like singing and laughing again. And now, she was going home, under the protection of a White soldier with red hair, Clark, who promised to handle her man if he dared to raise his hand to her again.

Did she really want to leave all that to go and live with the Shoshonis? Shouldn't Jean-Baptiste stay with the expedition in order for her mother's prophecy to come true? Would she find a man better than Charbonneau?

She was mulling over these questions in her head when, at a bend in the river, she caught sight of many Indians who were riding horses in their direction.

–Toussaint! Those men are Shoshonis, she cried out, leaping in his arms.

They started jumping for joy, singing and kissing. Clark, who followed a hundred yards back, noticed their open rejoicing, as if there had never been a strain between them.

Sacagawea turned to Clark and sucked her fingers as a baby would a breast. It was her way of making him understand that the men on horseback were from her native country. At this point, Charbonneau recognized Drouillard among the Shoshonis; he was dressed like an Indian and he came forward with a smile on his lips.

–Drouillard! exclaimed Charbonneau, also smiling. What on earth are you doing?

–Captain Lewis has sent me ahead with these Indians to meet up with you. He's waiting at the forks of the Jefferson. He's set up camp there with a Shoshoni chief who has horses.

–Horses! Hurray! Charbonneau did a little jig for joy. We'll cross over those damned mountains yet!

Drouillard summarized the situation to Clark who was immensely relieved to see the Shoshonis.

–Let's join Captain Lewis at his camp! he called out cheerfully.

He tacked a note to a tree for the benefit of the men who were towing the canoes, and set off for the camp, about a two-hour walk from there, with Drouillard next to him, Charbonneau and Sacagawea right behind. The Shoshonis went along, singing all the way, so happy were they to see a woman of their own nation among the strangers. Sacagawea sang with them, able at last to express herself out loud in her mother tongue. On her back, Jean-Baptiste was jumping up and down and clapping his hands. As for Charbonneau, he was glad to have the opportunity to act as interpreter with the Shoshonis. He didn't think at all about what his wife's return to her family would mean for him.

As they arrived at the encampment, a woman made her way through the crowd and ran to Sacagawea, who uttered a scream of disbelief: Butterfly Woman! Butterfly Woman! It was really she, the Shoshoni girl who had been abducted with her and Otter Woman by the Hidatsas. After enduring months of captivity in Le Borgne's house, she had been brave enough to run away and smart enough to outwit the warriors of the fearsome Hidatsa chief. After a long journey across the plain and the mountains, she had managed to get back to her people. She was just as amazed to see Sacagawea again; she had never thought it would happen, and yet, there she was, Sacagawea, before her very eyes, with a beautiful seven-month-old baby on her back. It was something of a miracle.

–I'm so happy to see you! said Butterfly Woman, pressing her friend to her heart.

–The only thing missing to make my happiness complete is Otter Woman, said Sacagawea.

The two young women continued kissing and hugging.

While the touching reunion took place, Lewis introduced Clark to the Shoshoni chief, Cameahwait, who welcomed the American by embracing him and pressing his left cheek against his.

–I'm very pleased, said Cameahwait in Shoshoni.

The chief was tall, with piercing eyes and an aquiline nose that gave him a noble profile. He was dressed in unadorned leggings and a fringed shirt, tightened at the waist by a leather belt and decorated on the chest with porcupine quills; he wore a necklace of grizzly claws.

–Welcome! added the chief.

He was escorted by twenty-eight men and three women, dressed in deer and wapiti skins like him. Some of the warriors had trimmed their moccasins with the skins of skunks whose tails trailed at the back of their feet.

After the first greetings, Cameahwait showed the captains to a shelter made of willow branches, and asked them to sit on antelope skins. He turned to Clark and proceeded to perform a ceremony that Lewis already knew. He laid on the Captain's head six small shells that looked like pearls, a much appreciated ornament the Shoshonis got from the Pacific coast Indians. He smeared his face with paint and grease; he then removed his moccasins and invited Lewis and Clark to do the same. Finally, he lit his pipe, puffed on it three times and passed it on to his guests.

Captain Lewis had met Cameahwait on August 13, four days before being joined by Clark. Accompanied by about sixty warriors mounted on fine horses, the Shoshoni chief had shown mistrust toward the Captain and his three companions, men from the East, the region where lived his sworn enemies, the Hidatsas, who had attacked his people again the preceding spring.

Cameahwait had nonetheless overcome his distrust and invited Lewis to his village, on the other side of the continental divide, on the Lehmi. This river flowed north as far as the main branch of the Salmon River, just as Seeing Snake and other Hidatsa chiefs had indicated. Upon arriving at the village, the Captain had been delighted to see hundreds of horses milling about the cone-shaped huts built out of willow boughs.

–I'm sure that we'll be able to buy enough of them to carry our baggage beyond the Rockies, he had said to Drouillard.

One expert look had been enough for him to notice that many of these animals would have given rise to favorable comments back in Virginia, especially south of the James River where horses were revered. Some had been branded by the Spanish who had a foothold south and west of Shoshoni country.

Even though they owned so many horses, a source of wealth and pride for them, the Shoshonis were not free from hunger and war. They lived west of the Rockies part of the year, on the banks of the Shoshoni River, where they fished for salmon, a succulent fish, but which did not provide for all their dietary needs. Once this resource was depleted by the end of the summer, they had to cross over the Rockies to go hunt the buffalo on the eastern plains, where they were often attacked by the Hidatsas who used firearms against them.

Lewis had noticed that the Shoshoni warriors only had bows and arrows, spears and shields. He had inferred that the Spanish, unlike the Canadians, refused to sell firearms to their Indian neighbors. Through Drouillard, he had tried to make Cameahwait understand that he could get him rifles if he helped the Corps of Discovery cross over the Rockies and reach its goal, the Pacific. All he had to do was sell horses to the expedition.

But before talking business, Lewis had had to persuade Cameahwait to accompany him with some of his men to the forks of the Jefferson, where Clark and the rest of the expedition were supposed to wait for him. These forks were forty miles from the

Shoshoni village, a distance the Corps of Discovery could not cover by canoe.

The Shoshonis had hesitated. They had been starving too long and some of them were eager to leave for the hunt, considering they had already wasted enough time. Others feared an ambush. In the end, only twenty-eight men and three women had accepted to follow the American Captain; Lewis had managed to arouse their curiosity by telling them that, among the members of the expedition, there were a woman from their nation and a man with black skin and frizzy hair.

When they had arrived at the forks of the Jefferson, on August 16, 1805, Lewis' heart sank. Clark and the others were not there. The Shoshonis had immediately shown their anger, seeing this hitch as proof of the White man's treachery. As a sign of good faith and so that the Indians would not disperse, Lewis had handed over his rifle to Cameahwait, and his men had done the same. The message was clear, but Lewis reinforced it by saying through Drouillard:

–I'm not afraid of dying. If I should deceive you, you can shoot me.

This gesture had inspired the Shoshonis with greater confidence, but Captain Lewis had resorted to another stratagem to convince them to camp right there and wait for Clark and the rest of the expedition. He had noticed that the note he had tacked to a tree was still there. He had asked Drouillard to fetch it and had read it in front of Cameahwait, letting him believe that Clark had written it.

–My brother informs me that he has been delayed by the river. He is not far downstream and is advancing slowly; he asks that I wait here.

Lewis had added that he would send a messenger to meet him the next morning.

–If you wish, you can send some of your own men along with him. I'll stay here with my other two companions.

The Shoshonis had accepted Clark's plan, except for one detail: they had insisted that Drouillard dress like an Indian. If he led them into a trap, he would also perish.

That night, Lewis hardly slept a wink. Not knowing what had held up Clark, he imagined the worst. What if Clark had stopped on the way because the Jefferson was too difficult to ascend? That meant the end of the expedition; the Shoshonis would never agree to go down the river; even the bravest among them would take the land route to go hunting, and the Corps of Discovery would find itself in the middle of the Rockies without a single horse.

Fortunately for Lewis, the paths of Drouillard and his Shoshoni companions and Clark's had crossed the very next day.

Cameahwait put down his pipe and signaled to the Americans that he was ready to talk. The captains sent for their interpreters, Labiche, Charbonneau and Sacagawea.

Labiche would translate from English to French, Charbonneau from French to Hidatsa and Sacagawea, from Hidatsa to Shoshoni. The process would unfold in reverse when Cameahwait spoke. It would take time, but it would work so much better than sign language. Up to that point, Lewis had to be content with Drouillard's gesturing to communicate as best he could with his hosts.

The interpreters sat to one side, between the captains and the chief. Lewis was delighted to play his part as a diplomat again, and he broached questions of sovereignty, commerce and peace with Cameahwait.

Taking over from Labiche and Charbonneau, Sacagawea started translating the first sentence of Lewis' speech. Suddenly, she stopped, jumped up and ran to the chief:

–Cameahwait! she cried out.

Seeing the chief close up, Sacagawea had recognized her elder brother. She threw her blanket on him and kissed him.

–Cameahwait! she kept repeating through her tears.

The chief was as moved as his sister, but he tried not to let it show, aware that the captains and the interpreters were observing him, witnesses to this unlikely reunion.

–If you are chief, that means our father is dead! said Sacagawea. What about our mother? Is she still alive?

–We'll talk about it after the conference, replied Cameahwait, and he asked his sister to return to her place.

Then he invited Captain Lewis to proceed, but Sacagawea interrupted again, unable to continue translating the Captain's words. Ignoring the circumstances, she insisted that her brother tell her what had happened to their parents during her long absence.

–I beg of you, tell me the truth! she pleaded.

She feared the worst. Her brother wore his hair very short as a sign of mourning. Too short. She suspected her father was not the only member of her family to have lost his life during the last Hidatsa raids. She wanted to know for sure.

The chief looked at her dolefully, and when he spoke, his voice was heavy with sadness:

–Our entire family is dead, except your elder sister's son, a little boy I have adopted.

When she learned the truth, Sacagawea burst into tears. She would never again see her parents whom she had missed so much these last years. Never again would she speak to her mother whose advice she needed so.

She wiped her tears and, turning to Charbonneau, she told him what she had just heard. Through Labiche, the interpreter hastened to inform the captains who had followed the exchange between brother and sister with inquiring eyes.

Charbonneau, as all the others, felt overwhelmed by the day's events. First, they had met the Shoshonis after looking for them across plains and mountains for days, a quest that had brought them to the brink of total exhaustion and despair. Then, Sacagawea had been reunited with Butterfly Woman and she had found her brother, who had become chief during her absence. And now, she had just learned that almost all the members of her family had died.

"You couldn't make up a story like that," thought Charbonneau, who made no bones about peppering his tales with extravagant additions. When he saw his son's mother crying, he wanted to comfort her, but Lewis didn't give him the time to go to her. He spoke again and insisted that they continue the conference where international diplomacy mingled with family drama.

The Captain made some changes to his usual speech. He gave as the official reason for the expedition the American government's desire to promote commerce with the Shoshonis. These words surprised Charbonneau. The Americans didn't even know about the existence of the Shoshoni nation before leaving St. Louis!

–Our government can supply you with any kind of merchandise, for your defense as well as your well-being, continued Lewis. Cameahwait seemed most interested by the Captain's proposal.

Of course, in order to obtain goods from the Americans, the Shoshonis had to accept the sovereignty of the United States, a powerful country, and help the expedition by providing a guide to cross over the Rockies and horses as needed. Lewis promised Cameahwait ample compensation for his help to his nation.

To the captains' great delight, the chief agreed to help the expedition in every possible way. He did not conceal his eagerness to see the Americans fulfill their promises.

–We need firearms and munitions, he said. The White men with whom we are in contact refuse to sell us any under the pretext that we would kill one another off. They prefer to leave us defenseless against our blood-thirsty neighbors, who have rifles and pursue us, kill us, irrespective of sex or age, and steal our horses every chance they get!

Even though her brother's cry from the heart intensified her sadness, Sacagawea translated his speech. His cheeks were hollow and he had a fierce look as he continued.

–If we had firearms, things would be different. We could live on the plains where the buffalo roam, eat our fill like our enemies, without having to hide out in those cursed mountains and eat berries and roots like bears. We're not afraid of our enemies, provided we're on an equal footing with them!

Clark spoke for the first time and promised a better future for Cameahwait and his people.

–After we return to our country, where the sun rises, the White men will bring you lots of rifles and all the other goods you want, he said in a solemn tone. You'll be able to obtain them at reasonable terms, in exchange for the skins of beaver, otter and ermine, which are plentiful in your region.

When he heard these words, Cameahwait expressed great pleasure.

–We have been waiting a long time to meet Whites who sell weapons. You can be sure of our friendship; we'll do everything in our power to help you.

Charbonneau translated faithfully the chief's words. He had never attended such a moving, harmonious conference of Whites and Indians. However, he wasn't naive, and he just couldn't see how the Americans would keep their promises. Who would be willing to cross the continent, face the Great Falls and the Rockies to sell firearms to a miserable band of Indians?

Toward the end of the conference, Cameahwait informed the captains that he didn't have enough horses to carry all the baggage of the expedition as far as his village, on the Lehmi River. However, he promised them to come back two days later with more men and more horses.

–That's all we need for the moment, said Lewis.

The Captain had already decided what to do next. He would stay a few days at the forks of the Jefferson with part of the troop, to unpack and air the goods and the supplies. For his part, Clark would follow Cameahwait to his village with a dozen men equipped with axes and other tools needed to build canoes. From there, Clark would explore the Lehmi as far as the Salmon River, a tributary of the Columbia. If he deemed it navigable and found the right kind of tree, he would start building boats. Otherwise, he would undertake negotiations to purchase the horses he needed, a ritual Lewis had little hope of avoiding.

Lewis also wanted Clark to take with him Charbonneau and his woman; their mission would be to make sure that Cameahwait would return to the forks with men and horses. In spite of the chief's reassurances, Lewis always feared that the Shoshonis would leave him in the lurch and decide to set off for the eastern plains before providing the expedition with the promised help.

He was careful not to show his concern to the Shoshonis. After the conference, he asked Cameahwait to introduce him to the other chiefs of the band. The time had come to distribute the gifts. They all went outside; the warriors formed a circle around the members of the expedition who had just arrived with the canoes and the baggage.

The Shoshonis showed great interest in the weapons, the boats, the men and in particular in York, Clark's servant, who stoically endured another full inspection, as if he were a freak in a traveling show. The chief of the White men had spoken the truth: there were indeed among them a Shoshoni woman and a black-skinned man. The prestige of the American expedition had gone up a notch in their estimation.

Cameahwait pointed out two of his chiefs. Lewis and Clark gave each one a small medal dating back to Washington's presidency, a shirt, leggings, a handkerchief, a knife and a small amount of tobacco. To the others, they offered a good quantity of paint, moccasins, awls, knives, necklaces and mirrors.

The mirrors made quite an impression on the warriors. One of them described them as "solid water that sometimes shines like the sun and that sometimes shows us our faces."

Clark and Lewis unintentionally made some people jealous by giving Cameahwait the most substantial presents: a United States flag, a medal bearing the effigy of President Jefferson, a tunic, a shirt, red leggings, a tobacco plug and some other articles. However, the Americans succeeded in appeasing the appetite of their hosts by preparing a hearty meal of boiled corn and beans, foods the Indians didn't know.

–I would like my people to live in a country where such food grows, said Cameahwait.

–In just a few years, the Whites will make it possible for you to live at the foot of the mountains where you will be able to grow corn, beans and squash, said Clark.

Charbonneau understood more than ever why Sacagawea and Otter Woman had wept the first time they had tasted his *boudin blanc.*

Sacagawea discreetly let her brother have a piece of sugar.

–I've never eaten anything this good, said Cameahwait to his sister.

That night, before retiring, Lewis and Clark agreed to name the site Fortunate Camp, because of the happy reunion of Sacagawea with Butterfly Woman and Cameahwait. They were also thinking of their own reunion. If Clark had not reached the forks of the

Jefferson on that day, the Shoshonis might have left the region and the expedition missed its last chance to cross over the Rockies.

The next day, in exchange for an old checkered shirt, used leggings and a knife, Charbonneau acquired a horse to carry Sacagawea and Jean-Baptiste. In his whole life, he had never clinched such a profitable bargain.

With his and Sacagawea's help, Captain Lewis also made some good deals with the Shoshonis. He gave a uniform jacket, a pair of leggings, some handkerchiefs, three knives and a few other small articles, no more than twenty dollars worth, to get three fine horses.

These horses were to be used to transport the equipment for the eleven men who would leave with Captain Clark. The group was to go over a mountain pass that the captains named Lehmi Pass. By passing through this narrow gorge, the troop would cross the continental divide and reach, forty miles further, the Shoshoni village on the Lehmi River.

Clark and his group left Fortunate Camp at eleven in the morning, accompanied by Cameahwait and the other Indians, except for two men and two women who stayed with Captain Lewis' group.

Sacagawea rode behind Butterfly Woman; the two women were overjoyed at having been reunited and told each other in great detail everything that had happened to them. Late that afternoon, Sacagawea finally asked Butterfly Woman the question that had been bothering her since her return:

–Has Swooping Eagle survived the Hidatsas' attacks?

–Yes, answered Butterfly Woman. He lives in the village with his two wives.

Sacagawea frowned. Just a few weeks before her abduction, she had been promised by her father to Swooping Eagle, who would claim her at puberty, around twelve or thirteen.

Perched on his mother's back, Jean-Baptiste enjoyed being rocked by the horse's rhythmic amble and discovering the world from above. Charbonneau walked behind them, with a nimble step and his head held high. He felt enthusiastic again, especially since the night before, Captain Lewis had entrusted him with an important mission. Taking him aside, he had said to him through Labiche:

–We're counting on you and your wife to make sure that the Indians come back here with enough horses to carry our baggage. It is of vital importance that you not let them leave for the hunt before they have helped us. Is that clear?

Charbonneau had told him not to worry. He would see to it that everything was done according to the Captain's wishes. He knew very well that the expedition, with the heavy loads it was carrying, could not possibly go through the pass without horses. And he suspected, like Lewis, that the Lehmi and Salmon Rivers would not be navigable. Going up the Jefferson had been sheer torture. They simply had to buy more horses from the Shoshonis.

After about fifteen miles, they set up camp near a brook that flowed in a rather desolate mountain prairie. Following Butterfly Woman's advice, Sacagawea didn't say a word to Charbonneau about the husband waiting for her in the village.

Meanwhile at Fortunate Camp, Captain Lewis celebrated his birthday, on August 18, by writing down in his journal these thoughts worthy of a son of the Age of Enlightenment: "This day I completed my thirty year, and conceived that I had in all human probability now existed about half the period which I am to remain in this Sublunary world. I reflected that I had as yet done but little, very little indeed, to further happiness of the human race, or to advance the information of the succeeding generation. I viewed with regret the many hours I have spent in indolence, and now sorely feel the want of that information which those hours would have given me had they been judiciously expended. But since they are past and cannot be recalled, I dash from me the gloomy thought and resolved in future, to redouble my exertions…"

When Sacagawea woke up, the grass was covered with white frost. A shiver went through her: summer was drawing to a close in the Rockies.

The explorers and the Indians set off very early, eager to see the sun come up over the snowy peaks and warm the depths of the valley. They crossed a region that was even hillier than the day before, along a series of small gorges and wet prairies, interspersed with brooks and potholes. Charbonneau and the others walked for so long in the icy waters that their feet were freezing.

Sacagawea observed the rugged landscape and remembered the harsh climate. During this second day's walk toward her native village, she remained silent for long periods of time, thinking about what lay ahead for her and the boy, and also for Toussaint.

They reached their destination the following afternoon. When she saw her village, Sacagawea shed more tears. On the bank of the Lehmi, where she was born seventeen years before, there remained only miserable huts built with willow branches. All the permanent structures had disappeared, except for a large cabin in the middle of the village square.

–What happened here? asked Sacagawea.

–The Hidatsas destroyed everything last spring, replied Butterfly Woman. They weren't content with killing our men, taking our women and stealing our horses. They had to destroy our homes.

The village now consisted of only thirty huts for a population of a hundred warriors, three hundred women and children and a handful of old men.

Cameahwait had the troop stop outside the village, where he smoked several pipes with Captain Clark and his entourage. After the welcoming ceremony, he led the visitors to the big cabin. He was about to light another pipe, when a man stood in the doorway. It was Swooping Eagle, Sacagawea's "husband." Taller and more muscular than the average Shoshoni, he was one of the bravest warriors in the village.

Speaking to Cameahwait, he asked for Sacagawea.

–She belongs to me, he said in a peremptory tone. Your father gave her to me before she was abducted by the Hidatsas. She is now pubescent; therefore I shall make her my third wife.

Cameahwait didn't know how to respond. He remembered well the day when his father, the village chief, had promised to give his youngest daughter in marriage to the valiant warrior who was attracted by her beauty. Taking his silence for assent, Swooping Eagle walked up to Sacagawea, but Charbonneau stood in his way. The French-Canadian had guessed what was happening; he turned to Sacagawea and declared firmly:

–Tell that Snake that you are my wife and that the child on your back is our son.

Sacagawea complied. She knew right there and then that she would not stay in her native country and that she would continue on the journey to the Pacific with Charbonneau and the expedition.

When he learned of her situation, Swooping Eagle shrugged his shoulders.

–You can keep her, he said to Charbonneau contemptuously; he turned on his heels and went back to his two wives.

Two days later, shortly before noon, Charbonneau and Sacagawea brought back the Shoshonis to the forks of the Jefferson River. Cameahwait led a delegation of fifty warriors, thirty women and as many children. Charbonneau and his woman had fulfilled their mission: the Shoshonis had returned to Fortunate Camp to help carry the baggage of the expedition to the Lehmi.

Lewis ordered his men to get ready to leave. He bought nine horses and a mule and hired two other horses. He had the baggage loaded on the animals. The Indian women took the rest on their backs; not one of the warriors touched the equipment.

When he saw how heavily loaded the horses were, Charbonneau estimated that they would need at least twenty-five of them to carry the baggage beyond the Rockies, to a navigable branch of the Columbia. Lewis came to the same conclusion and his face clouded over, but at the same time, he felt great satisfaction in leaving Fortunate Camp, on August 24, 1805, under blue skies and bright sunshine. The Corps of Discovery was on its way again at last.

All the members of the expedition walked, except Sacagawea, little Jean-Baptiste and Captain Lewis. The Shoshoni woman rode the horse that Charbonneau had bought a few days earlier. As for the

American, he mounted one that a Shoshoni had been kind enough to offer. He would thus be spared the fatigue of the journey and also be in a better position to supervise the advance of the troop toward the Indian village.

The expedition, together with the fifty warriors, entered Lehmi Pass. Many of the Shoshoni men couldn't help eying Sacagawea in disbelief; they were stunned to see a Shoshoni woman riding the horse, while Charbonneau, her man, was walking. They would never have tolerated such a humiliating situation.

Sacagawea, aware that her fellow countrymen were looking at her, kept her eyes on the path ahead. However, she pricked up her ears, trying to grasp the comments they made and she noticed a certain level of tension among the band. Apart from her brother, the Shoshoni delegation included two other chiefs who made no secret about the fact that they were impatient to leave for the buffalo hunt on the prairie. While they rode across the pass, some of the men expressed their displeasure out loud.

–We're hungry, said one warrior.

–Let's go down to the plains immediately, suggested another.

Although he was the most important chief of the band, Cameahwait could not ignore the other men's opinions.

The Shoshoni women brought up the rear, loaded with the baggage or their children. Sacagawea noticed among them a pregnant woman who, judging by the size of her belly, was close to giving birth. Jean-Baptiste's mother felt guilty about being on horseback.

As they reached the bottom of the gorge, a Shoshoni caught up with Lewis and informed him that, at the rear of the line, one of his men was quite ill and could not go on anymore.

–Stop here and wait for me, said Lewis to the troop.

His orders were translated by Labiche, Charbonneau and Sacagawea.

Without losing one moment, Lewis galloped in the opposite direction and, two miles uphill, rejoined one of his soldiers, Wiser, who had a severe stomach ache. He sent Sergeant Ordway, who had stayed at his side, to fetch some water. In the meantime, he gave Wiser some mint essence and a dose of opium. In less than half an hour, the soldier was on his feet again and ready to ride on Lewis' horse. The Captain continued on foot.

There was one hour of daylight left when Lewis met up with his men where he had left them, in a little ravine that opened out in the gorge. The Captain was annoyed when he saw that the Shoshonis had already set up camp and that his own men had followed their example and unloaded the horses. The troop had covered only six miles in one day!

Lewis realized that there was no point in protesting. He sent Drouillard hunting to feed his men, the fifty warriors, the thirty women and their children, who had nothing to eat except for a type of fennel that grew in wet soil. Drouillard came back empty-handed. The Captain then decided to give some corn to the women who had carried the baggage. While they were eating their scanty meal, he sent for his interpreters and Cameahwait, to whom he announced:

–We cannot provide enough food for all your people. We advise you to tell those who are not needed to go ahead to the village.

Cameahwait promised to pass on the message, but he failed to persuade anyone. His men didn't want to go any further; they were eager to feed their starving children and, for that, they wished to join the Shoshoni bands that had already left for the hunting grounds of Upper Missouri. That was why they had set up camp after only six miles.

Under the tepee, while she breast-fed Jean-Baptiste, Sacagawea explained to Charbonneau the difficult situation that her brother was facing.

–Cameahwait is thinking of sending messengers ahead to tell the rest of the band to meet them here and then leave for the hunt.

–But he can't set off for the plains! He promised the captains he would help the expedition cross over the Rockies! exclaimed Charbonneau.

–Our people are hungry, she answered in a steady voice. The children have nothing to eat but roots. Did you see their inflated tummies?

Charbonneau didn't say anything. That night, he could hardly sleep. Yes, he had seen the children: they were in a pitiful state, like their mothers. He understood that Cameahwait was thinking of the good of his band before the good of the expedition. But how could he go back on his word, after smoking several pipes?

The next morning, after the horses had been loaded, Sacagawea confirmed that Cameahwait had sent two messengers to the village on the quiet.

–They'll probably get back tomorrow, said Sacagawea.

–I must tell the Captain, replied Charbonneau.

–My brother has no choice, added Sacagawea even more firmly than usual. He must leave for the hunt; he cannot let the women and children starve to death.

Charbonneau started out again with the rest of the troop, shortly after sunrise, with an empty stomach and a knitted brow. It was extremely cold; the ice was a quarter of an inch thick at the bottom of the cooking pots.

Should he inform Lewis of what the Shoshonis were plotting? Charbonneau gave it some thought as he moved across the gorge. It seemed to him that he had to reveal such a crucial piece of information. If Cameahwait deserted the expedition now, the consequences would be disastrous.

On the other hand, the French-Canadian was not impervious to the suffering of the Indians. Had he been in Cameahwait's place, he might have done the same. A chief could not be blind to the children's distended stomachs. But Charbonneau wasn't a chief. He was a member of the Lewis and Clark expedition and he wanted to reach the Pacific.

The hunters killed three deer that were shared with the Shoshonis at the noon stop. After the meal, Charbonneau walked up to Lewis with Labiche. Without letting on about what he had known for a while, he said:

–I expect to see all the Indians leave for the plains tomorrow.

–What makes you say that? asked Lewis, sounding alarmed.

In a neutral tone, Charbonneau told him that Cameahwait had sent messengers to the village to summon them to the middle of the gorge.

–They want to go hunting.

–How long have you known? said Lewis, his heart pounding in his chest.

Charbonneau could have lied, but he told the truth.

–Sacagawea warned me this morning.

When he heard that, Lewis blew up.

–You fool! he uttered, glaring at Charbonneau. And you managed not to say anything until now! Don't you have the good sense to see the consequences of that? Only a French-Canadian would do something that stupid!

When he heard the insults translated, Charbonneau's face flushed with anger. He nearly flew at the Captain's throat, that arrogant, ungrateful, insensitive American. But he swallowed his pride and controlled himself. After all, in the Captain's place, he would have had a fit too; the expedition was in grave danger.

There was no time to waste; Lewis had to revoke Cameahwait's orders. He immediately called the three Shoshoni chiefs to a meeting. He first smoked a pipe with them; then, through his interpreters, he asked them a direct question:

–Are you men of your word?

–Yes, answered the chiefs as one.

–Didn't you promise to help me carry our baggage as far as your village and beyond the Rockies?

Once again, the chiefs answered in the affirmative.

–So, then, why have you sent messengers to tell your fellow countrymen to meet you in the middle of the gorge?

The chiefs remained silent. Lewis continued:

–If you had not promised to help me, I would never have attempted to cross the pass on foot. I would have gone down a river. In that case, you would never have seen Whites in your country again. If you wish Whites to be your friends and to supply you with weapons, you mustn't promise what you have no intention of doing. If you are men of your word, you must send a counter order to the village immediately.

Cameahwait retreated into silence. Lewis looked at the other chiefs questioningly.

–It's the first chief who sent the messengers to the village, they said, referring to Cameahwait. We were against his decision; we wanted to help you.

Sacagawea's brother had to exert incredible self-control not to react to this lie. He had sent the messengers because the two chiefs had insisted. After a while, he broke his silence and stared at Lewis.

–I promised to help you and I will keep my word.

He paused, then added:

–Maybe I was wrong, but I didn't want my people to starve to death.

Lewis didn't flinch. Charbonneau and Sacagawea exchanged meaningful glances.

Cameahwait sent a young man to the village to tell everyone to wait there. Lewis gave the messenger a handkerchief to persuade him to defend the interests of his expedition.

When the troop got under way again, Charbonneau said to Sacagawea:

–I had to tell the Captain.

His wife turned away, and for the rest of the day, she wondered if she had not betrayed her brother's interests by confiding in Charbonneau.

One day's walk away from the village, the pregnant woman who helped carry the baggage stopped at the edge of a brook, about a mile behind the troop. Having lost sight of her, Lewis inquired as to the reason for her delay. The chief answered:

–She has stopped to give birth. She will catch up.

And indeed, an hour later, the woman caught up with them with her newborn in her arms. To Lewis, she looked in as good a shape as before. That night, the Captain demonstrated his insensitivity once more by writing down in his journal: "It appears to me that the facility and ease with which the women of the aborigines of North America bring fourth their children is reather a gift of nature than depending as some have supposed on the habitude of carrying heavy burthens on their backs while in a state of pregnancy."

The time for bargains had passed. At the Shoshoni village, prices were soaring. A single horse cost Captain Clark a pistol, a hundred bullets, gunpowder and a knife. Another horse was exchanged for a musket in perfect condition. The expedition got twenty-nine horses this way to get beyond the Rockies.

The haggling took three days; when it was over, Charbonneau inspected the animals. He realized that the Indians had passed off their worst mounts, young, skinny horses with sores on their backs due to the hard saddles of the Shoshonis. He decided to go and see Clark with Labiche to give him his opinion on the acquisitions. They found him fishing on the riverbank. Desperately hungry like everyone else, the Captain was hoping to catch a few fish for the next meal. Most of the other men were busy making packsaddles for the horses that would carry the baggage.

–They've sold you miserable nags, Charbonneau said to the Captain.

–They'll have to do, he answered without looking at him.

–Make sure you don't overload them, or you'll lose them after the first day, Charbonneau insisted.

The American turned around to face the French-Canadian. Under normal circumstances, he would have rebuffed him and advised him to mind his own business. But he was happy to see him again, and Sacagawea too, whom he now called Janey, and little Jean-Baptiste, who had danced a few steps for him when he had returned from his exploration of the Lehmi and Salmon Rivers.

As he cast his line in the water again, Clark said to Charbonneau:

–The animals won't be the only ones to suffer. We're beginning the toughest part of the journey. Judging by what I've seen these past few days, the portage to get beyond the Great Falls was a walk in the park compared to what lies ahead. I'm wondering if you'll even last one day...

–Don't worry about me, interrupted Charbonneau. When you get to the great salted lake, I'll be right there with you.

–We'll see, said Clark, amused.

At this very moment, something bit at the line and Clark pulled a beautiful trout out of the water. One last time, Charbonneau made his point:

–Anyway, when it comes to the horses, you were taken for a ride.

And he was all the more emphatic as most of the deals had been made by Lewis.

Clark was not exaggerating when he spoke of the difficulties of the next stage. While exploring the region with his small team, he became more convinced than ever that it would be impossible to sail the waters of the Lehmi and Salmon Rivers. To cross over the Rockies and reach a navigable branch of the Columbia, there was only one solution: follow the trail of the Nez Percés, a nation that, like the Shoshonis, came over the mountains once a year to go and hunt the buffalo on the plains.

Cameahwait had been the first person to mention this route while they were crossing the Lehmi Pass together. The second was Toby, a seventy-year-old Indian whom Lewis had met in the village of another Shoshoni band while exploring the Salmon River.

His real name was Pi-Kee Queen-Ah, but Clark had not been able to resist his habit of giving everybody a nickname. From then on, Pi-Kee Queen-Ah was known as Old Toby to the members of the expedition.

Old Toby had already followed the trail of the Nez Percés, and he strongly advised Clark against taking it.

–It's a very bad route, said the old man, whose body was still sturdy, despite his years and white hair.

Using sign language, Old Toby explained that his family had nearly starved, having nothing but berries to eat for days. No game was to be found in this region of jagged mountains, unstable rocks and snowy paths.

–Don't the Nez Percés travel that way every year to go hunting on the eastern plains? asked Clark.

–The Nez Percés are even more desperate than the Shoshonis, replied the old man with signs that Pierre Cruzatte managed to understand and translate.

–If the Nez Percés can cross those mountains with their women and children, so can we, declared Clark.

Old Toby spoke of other trails leading to the Pacific, but it seemed to the Captain that the trail the Nez Percés took was the only one that could lead the expedition quickly to the Columbia River.

Clark had spent the rest of the day smoking with Old Toby, gathering all the information he could on the awesome mountain range they were about to cross, a range he named Bitterroot, because, according to the old man, nothing grew there except bitter roots. At the end of the day, Clark had offered the old Shoshoni a generous reward if he was willing to act as a guide as far as the plain where the Nez Percés lived, on the other side of the Rockies. Old Toby had accepted.

Chapter Twelve

The Trail of the Nez Percés

On September 1st, 1805, under a gray and menacing sky, the expedition left the Shoshoni village on the Lehmi River and started out on the trail of the Nez Percés. At the same time, Cameahwait and his band set off in the opposite direction, toward the eastern plains where the buffalo roamed. And also their enemies, the Hidatsas.

Sacagawea was in tears; she waved to Cameahwait and Butterfly Woman; her friend waved back, her brother merely nodded. She had promised to return to the village with the expedition on its way back, the following summer, but something told her she would never see her family and friends again. She dug her heels in the sides of the horse and rejoined the expedition. She was fulfilling her destiny and that of her son.

–We are leaving for the great waters, she told Jean-Baptiste in the Shoshoni language.

The child didn't hear because he was sound asleep in the baby-carrier on his mother's back. Charbonneau walked behind with York; they envied the men who, like the captains, rode their horses. However, Toussaint did not envy the beasts of burden that would surely collapse under their heavy loads. He looked at his wife whom he found more beautiful than ever; she had dried her tears and smiled at him. Until the last minute, Toussaint had feared she might stay with her people, but she had chosen to follow him. Could it be that she really loved him? He promised himself he would never raise a hand to her again. Ill at ease, he turned away.

He became aware of the gloomy atmosphere that reigned all around him; he had never been part of such a silent, serious departure. Usually, the challenges of the journey spurred on the voyageurs, prompting them to sing, to encourage one another, as had been the case before and during the portage of the Great Falls, which had united the troop. Today, the members of the expedition were exhibiting grave faces as they followed close behind Old Toby. They were afraid of not coming out of the Rockies alive. Starvation was a real threat during the crossing that could last more than three weeks, according to their guide.

It started to rain. The path ran alongside the Lehmi River at first, going west; then it branched off to the north along the Salmon River. The rain kept on falling, making the ground unsteady. No one spoke; everyone watched carefully where they stepped. Toward the end of the afternoon, Drouillard broke the silence and pointed out to Charbonneau that it was snowing on the peaks of the Bitterroot Mountains.

–That's promising! grumbled Toussaint, looking in the distance.

That night, under the leaking tepee, Lewis did not write anything personal in his journal, confining himself to his observations on the fauna and flora. The Captain was not only weary from all the hardships of the preceding weeks, but also unhappy about the way the expedition was going. More than ever, he understood that President Jefferson's dream was dead: there was no navigable route from the Mississippi to the Pacific. The legendary Northwest Passage that all explorers of North America had been searching for, ever since Jacques Cartier, had been nothing but a pipedream. The expedition had just lost most of its commercial significance.

It had been pouring for hours. Pulling on the reins of his wife's horse, Charbonneau was carefully negotiating the steep and rocky side of a hill. Many horses had already slid down the slope, ending up a hundred feet below, in the torrent formed by the west branch of the Salmon River.

–Goddamn it! swore Charbonneau who had just stepped on a shifting rock. This trail is terrible!

–If you can call it a trail, replied Sacagawea who was shivering on her horse.

Earlier in the day, Charbonneau had lost his walking companion, York, whose feet were so scraped that he had to continue on horseback. Three exhausted horses had refused to take one more step. The others struggled along; they were not shod and thus injured themselves on the stones and the many fallen trees that blocked the path.

Despite their efforts, the troop covered only seven miles that day and spent a miserable night under the rain. The following afternoon, Charbonneau, who walked at the head of the line with Old Toby, reached the top of a hill from which his eyes swept the Bitterroot range. High, jagged mountains, with snow-capped peaks rose in tiers as far as the eye could see. As he gazed at the imposing scenery, he felt his heart beating wildly. God! How would they ever cross this horrible mountain desert? Each member of the expedition wondered about the same thing, and the distressing question weighed heavily on every step they took that day.

At dusk, it started snowing and, adding to the list of mishaps, Clark deplored the loss of the last thermometer. The troop ate a meager dinner of a few grouse and a little corn. Under the torn tepee, Charbonneau and Sacagawea, wet and chilled to the bone, curled up against each other to keep warm while they slept. Snuggled between them, Jean-Baptiste was the only one who didn't suffer too much from the cold.

When the troop woke up, snow blanketed the ground. They had to postpone their departure to let the baggage covers thaw out. They finally set out by mid-morning. The trail led to the top of a mountain, then along a ridge for several miles. For their next meal, they roasted a deer that Drouillard had shot, the first in a while; the hunter didn't get many opportunities to use his rifle. While they ate, they forced themselves to laugh and be cheerful, but all along Charbonneau was thinking of what Clark had said on the bank of the Lehmi: crossing the Bitterroot massif would be even more difficult than the portage of the Great Falls. The Captain had certainly not exaggerated.

In the afternoon, the expedition advanced along the torrent as far as its forks, where stood an Indian village.

–They are Tushepaws, friends of the Shoshonis, announced Sacagawea; Charbonneau conveyed the information to the captains.

The Tushepaws were an important nation. Explorers called them Flatheads because of the gesture they made to identify themselves. That particular band lived in a village of about four hundred inhabitants and five hundred horses that represented the bulk of its wealth.

The Tushepaws were getting ready to join their allies, the Shoshonis, on the buffalo plains. They put off leaving and heartily welcomed the exhausted travelers.

Three Eagles, the most important chief in the village, showed the captains and the interpreters into a tent made of skins. There, he had blankets thrown over the shoulders of his guests. Then he smoked the pipe of peace and shared what little food he had with them, some berries and roots. As the other men of his nation, he wore a bonnet made with the skin of an otter whose tail hung down to his shoulders. His complexion was fairer than that of the other Indians the expedition had encountered.

–You are the first Whites to come along the Salmon River, said Three Eagles, beginning a speech that lasted late into the night.

A young Shoshoni, whom the band had adopted a few years earlier, helped translate the chief's words. The chain of interpreters was longer than ever: Three Eagles spoke Tushepaw to the boy, who translated into Shoshoni to Sacagawea, who in turn translated into Hidatsa to Charbonneau, who translated into French to Labiche, who translated into English to the captains. Despite all this, the message was understood.

–I've seen you coming from afar, continued the old chief. I quietly came near you. At first, I was surprised to see that you did not wear blankets over your shoulders, like my Indian brothers. Then I wondered why one of your men had his face painted black. Was it a sign of war? I concluded that it wasn't, because a party of warriors doesn't travel with a woman.

And Three Eagles motioned in the direction of Sacagawea with his chin. The Tushepaw chief could have talked forever. He told the history of his people in great detail, yielding to the captains only rarely. Charbonneau was struck by his pronunciation: the words of the old Indian sounded strangely guttural. Without knowing it, the expedition had just entered a new linguistic region, different from the one occupied by the Great Plains Indians, the Salish region, which extended to the Pacific.

Lewis spent the next morning compiling a lexicon of the Salish language with the help of his team of interpreters. Even in an isolated village in the middle of the Rockies, he remained faithful to the scientific objectives of the expedition. Charbonneau, who took his role as interpreter seriously, admired the persistence of the Captain whose qualities were certainly as great as his faults.

In the meantime, Sergeant Ordway bought twelve horses and exchanged seven of the troop's tired animals for as many frisky ones. The expedition now owned forty horses. Whether out of naivety or generosity, the Tushepaws asked only for a fraction of the price exacted by the Shoshonis for their nags.

At two o'clock in the afternoon, the Tushepaws said goodbye to the Corps of Discovery and left their village to join the Shoshonis at the forks of the Missouri. The expedition went its own way.

In spite of the heavy rain, Charbonneau felt happy; he was riding a horse for the first time. As he looked at his wife and son riding beside him, he couldn't help smiling.

–We'll make it out of these damned mountains!

–Are you sure? asked Sacagawea, staring at the snowy peaks.

–As sure as my name is Toussaint Charbonneau. We'll taste the water of the Pacific and then we'll go back to our village.

He had stressed the word "our" and watched for her reaction. She nodded approvingly.

The trail was getting easier. They now walked in a lush, green meadow; it stretched over a six-mile valley, surrounded by mountains that rose more than seven thousand feet. A crystal-clear river, the Bitterroot, wound its way between banks lined with poplar trees. It was about a hundred yards wide and certainly navigable, but the captains did not deem it advisable to have canoes built.

That day, the expedition covered twenty-two miles, twenty-three the next, twenty-one the day after that. On September 9, it set up camp near a wide brook that babbled on its bed of polished pebbles. The weather had finally turned fair; Lewis decided to spend two days there to let the men and horses rest, and give himself the time to engage in some astronomical observations. He called the spot Travelers' Rest.

In the evening, under the tepee now in shreds, he called together Clark, Old Toby and the interpreters. He questioned the guide about the Bitterroot River, trying to find out if it flowed into the Columbia. The old man couldn't say for sure. However, at the end of the meeting, he revealed a stunning piece of information. In an even tone, he announced:

–From this camp, a man on horseback can follow a trail that will take him to the Missouri in four days.

Four days! When she heard her fellow countryman, Sacagawea stared at him wide-eyed. It had taken the expedition fifty-five days from the Gates of the Rockies to Travelers' Rest. Four days instead of fifty-two! Charbonneau had the same reaction when Sacagawea translated Old Toby's declaration and he saw the same stunned look on the faces of Labiche and the captains.

Four days... Maybe Seeing Snake was right after all…

Some time later, Old Toby led the troop astray, only realizing his mistake after three miles. To everyone's great relief, the guide managed to find his way again. He apologized profusely to Clark, who downplayed the incident: the expedition depended entirely on him to make it through the Rockies.

The trail seemed to go on forever through scenery that appeared similar to the landscapes previously crossed. The members of the expedition were all very hungry; Drouillard's rifle wasn't of much use, for no game was to be found in these arid parts, except for some rams that took off as soon as a hunter tried to get closer.

The next day, the trail went down steep slopes where the horses slid again and scraped their sides. The one that was carrying Clark's desk tumbled down forty yards. A tree stopped its fall; the animal came out of it unharmed, but the desk was smashed to pieces. The expedition lost two horses; injured or exhausted, the mounts refused to go on.

They set up camp for the night on a wind-swept hill. After pitching the tepee, Sacagawea went to the top of a rise where she could see the entire region. The young woman thought that she could have been on the banks of the Missouri, laying beaver traps with Otter Woman, while Toussaint prepared *boudin blanc* in their nice, warm home. She could almost taste the berry-flavored pemmican, and her empty stomach gurgled. Right behind her, Jean-Baptiste's cries of excitement signaled the arrival of his father who started teasing the baby by rubbing his nose with a feather.

–You're still in a mood for laughing? Sacagawea said in a surprised tone. Do you really think that we'll make it out of these bitter mountains?

He put his arm around her waist and drew her to him.

–Of course, we will. Otherwise, your dream wouldn't make any sense. Remember what your mother told you. She came back from the dead to announce that we would become part of the legend. That was no ordinary dream.

Sacagawea remained silent for a moment, as she thought of her family who had been slaughtered; then she said in a disheartened voice:

–But we have nothing to eat; we have no strength left and winter is coming.

–All the more reason to trust in our *bonne sainte Anne*, answered Charbonneau, holding her tight. She has always protected us.

–That's true.

In the morning, they woke up under the snow. It had started falling three hours before sunrise, and it looked as though it would continue snowing all day. Old Toby had trouble locating the trail under the thick white cover, and he stopped every few steps to make sure he wasn't leading the troop off course.

They stopped at noon to warm and dry themselves, and especially to allow the animals, even more tired than the men, to rest a while. Charbonneau, who had faced the worst possible winters in the North Country, was soaked to the skin; he had never felt so cold. He feared that his feet would freeze inside his thin moccasins and he shuddered as he remembered the amputations he had witnessed at Fort Mandan. In front of the fire, Sacagawea was stamping her feet to keep warm while she rocked Jean-Baptiste, wrapped in a buffalo skin in her arms, to calm his tears.

Later that afternoon, Clark walked up to Charbonneau, who was also on foot to spare his mount. The Captain held a colt by a halter. He laid his hand on Charbonneau's shoulder and said in English:

–Follow me, we'll go on ahead.

The French-Canadian was beginning to understand snatches of English and guessed the Captain's intentions. He looked at his wife reassuringly and followed close on Clark's heels. The two men walked as fast as they could in order to outdistance the rest of the expedition. Toussaint pointed to the colt and shook his head.

–It will be good, he said, rubbing his stomach.

Clark smiled. Six miles further, they stopped near a brook and started several fires. They killed the colt, cut it up and cooked the evening meal while they waited for the others to arrive. Under all other circumstances, they would have conversed as best they could, mixing English, French and signs. Clark was always curious about the experiences the trader had lived. But instead, they butchered the animal in silence, as if it were a solemn occasion. When the colt was reduced to bleeding pieces of meat, a kind of happiness washed over Toussaint. Even if he lacked many ingredients, he surpassed himself as a cook; the members of the expedition enjoyed the horsemeat, which they found excellent.

The captains named the brook Colt Killed Creek.

On the morning of September 18, Lewis and Clark had a serious private discussion. Through the previous nights, they had heard the howling of wolves getting closer to the camp. The howling made the men's blood turn cold; some of them were losing heart: they were in the middle of a boundless mountain range, surrounded by wild beasts; they would never pull through. The captains were quite aware of the fact that the troop was close to the breaking point. They had left Cameahwait's village eighteen days before; there was no turning back now, but something had to be done to feed the men, left thinner by the deprivations, and to lift their spirits.

The captains agreed on a plan. Clark would go ahead with six men to a less mountainous region to find game. As soon as he had stocked up enough meat, he would rejoin the others. In the meantime, Lewis would do his best, with the rest of the expedition, to go as far as the horses would permit.

Clark set out with Drouillard, York, Charbonneau and Privates John Colter, Reuben Fields and John Shields. Charbonneau was by far the worst hunter of them all, but the Captain took him along anyway, as if he wanted to bring upon them St. Anne's protection. After all, she was supposed to watch over all voyageurs. In the spring, the Americans had made fun of Charbonneau's devotion to his patron saint, but at the beginning of fall, in the hellish world of the Rockies, they had all learned to invoke her name.

Clark and his men left the camp early and crossed over two nearly impassable mountains, climbing up steep slopes and stepping over uprooted trees everywhere. Unfortunately, Charbonneau had nothing for the famished team, not even a humble hake. They named Hungry Creek the torrent near which they slept out in the open, wrapped in frayed buffalo skins. All around, the wolves howled all night.

The next day, they traveled through yet another hilly region. For weeks, there had been no change in the scenery. Was it endless? With each peak they climbed, they hoped it would be the last, only to find more mountains on the other side. Then, on September 20, 1805, they reached the last peak of the Bitterroots. At the foot of the low mountain stretched out a vast plain planted with pine trees. The nightmare of the Rockies was coming to an end, after a forced march of one hundred and sixty miles.

Clark and his companions went wild with joy, like the passengers on a ship who catch sight of land at last, after a long and perilous sea voyage.

–The plain! they cried out jumping for joy. The plain!

Charbonneau surprised Clark by hugging and kissing him on both cheeks:

–We made it! We made it! We have overcome those damned mountains!

Then, Charbonneau did a little jig with York, who burst out laughing. Gazing at the lovely prairie that extended far to the west, Clark's servant experienced, like the others, a deep sense of pride. He felt as tall as the mountains he had just crossed.

–Let's give thanks to good St. Anne, he said.

After expressing their joy, they climbed down the last mountain, constantly turning around to see the western slopes of the Rockies. An enormous weight had been lifted from their shoulders and they now advanced with ease across the plain. Five miles further, they spotted three young Indians who fled at the sight of the strangers and hid in the tall grass.

–Nez Percés, commented Charbonneau, pointing to the boys.

The Captain nodded and handed over his horse and his rifle to Charbonneau. He quickly walked over to the place where the boys had hidden themselves and, to reassure them, gave them bits of ribbon. The children were tamed in no time, and Clark asked them through signs to run to their village and announce their arrival in the region. The children bolted off through the yellow grass.

A few minutes later, a man came to meet the strangers hesitantly. He was quickly reassured by their friendly attitude and what seemed to be their peaceful intentions. He guided them to his village, which consisted of about thirty tepees, and invited them to follow him under a big tent in the central square.

All the inhabitants gathered to observe the strangers. Charbonneau could read in the eyes of the women and children a mixture of fear and pleasure. He didn't mind having such an effect on the Nez Percés who had never met Whites. Sitting tall on his horse, he threw out his chest and raised his head like a conquistador.

Before entering the big tent, he noticed that only a handful of men defended the village. He used the signs Drouillard had taught him to inquire as to the whereabouts of the men. The Nez Percés explained that the warriors had gone to attack some of their enemies in the South West and that they would not be back before a couple of weeks. Meanwhile, the strangers could make themselves comfortable in the tepee of the great chief of the band, Broken Arm.

The people of the village didn't have much food, but what they offered seemed a feast to the explorers who hadn't eaten in two days. The women served them a small piece of buffalo meat, some dried salmon, berries and many kinds of roots, such as quamash root, a sweet, mild bulb that the Nez Percés ate raw, boiled or made into bread.

–It tastes like pumpkin, said Charbonneau to Drouillard, as he savored the root that looked a lot like an onion.

Drouillard nodded.

The members of the expedition ate of everything greedily, eager to appease the hunger that gnawed at their stomachs. That night, they were all sick.

Watkuweis camped with her band on the banks of the Clearwater River where they had been fishing for salmon with big nets. In the language of the Nez Percés, her name meant Woman Back From a Faraway Land. She had just dozed off under a shelter of bark and branches when she heard one of the lookouts shout:

–Wake up everybody! Wake up! Some strangers are riding this way! Some have faces as pale as cold ashes! One of them has skin as black as a crow's feathers!

In a second, everybody was up and formed a circle around the warrior who was making frantic gestures in the middle of the moonlit camp. Watkuweis found herself next to the chief of the band, Wallamottinin, or Twisted Hair, as he was known on account of the magnificent coil of hair that hung down his back.

–They carry firearms! added the sentry, whose watch post was about half a mile away from the camp, uphill from the river.

As soon as he had seen the members of the expedition, he had jumped on his horse and galloped flat out to warn the village. The chief of the Nez Percés frowned while considering the matter for a few moments. He could count on thirty warriors; he didn't want to let such a chance to obtain rifles slip by.

–We'll seize their firearms, said Wallamottinin to his men. If they resist, we'll drive our spears through them.

The warriors approved of Twisted Hair's plan and went to get their weapons. Just like the Shoshonis, the Nez Percés owned no guns to defend themselves against their enemies, the Black Feet, who could get firearms from British traders. Every year, because of their inferior weapons, they lost many of their men, women and horses.

At eleven o'clock at night, Clark and his party arrived at Twisted Hair's encampment, whose position they had learned the day before while talking to the Nez Percés of the first village. Earlier that same day, they had bought as big a quantity of smoked salmon, berries and roots as they could with the few articles for exchange they had left. Clark had the food brought to Lewis and the rest of the troop by Fields and a Nez Percé.

–Tell Captain Lewis to come and meet us at Twisted Hair's fishing camp, Clark had said to Fields. Let him use one of the Nez Percés of the first village as a guide.

Fields would have well done without this mission that obliged him to go back into those cursed Rockies, but he had set out without wasting any time, for he suspected the rest of the troop probably hadn't eaten in a few days.

At around four o'clock in the afternoon, Clark and his men had started toward the Clearwater River camp, still suffering from nausea and stomach aches. They would have arrived at their destination much earlier had they not lost their way. Showing up so late at the camp, they were aware that the Nez Percés would not exactly make them welcome. However, they did not expect to come face to face with thirty warriors armed with spears.

–Make no abrupt gestures, said Clark to his men when he saw Twisted Hair's warriors. We need help from these Indians.

The explorers were only fifty feet from the warriors when the Woman Back From a Faraway Land eased the tension by intervening between the two groups. Pointing a finger to the four pale-skinned men, she said to her fellow countrymen:

–These are the people who helped me! Don't harm them!

The warriors looked at each other in amazement, not knowing how to react to Watkuweis' revelations, while Twisted Hair started weighing their implications. What the old Indian woman had just said was worth considering. Many years earlier, she had been abducted by the Black Feet who had made her their slave and later sold her to a White trader. She had lived among Whites for five years before returning to her people. Since she had been treated much better by the fur traders than by the Black Feet, she had happy memories of the Pale Faces.

As all the other members of his band, Twisted Hair knew Watkuweis' story in detail. However, he had his doubts on that particular day.

–Are you sure these are the people who helped you? asked Twisted Hair.

–Yes, answered Watkuweis firmly. Look, they have blue eyes and hairy faces.

Watkuweis couldn't distinguish between the French-Canadians, the British and the Americans. She believed that all Whites were the same as the ones she had lived with, that is, industrious, greedy, cheerful and relatively nice to Indian women.

Twisted Hair thought for a minute, then said to his warriors:

–If indeed these are the men who helped the Woman Back From a Faraway Land, we must treat them as friends. Put your spears away.

The warriors obeyed. The explorers heaved a sigh of relief. Twisted Hair motioned the strangers to follow him to his hut, where he smoked with them until one in the morning. Using sign language, the chief of the Nez Percés appeared cordial and sincere to Clark and his companions. He told them Watkuweis' story, leaving out the fact that she had intervened to prevent his warriors from killing the members of the American expedition.

Later, when it was time to go to bed, Drouillard asked Charbonneau:

–Do you think that the old woman has lived with Canadians?

–For sure, replied Charbonneau. And maybe they were fellows we know!

The next morning, at Clark's request, Twisted Hair drew the course of the rivers of the region on a whitened wapiti skin. According to the chief's information, the Clearwater River flowed into the Shoshoni River, which in turn flowed into the Columbia.

–When you get to the river where the Shoshonis fish for salmon, you'll be only five nights away from the big river that runs from the northeast, said Twisted Hair, referring to the Columbia.

–How many days between the Clearwater and the Shoshoni Rivers? inquired Clark.

–Two, replied the chief.

Once they understood the meaning of Twisted Hair's signs, Clark, Charbonneau and Drouillard smiled at one another. If they were to go by what he said, it would take the expedition only one week by canoe to reach the Columbia. They were drawing near the great river at last, and consequently, near the ocean, the ultimate destination of this endless journey across the continent. In less than a month, they would see and hear the waves crashing against the coast.

–I've never been so anxious to get back in a canoe, said Charbonneau to Drouillard.

–Me too, he answered.

Afterwards, Captain Clark explained to the chief of the Nez Percés the goals of the American expedition. Through Drouillard, he spoke of peace and trade, two concepts that seemed to please Twisted Hair. He had enough of wars with the Black Feet and of his people's precarious way of life. Just like the Shoshonis, his tribe wanted to live on the buffalo plains, without fear of being attacked by its enemies.

However, for the first time in the journey, Clark did not broach the question of United States sovereignty with an Indian. The fact was that the Captain and his small troop, after climbing down the western slope of the Rockies, had entered a new country. They no longer were in Louisiana, the vast territory they had just crossed. They were in the Oregon territory, which extended from the northern border of California to the southern border of Alaska. Inhabited by many Indian nations and rich in fur animals, this territory was coveted simultaneously by the Americans, the British, the Russians and the Spanish.

Thanks to the expedition he had sponsored, President Jefferson hoped to claim at least the territory bathed by the Columbia River and its tributaries. It was much too early to ask Twisted Hair and the other chiefs to pledge allegiance to the United States. That didn't prevent Clark from presenting the chief of the Nez Percés with the star-spangled flag of his country and a medal bearing the effigy of Jefferson.

Charbonneau and Sacagawea were lying under a pine tree that rose above the Clearwater River, near the expedition's encampment. Clark, who was overseeing the building of the canoes a little further downstream, had taken Jean-Baptiste with him. Lying on her back, Sacagawea had a bloated stomach and it made her breathing difficult.

–I have a stomach ache, she moaned.

Overwhelmed by the heat and humidity, Charbonneau did not react to her complaint. There wasn't much to say: what ailed her wasn't so unusual; all the members of the troop were suffering from serious stomach upset. Clearly, the smoked salmon and the roots of the Nez Percés did not agree with them, but that's all there was to eat, day after day, until the expedition moved on to the Columbia River and the Pacific. They would have given anything for a piece of grilled meat!

After a moment, Sacagawea made a supreme effort to get up.

–I'm going to get Jean-Baptiste. He must be hungry.

Charbonneau replied with a grunt.

His wife started with a heavy step toward the construction site. She felt as if she were carrying a hundred pounds on her back. She had an urge to vomit, which she proceeded to do in the middle of the camp. And to think she had been so delighted, just five days earlier, to see Private Fields arrive with the supplies bought by Clark's group. She had literally devoured her portion of dried salmon, enjoying the taste she remembered from childhood. She had then stuffed herself with quamash.

However, her stomach had become accustomed to the Upper Missouri diet, and she had reacted no better than Whites to the radical change. Only a few hours after eating the food of the Nez Percés, she had been violently sick to her stomach and had thrown everything up. In her pitiful state, she had not been able to enjoy the spectacular view from the top of the last peak of the Rockies. There, right before her, was the plain they had longed to reach, with its promise of plentiful game, but she was bent over with cramps and hadn't seen anything! At any rate, it was a false promise. In the Weippe plain where the Nez Percés lived, game was as rare in the fall as in the Bitterroot Mountains. That is why the Indians crossed over the Rockies to go and hunt the buffalo on the eastern plains. Like the Shoshonis and the Tushepaws, the Nez Percés lived in constant insecurity on another continental divide, the one that separated the world of the buffalo from that of the salmon.

Sacagawea wiped her mouth and started walking again; she stepped over Drouillard who was lying on the ground. Among the sick of the expedition, the brave hunter was hit hard; he couldn't get up, even less take part in the building of the canoes. He had been "treated," like the others, by Clark who had given him the "Rush pills," a universal drug named after Benjamin Rush, the medical consultant of the expedition and friend to President Jefferson. Unfortunately, the medicine of the eminent doctor from Philadelphia had not contained the widespread diarrhea, quite the contrary.

Many other men lay about the camp, among them Lewis himself. Not only did they have severe cramps, but after two months of epic hardships in the Rockies, they also suffered from exhaustion. And the oppressively hot weather didn't help.

Sacagawea heard Drouillard's voice come from behind. She turned around and saw him bringing his hand up to his mouth, as if to drink.

–Water. Bring me some water.

–I'll be right back, she said in French.

Raising his head, he saw the beautiful Indian girl going toward the river, and was surprised that she was even able to walk. She came back and gave him a drink of water, then went over to the other end of the camp, where Clark appeared to be sleeping against a tree, his head tilted back. At his feet, Jean-Baptiste crawled around in the yellowed grass. Six other men were sleeping in the shade. Not a sound came from the work site, as if the men had been struck by lightening.

Five trees from the pines surrounding the camp had been chopped down. The men were supposed to carve canoes out of the trunks that lay on the ground, but they were so tired, and their axes so bad, that they had barely made a dent in the wood. "At this pace, the expedition will spend Christmas with the Nez Percés," thought Sacagawea.

She bent down to pick up Jean-Baptiste who was coming to meet his mother on all fours, screaming with joy. Since he ate neither salmon nor roots, he was the only member of the expedition who could still smile.

On the last day of September, it got cooler, to everyone's great relief, since people had been complaining as much about the weather as about the food.

Drouillard went hunting again, but he didn't see a ghost of a deer either on the prairie or on the foothills of the Rockies, where the parched grass was of no interest to the game. Desperate for food, the troop killed another horse, but they soon got back to their diet of salmon and roots; they couldn't afford to kill the very animals they needed to cross over the Rockies on their way back.

On October 1st, at the break of dawn, Charbonneau went outside to relieve himself on the riverbank. The Clearwater was seventy yards wide and its name suited it well. He looked up at the pinkish sky and saw a flight of ducks migrating south. He recalled his first encounter with the Americans, the preceding fall, in Upper Missouri. So many things had happened since then. He had wanted to be part of the legend and he was paying the price for it.

He shook his penis, which he had not used for his pleasure in a long time, far too long, and tucked it back in his pants. In the winter, on the shores of the Pacific, he would surely get the chance to bring it into service again with Sacagawea and the local Indian women.

Later that day, after examining his clothes and putting them out to dry, Charbonneau went to the work site to check the progress of the canoes. Nearly all the men were at work, including some Nez Percés, among them Twisted Hair himself who had promised to accompany the expedition as far as the Columbia, together with Tetoharsky, another chief of his nation.

Twisted Hair was involved in an animated discussion with Clark. Using his hands, he was explaining to the American and his men that they were going about it all wrong.

–You must use fire instead of axes, said the Indian, whose sign language was translated by Drouillard to the Captain.

Twisted Hair offered to demonstrate the method used by the West Coast Indians to build their pirogues. The Captain agreed with pleasure. At their chief's command, the Nez Percés got down to work, using controlled fires to hollow out the inside of the tree trunks. By adopting this method, the men of the expedition finished building the boats on October 5, 1805.

On that day, Captain Clark had all thirty-eight horses rounded up and branded; the Nez Percés had agreed to take care of them until the return of the expedition. Only two weeks earlier, these Indians had planned to kill the strangers in order to steal their rifles. Watkuweis had stopped them just in time, and now they had become the most valuable allies of the explorers after the Shoshonis.

Cruzatte and a few men dug out a cache to bury the saddles, as well as a powder keg and a bag of bullets. The next morning, under overcast skies, Captain Clark had the pirogues lowered into the river and supervised their loading. He took care of all the preparations for the trip without Lewis, who was sick for the tenth consecutive day. Clark was barely feeling better. During the night, he had complained of a stomach ache and intestinal cramps.

At three in the afternoon, after waiting in vain for Twisted Hair and Tetoharsky, the expedition decided to set off. A familiar song rose from the Clearwater River:

M'en revenant de la jolie Rochelle
M'en revenant de la jolie Rochelle
J'ai rencontré trois jolies demoiselles.

This time, some American soldiers joined Charbonneau and his countrymen in singing the favorite song of the French-Canadian voyageurs. They had heard it so many times since they had left St. Louis that they were now able to pronounce the words and let their joy burst forth. For the first time since the middle of August, the expedition was sailing once more. It felt good to float on water again after that terrible crossing of the Rockies!

C'est l'aviron qui nous mène, qui nous mène
C'est l'aviron qui nous mène en haut.

Charbonneau's paddle went effortlessly in and out of the crystal-clear water; the current was so strong that the canoe seemed to move forward by itself. Interrupting his singing for a moment, Charbonneau turned around and said to his wife triumphantly:

–It's so much easier to go down than up the river!

Sacagawea sat at the bottom of the canoe with Jean-Baptiste. She listened in silence, still very much on her guard, remembering what Twisted Hair, the chief of the Nez Percés, had said: on the way to the Columbia, the expedition would come across many dangerous rapids.

Charbonneau could not suppress his excitement. The Clearwater River was the first he was sailing down since Fort Mandan. He had ascended the Missouri and the Jefferson, struggling against the current, having to tow the boats as far as the Lehmi gorge where the expedition had bought its horses. Now, he could finally let the current carry him to the Pacific. That was enough to make him want to sing his head off:

C'est l'aviron qui nous mène, qui nous mène
C'est l'aviron qui nous mène en haut.

Charbonneau traveled with seven members of the expedition, with Cruzatte at bow and Clark at stern. Old Toby, their Shoshoni guide, sat behind Sacagawea and did not paddle. On his face, one could read his displeasure at being in a boat rather than on horseback.

An hour of easy sailing went by when suddenly Cruzatte called out:

–Rapids ahead!

The paddlers had no trouble riding these first rapids, which were brief, nor the second that provided wide free passages. However, things got tough at the third rapids, which required precise maneuvering on account of the impressive waves, the numerous rocks that showed on the surface, the foaming whirlpools and especially the narrow passes.

Cruzatte did his best to steer the canoe, trying to interpret each rapid from its position just above the water.

–Rock on the right! he shouted.

The men paddled to the left.

–Rock on the left!

Down went the paddles on the right.

Unfortunately, Cruzatte did not see the next obstacle in time, an irregular rock which the canoe hit full force. Under the impact, it almost overturned. Still fearful of the water, Charbonneau turned as white as a sheet. As for Old Toby, he was green; despite his advanced age, he had never traveled in a canoe.

Suddenly, Charbonneau's voice was heard:

–The canoe is letting in water!

Cruzatte also felt the water at the bottom of the boat and immediately informed Captain Clark, who ordered the men to paddle ashore. While the other four pirogues negotiated the rapids without incident, Clark and his team unloaded the canoe on the bank. They discovered a little leak on one side, which they sealed off with pine resin and bits of wood. They reloaded the baggage and started out again on the choppy waters of the Clearwater. This time, nobody sang.

Altogether, they rode ten rapids that day, spread out over ten miles of river. It was good preparation for what lay ahead: according to Twisted Hair, the Columbia and the Shoshoni Rivers presented even greater difficulties. Was that why the chief of the Nez Percés had not shown up?

–Cruzatte, Charbonneau called out, come with me; we're going to buy some dogs.

–Dogs? Where?

–At the last Indian camp.

All through the day, the troop had passed by Indian camps established on the islands and near the rapids where the Nez Percés fished for salmon. In some of the camps, Charbonneau had seen dogs, and he had told himself that he would attempt to buy some that evening. He was literally fed up with the salmon and roots they had been eating, and especially with the indigestion that invariably followed. He had a craving for roasted meat. And dog meat was as good as horsemeat. He had already eaten some during the food shortages that were rampant in Upper Missouri.

–I'm right behind you, said Cruzatte, as he packed some articles for trading.

The idea of roasting a dog didn't disgust him. They started walking toward the closest camp of the Nez Percés, half a mile upstream. The Indians greeted them in a friendly manner. Pleasant-looking men and women both wore clothes made of buffalo or wapiti skins, adorned with mother-of-pearl beads and sea shells. Some were sporting feathers, others paint for which they found the white, green and light blue pigments in their own region. When he saw the women in their tight-fitting clothes, Charbonneau felt his member coming to life. If hunger hadn't gnawed at him, he would have gladly spent the night at this encampment; the legend of his sexual prowess could thus have spread to the West Coast. However, he had come to buy dogs, which he did with Cruzatte's help. The fiddler used sign language to offer a deal to the young chief who came to meet them with his genitals exposed, as was the custom for men in their own camp.

They traded two dogs for a tin box, a handkerchief and a little tobacco. Back at camp, they got the animals ready for roasting. When the meat was done just right, the cook announced:

–Dinner is served!

–Only a Frenchman or a Sioux would roast a dog, said Sergeant Gass.

As for Joseph and Reuben Fields, they made fun of the French-Canadian by imitating the bark of a dog:

–Woof! Woof!

They managed to infuriate Charbonneau who threatened to poke one of their eyes out with his knife. Clark intervened in time:

–Come now, Charbonneau, it's a joke!

Cruzatte, Drouillard, Labiche, Lepage and Sacagawea accepted Charbonneau's invitation.

–It's not bad, said Drouillard.

–Of course it's not bad, chimed in Lepage.

–It'll set our stomachs right, added Cruzatte, biting into the meat with gusto.

After the meal, Cruzatte felt well enough to play his fiddle; the dog meat eaters sang and danced. Drawn by the music and the singing, some Nez Percés from the neighboring camp joined the explorers and shared in the general rejoicing.

One woman among them caused a disruption. At some point, she started singing a strange song in her native tongue while she went around distributing roots and bracelets that were hanging from her clothes. When a soldier refused one of her gifts, she became furious and threw the objects in the fire. Then she rushed at her husband and snatched from his hands a piece of flint and slashed her arms. Nobody budged. She started licking the blood that was running down her arms, before going into a trance that lasted a good half-hour. The explorers concluded that she was raving mad, but in fact the Indian was under the influence of Wyakin, her guardian angel.

Old Toby took advantage of the commotion to flee in the night.

The incident on the rapids and the near wreck of the canoe had unnerved the old man; the Shoshoni guide had no intention of accompanying the expedition in its crazy venture. When Clark noticed he had gone, he regretted not having had the chance to reward him for his invaluable help during the crossing of the Bitterroot Mountains. At the end of the evening, however, he was glad to see Twisted Hair and Tetoharsky arrive; they had been delayed by their affairs.

The expedition reached the Shoshoni River on October 10. That night, the American soldiers overcame their distaste for dog meat and bought some animals at the nearest encampment of Nez Percés. Sick of dried fish and roots, they discovered that they actually liked the meat of man's best friend. Only Clark refused to touch such food, not wanting to be regarded as a dog eater by the Nez Percés.

Charbonneau couldn't resist the temptation to make fun of the Fields brothers and give out pathetic little cries: "Woof! Woof!"

Chapter Thirteen

Down the Columbia River

The Shoshoni River flowed across wide plains where not a single tree grew. Its flat, even banks contrasted with the picturesque grandeur of its course, with its islands, rocks and rapids. Had Charbonneau been riding or walking along its banks, he might have appreciated its beauty, but he was too busy trying not to capsize in the frothing waters to enjoy the scenery.

Fortunately, the pirogue in which he traveled with his family did not sustain any other damage, riding successfully the numerous rapids, some of which extended over a distance of two or three miles. The passengers were terribly indebted, not only to St. Anne, whose name the French-Canadian continued to invoke regularly, but also to Cruzatte who had become quite the expert in the art of sailing between reefs.

Despite the obstacles and the dangers, the troop succeeded in covering up to thirty miles a day, making good progress toward the Columbia. Following the current, they had passed many fishing establishments deserted by the Nez Percés who had left the region to go hunting on the eastern plains. They did, however, meet some Indian bands from whom they bought dogs, fish and roots. Twisted Hair's countrymen also acted as pilots to help them over some of the worst rapids, which they rode laughing in their little canoes.

But not all the boats were so lucky. Several of the expedition's canoes hit some reefs and capsized. In the afternoon of October 14, a cloudy, cold day, the canoe steered by Drouillard came within a hair's breadth of a catastrophe. As it was entering a difficult passage, it bumped into a big black rock, heaved to the current and began letting water in as the waves flowed over it. The whole crew climbed onto the rock, and using only their arms, managed to keep the boat afloat. When he saw this, Clark rushed ashore and unloaded his pirogue before going to the rescue.

He and his men retrieved the boat, the passengers and nearly all the baggage, with the exception of the bedding for two soldiers and a tomahawk that drifted away on the current.

They had had another narrow escape, but they had now cleared the dangerous passages down the Shoshoni River.

–We should do more portages, said Charbonneau to Drouillard as they drew alongside an island.

–Time is too precious, commented Drouillard.

His answer reflected the opinion of the majority. Undoubtedly, they could have done more portages, but they were in a hurry to get to the Pacific. Even those who could not swim were ready to leap into the worst rapids, so eager were they to catch sight of the sea they could almost smell.

There wasn't a single tree on the island where the expedition was about to spend the night. In order to start a fire, the men had to break a rule they had set for themselves: never take anything that belonged to the Indians. When landing on the island, they had noticed some boards intended for a fishing hut; the Nez Percés had piled stones on the wood so that it wouldn't be carried away by the rising water. They decided to use part of the boards.

–If we find the owner of the hut, we'll compensate him, Captain Clark told Twisted Hair.

The expedition had only covered fourteen miles, but Clark soon got over it by having his best meal in three weeks. He had shot a big wild duck and asked Charbonneau to cook it. He shared it with Charbonneau and his family; Sacagawea chewed on some small pieces of meat and fed them to Jean-Baptiste who seemed to enjoy them.

–Pomp is right to smile; it's much better than dog, declared Clark, winking at Toussaint.

At noon, on October 16, 1805, a cool, sunny day, the Corps of Discovery finally arrived at the confluence of the Shoshoni and the Columbia Rivers.

–Look, Toussaint! called out Sacagawea, as she pointed to the Indians assembled on the bank.

Charbonneau stared in amazement. He estimated that there were about a hundred men, women and children on a bare strip of land. No one expected to see as many Indians upon arriving.

The two major Indian nations who lived at the gateway of the salmon kingdom, the Yakimas and the Wanapams, had been warned of the expedition's arrival by Twisted Hair and Tetoharsky, who had been sent ahead as emissaries by the captains two days earlier. The chiefs of the Nez Percés had fulfilled their mission; informed of the explorers' friendly intentions, the people of the region had promised their hospitality.

The Indians moved away from the water to allow the canoes to come ashore, all the while examining the bearded, white-skinned men, a race they had never seen before. They looked closely at their clothes, their weapons, their baggage, and exchanged lively comments. Some of the men were bold enough to come closer and the visitors took this opportunity to invite them to smoke. The Yakimas and the Wanapams did not use tobacco, but they were happy to participate in a ritual they associated with the Indians of the Great Plains.

After smoking, the explorers set up camp near a place where pieces of wood had washed up on the shore. They lit fires, still under the close scrutiny of the Indians who were fascinated by their equipment. The French-Canadians sang while they worked, expressing their joy at having reached the Columbia at last. This river had never been explored east of the Cascades, the mountain range to which Mount Saint Helens belonged.

They knew the St. Lawrence, which flowed through the valley where their ancestors were born and into the gulf by the same name; they knew the Mississippi that flowed into the Gulf of Mexico after tracing the border of the United States from north to south. And now they were going to discover the Columbia, a river where no French-Canadian had plunged his paddle yet. One more reason to feel like singing. The Yakimas and the Wanapams were surprised to hear their voices modulating in unison incomprehensible words:

C'est l'aviron qui nous mène, qui nous mène
C'est l'aviron qui nous mène en haut.

However, the men stopped just as they were beginning their third song to watch in amazement a spectacle much more colorful and noisy than their *a cappella* concert. Cutssahnem, a chief of the Wanapam nation, looking majestic under his plume, arrived at the head of two hundred warriors singing and beating the drums. In rhythm with the music, they formed a circle around the explorers and continued to sing for a good half hour.

Never had the members of the expedition been welcomed with such pomp. It made them forget the ordeals and loneliness they had experienced in the Rocky Mountains. There, at the confluence of the Shoshoni and the Columbia Rivers, they were discovering a new civilization, the culture of the West Coast, very different from the culture of the Great Plains, which was entirely based on the buffalo.

Lewis and Clark communicated with Cutssahnem through signs. They thanked the chief for his warm reception and expressed their delight at finding themselves among their "children." Drouillard, who was translating the words of the captains, took the liberty of replacing the word "children" with the gesture meaning "friends." Cutssahnem welcomed the visitors, never suspecting that one day the Whites would destroy his kingdom.

The encampment was located on a strip of land where the Yakimas and the Wanapams used to meet to fish, trade and fraternize. The captains decided to remain there for two days so that the men could mend their clothes and rest. On the second day, Charbonneau and Sacagawea accompanied Lewis and Drouillard to Cutssahnem's village, half a mile from the Columbia River. The

Captain wanted to compile a lexicon of local terms. He didn't need Charbonneau and his wife, but he agreed to their request to join him.

It was Sacagawea who had insisted on visiting the village. She was curious about the customs of the Indians from the great river that flowed to the salted waters. When she arrived at the village, she observed that the dwellings were not covered with skins but with reed matting. Oblong in shape and supported by stakes, they measured from fifteen to sixty feet in length. They were topped by flat roofs, which suggested to Sacagawea that it didn't rain very often in the region.

While Lewis and Drouillard worked on the lexicon of the Wanapam language with Cutssahnem's help, Sacagawea continued her visit with Charbonneau. As she watched the Wanapams performing their daily chores, she noticed men and women busy cutting up and laying out the salmon to dry on racks. She was surprised to see that the men did the same work as the women.

Charbonneau was just as surprised as she was, for he had never seen Indian men engaged in activities other than hunting or war. They saw many white-haired heads in the village; less numerous than the children, the old people seemed nonetheless to hold an important place and to be revered by all. This accurate observation was later confirmed when they were shown inside a house by two young girls with eyes as black as their braided hair that hung down the middle of their backs. Charbonneau couldn't take his eyes off these Indians girls who only wore a piece of leather around their waists, which barely concealed their private parts. Sacagawea became aware of her man's interest for them and showed her displeasure by nudging him hard but discreetly. Charbonneau was surprised again, this time by Sacagawea's reaction, which looked a lot like jealousy.

Inside the house, the couple found a totally blind old woman; she sat in the best spot, surrounded by women and children. When she was informed of the presence of visitors, she began to speak in a lively voice that commanded everyone's attention and imposed silence upon all those who were present.

Using sign language, a young girl explained that the old woman had lived more than a hundred winters. Sacagawea and Charbonneau looked at each other in disbelief: on the Great Plains, Indians often died before the age of thirty.

–I hope to live as long as the old blind woman, said Sacagawea to Charbonneau as they left the house.

Sacagawea and Toussaint returned to camp, leaving Lewis and Drouillard to their vocabulary studies. On their way, they found an idyllic spot on the bank of the Columbia, where the Shoshoni girl made the French-Canadian forget the lovely Wanapam women. Jean-Baptiste babbled happily during their lovemaking.

Before the expedition started again down the Columbia, the Americans purchased about forty dogs for their food stocks. Charbonneau was almost sorry that he had introduced the troop to dog meat, for he found it difficult to bear the sight of the poor animals being slaughtered, struggling, howling and biting. He soon forgot all about it when he was back on the river.

Indeed, soon after the departure, Charbonneau stopped paddling and bent over the water.

–Look! he called out to Sacagawea.

The water was so limpid that they could see the salmon at a depth of fifteen to twenty feet. A little later, however, she wondered why so many of them washed up dead on the shore or floated on the surface.

–What are they dying of? she asked.

Charbonneau couldn't answer. He didn't know that salmon die after spawning.

The flotilla came across many fishing establishments that consisted of cabins and stands on which were drying great quantities of fish. The Wakimas were motioning the travelers to stop, but the expedition continued on its way, in a great hurry to see the Pacific.

After sixteen miles, the Columbia changed in aspect and became swifter. The river left the plain and entered a region of cliffs that towered nearly two hundred yards over the water. Charbonneau could see a cone-shaped mountain in the distance; its snow-capped peak strangely seemed to be level with the pirogue. "The river will drop steeply," he thought to himself.

Many Chinooks had gathered at the top of a cliff that offered an unrestricted view over a narrow pass of the river and its roaring rapids. The White explorers were about to launch their flimsy little pirogues in the midst of it. Charbonneau, Sacagawea and the other members of the expedition who couldn't swim climbed up the cliff and, all out of breath, mingled with the Indian spectators.

From up there, they could assess the seriousness of the challenge confronting the paddlers. At that point, the Columbia was funneled into a channel of no more than forty-five yards. The current had to pass through it, after tumbling down a series of falls that had forced the expedition to do a portage. In that narrow passage half a mile long, whirlpools and huge waves combined in a violent surge.

–They won't make it, said Charbonneau to Labiche, raising his voice above the noise of the water that caused the cliff to vibrate beneath their feet.

–It's time to pray to *sainte Anne*, replied Labiche in earnest.

The two men collected their thoughts to pray to their patron saint.

The captains had deemed unfeasible the idea of transporting the canoes beyond the cliff where the observers stood. And so, before taking the narrow passage in the river, they had entrusted to the men who couldn't swim the most valuable possessions of the expedition and had arranged to meet at the end of the channel, where the river widened and became calm again until the next rapids two miles down.

Charbonneau carried on his back the captains' papers among which were, not only the journals and the charts, but also the letters of credit signed by President Jefferson. These letters were just as precious as the other documents; if ever the explorers were lucky enough to come across a commercial ship at the mouth of the Columbia, the papers would allow them to buy their passage on board and return to the United States by sea, either through Cape Horn or the Cape of

Good Hope. All the members of the expedition were ready to sail a whole year rather than having to cross the Rockies again.

These letters of credit, however, would be useless if the pirogues didn't make it through that very dangerous passage of the Columbia, something even the local Indians, the Chinooks, had not attempted in their sleekest boats. That explained their surprise at the recklessness of the explorers, a surprise that turned into astonishment when they saw the five canoes emerge from the frightening channel unscathed. Shouts of joy burst forth among the members of the expedition who had mingled with the Indians.

–I told you they would make it! exclaimed Charbonneau, nudging Labiche in the back.

–No you didn't, you idiot! You said they wouldn't! retorted Labiche, pulling a wry face.

–That was before we prayed to *sainte Anne*!

They started walking again to rejoin the canoes downstream from the channel. As they headed down, Charbonneau held his wife's hand; she admitted she had feared for their companions. On her back, Jean-Baptiste was wriggling with joy; everything he saw aroused his curiosity.

–If he doesn't become an explorer, my name isn't Toussaint Charbonneau.

–He'll go even further than us, added Sacagawea.

That day, the members of the expedition set up camp near Nixluidix, a village inhabited by the Wishrams, a group of Indians belonging to the great family of the Chinooks. Charbonneau had just put the baggage down when he started complaining about the bad smell in the air.

–It smells of rotten fish, he said to Drouillard, who had arrived at the camp before him.

–Go and see below the village and you'll understand, replied the hunter.

Charbonneau finished unpacking and started, with Sacagawea and Jean-Baptiste, in the direction indicated by Drouillard. Walking along the river, he passed by the village; it consisted of about twenty large dwellings that could accommodate many families. For the first time since he had left Illinois, he saw wooden houses inhabited by Indians. Illinois... such a long time ago.

Built over rectangular excavations, the houses, made of wooden boards, were decorated with painted animal designs. A small door that opened no more than two feet above the ground served as the only entrance. In front of one of these houses, a man motioned them in. They accepted the invitation and slipped inside by pushing back a mat hanging in front of the door. Then they had to go down a small wooden ladder, as the house was partially underground.

Half of the space inside was used to store large quantities of dried fish that gave off a strong odor. In the other half, the living space, small beds, made of mats laid on trestles, were lined up against the walls. The fireplace was in the middle and the man invited his guests to sit by it. He offered them boiled salmon and berries, which they ate heartily.

–This is very good fish, said Toussaint.

His wife nodded in agreement and added:

–Did you notice how big and comfortable the house is?

She thought these people must have a pleasant life, much easier than the Shoshonis', even easier than life on the Great Plains. The world she was discovering filled her with wonder for its great diversity of scenery and people. Before leaving, she presented their host with the blue beads she had on.

They made their way again toward the stench that grew worse as they got closer. Finally, two miles down the road, they saw, in the middle of the Columbia, tall scaffoldings on which the Indians laid the fish to dry. The bed of the river was strewn with rocks, which the water submerged when it rose in the spring, but were uncovered this time of the year. Dried salmon were stacked on each one, about a hundred piles in all. Toussaint calculated that the whole thing amounted to approximately ten thousand pounds of fish. Swarms of flies buzzed around the foul smelling guts of the salmon.

–Yuk! said Charbonneau, holding his nose.

–These people have so much food that they don't know what to do with it, commented Sacagawea, as she followed her man back to camp.

They had just glimpsed at the market of Nixluidix where every year, three important fairs where held, the last of which had taken place two weeks earlier and had ended with a great celebration. Coming down from the Columbia plateau, the Nez Percés arrived with buffalo and wapiti skins, hoping to exchange them for the products from the coast: fish, shells and various objects obtained from the White merchants who traveled to the mouth of the river in their big sail boats. Other tribes, such as the Yakimas and the Walla Wallas, also came to this trade hub, where the Chinooks played a major role, a bit like the Sioux at the gateway of Upper Missouri.

When Charbonneau and Sacagawea arrived at the camp, Cruzatte was playing his fiddle and York danced to his music to the great amusement of the Wishrams.

The Skilloots were heading straight for the explorers' encampment, located in a lovely meadow surrounded by woods on the right side of the bank. The members of the expedition put their plates down on the ground and stood up when they saw the twenty or so proud representatives of the Chinook family coming toward them.

The Skilloots were sailing aboard large canoes, beautifully built, streamlined at both ends, decorated on the bow with a bear figure and on the stern with an eagle's head. They were colorfully dressed in a combination of their traditional costumes and Whites' clothes: sailor's pants and jackets, shirts, hats, red and blue blankets. That clearly indicated their multiple contacts with Spanish and English merchants, and thus the proximity of the coast. Like the other members of their nation, they had deformed heads, the result of a local practice that consisted in compressing the heads of newborns between two boards, which flattened the skull laterally, making it jut out lengthwise.

They drew alongside the riverbank and got out of their canoes, armed with tomahawks, spears, bows and arrows. Some carried muskets and pistols.

Clark and Lewis were not overly alarmed at their being armed.

They said to themselves that the Skilloots had worn their favorite outfits to pay them a friendly visit. They invited them to sit by their fires and offered them tobacco to smoke and wapato roots to eat, a kind of potato, roasted in hot ash until tender. Of about the same shape and size as the Irish potato, this root had a pleasant taste and replaced bread as a starch.

The captains spared the Skilloots the trouble of making speeches, communication between them being impossible. Four days earlier, Twisted Hair and Tetoharsky, their Nez Percés guides, had left the expedition and gone back to their country. During the descent of the falls and rapids of the Columbia river –fifty-miles of perils and toils over seven long days –the two chiefs had acted as interpreters with the Chinooks of the area, who had helped them over the most difficult passages, on top of selling them fish, dogs and roots. The Chinooks had been of great service to the expedition, but they had also taken advantage of the portages to steal some articles, arousing the victims' anger. In the name of peace, the captains had preferred to turn a blind eye to these petty thefts.

But the Skilloots went too far during their visit to the expedition's encampment on November 4, 1805. The explorers put away their pipes and continued eating, while keeping an eye on the visitors who hovered around the baggage of the expedition. All of a sudden, Clark saw one of the Indians smoking his peace pipe. He jumped up and snatched it away from him:

–Give me that! he ordered, and he put the pipe back in his bag. He then noticed that his tomahawk had disappeared.

–They stole my tomahawk! he cried out in an exasperated tone.

The other members of the expedition, who looked on apprehensively, stood up together and grabbed their weapons; most of the Skilloots closed ranks. Clark moved closer and glared at them.

–Who took my tomahawk? he asked in English in a threatening voice.

The Skilloots pretended not to know what he was talking about. It would have been pointless to ask Drouillard to translate; the West Coast Indians didn't understand the sign language used by the Great Plains Indians. Clark searched the Skilloots one by one, then their canoes, but he didn't find his tomahawk. He was furious when he went back to the fireside.

Charbonneau lost his temper too: his blue coat, the Christmas present from Sacagawea and Otter Woman, had also vanished.

–Somebody stole my coat!

He clenched his teeth and aimed his gun at the Skilloots; the rest of the troop followed suit. They were getting seriously annoyed at these Chinooks. The visitors felt the ire of the explorers and, being outnumbered, decided it was better to just go.

–What a nuisance these Skilloots are! exclaimed Charbonneau, expressing the general feeling.

Sacagawea, who had kept out of the way during the incident, called out to her husband:

–Toussaint, your coat is right here!

She was pointing to a big tree root under which one of the Indians had stuffed Charbonneau's blue coat.

Fearing the Skilloots might come back, the expedition made the most of the remaining daylight to find a new place to camp. They passed a village with large houses and, three miles downstream, they came to a spot with a magnificent view of Mount Saint Helens, which they had glimpsed for the first time on October 19.

–It could be the highest peak in North America, said Clark to the paddlers of his canoe.

Charbonneau turned to the southwest and gazed at the sugar-loaf mountain.

–We're getting near the coast, he said to Sacagawea. It's the last mountain.

–Have you ever seen a great salted lake, Toussaint?

–No more than you, but I've been told that it's much like the Great Plains: you don't see the end of it.

The canoes were floating down the river along high, steep hills; the mist was so thick that the explorers couldn't even see the opposite bank.

In a few days, the landscape had changed completely from the barren plateaus of the upper Columbia. Since the village of Nixluidix, which marked a kind of ecological boundary, the expedition had been crossing a forest region where yews, fir trees and spruce grew to incredible heights.

Charbonneau had to tilt his head back to see, when they weren't shrouded in mist, the tops of some of the trees, which had trunks as big as the huts of the Mandans. He had no doubts about the reason for such lush vegetation: the soil was fertile and it constantly rained or drizzled. Drenched and chilled to the bone, he couldn't get warm in spite of the energy he expended paddling toward the Pacific Ocean. He was in a bad mood and cursed the country, its damp climate and the bugs that he picked up when they camped near the Indian villages.

As most members of the expedition, Charbonneau had come to cordially detest the Chinooks whom he called thieves and criticized about everything. He found them too short and badly built, poorly dressed, some of them wearing only a loincloth. The local women seemed particularly ugly to him, with their chubby legs and big, sagging breasts. He also made fun of their deformed heads. He couldn't even appreciate the beauty of the big Chinook canoes that clove majestically through the waters of the Columbia.

And this permanent mist that hid even the sun! It made the region look mysterious, to the point where Toussaint soon started to feel that he was entering a disquieting world where earth, water and air seemed to meld into one.

Behind him in the boat, Sacagawea was shivering in his blue coat, which he had given her since her tunic was tattered, the dampness and the water having rotted the leather. Jean-Baptiste also shivered in her arms.

–This is the Pacific? she asked in a weary voice.

–No, we're still on fresh water. Are you cold? What about Jean-Baptiste?

The young woman smiled.

–Don't worry about us! Just go on.

Charbonneau resumed paddling with greater zeal.

On November 7, 1805, around eleven in the morning, the rain let up and the mist cleared away. Cruzatte was the first to shout:

–The ocean!

As the curtain in a theater rises, revealing the stage, the fog was lifting and, before the explorers, filled with wonder, the water stretched away endlessly into the distance. The Pacific! The ultimate destination of their long journey to the ends of the North American continent.

–The Ocean! The Ocean at last!

Each man in turn uttered those magic words, and each experienced the greatest satisfaction of his life. The expedition had headed up the Missouri as far as its source, crossed over the Rockies and sailed down the Columbia River to the Pacific, completing a journey that no other human being had made before them.

–The ocean!

Charbonneau was ecstatic; he clasped Sacagawea and Jean-Baptiste in his arms. His place in the legend of the West was now ensured! His name would still be known in seven generations, as well as his wife's and son's!

His eyes met Clark's, who seemed lost in thought. After a rush of joy, the Captain was calculating in his mind the distance between the mouth of the Missouri and the Pacific: four thousand one hundred and forty-two miles! He was also proud of their feat, but Lewis' sullenness spoiled his pleasure. They had both known since going over the Rockies that the expedition would not have the economic repercussions hoped for by President Jefferson. Still, there was the glory of the discovery. And the satisfaction of surpassing oneself.

That evening, the troop set up camp on the shore, where they could hear the sound of the waves crashing against the cliffs, a bit to the south. The mood was one of general rejoicing.

–I would certainly drink to that, reflected Drouillard as he remembered nostalgically the glassfuls of rum the captains used to serve them at the beginning of the expedition.

–So would I, Labiche chimed in.

–Come now, gentlemen, we can at least have some fun, said Cruzatte, getting his fiddle.

And, with a powerful bow-stroke, he launched into *La Gigue de la Rivière Rouge.* Carried away by the music, Charbonneau started to jig in front of what he believed to be the Pacific; York followed suit defiantly. The rest of the troop formed a circle around the dancers, making bets on who would tire first. The first jigging competition on the West Coast had just begun, when it was interrupted by the arrival of two Chinook canoes with ten men and a woman aboard. Leaving the woman in one of the canoes, the Chinooks came ashore and walked up to the Americans. The one who seemed to be their chief greeted them in English:

–Welcome, bastards!

The members of the expedition were so surprised to hear English words that they didn't even take offense. Smiling broadly, the chief took advantage of the stunned silence to let out all the bad words he knew in English, insults, swearwords, obscenities. When Lewis finally got over the shock, he said to the chief:

–Who taught you to speak English so well?

–Mister Haley, the biggest merchant on the coast.

And pointing to the woman in the canoe, he added:

–Mister Haley really likes that woman. Do you want to try her?

–No, thank you, replied Lewis. Tell me, where is Mr. Haley's ship?

–Somewhere along the coast, answered the chief, motioning vaguely towards the ocean.

–But we are on the coast! exclaimed Lewis.

–The coast? Coast, not here. Coast, over there.

The chief pointed far into the distance. Lewis then realized that the expedition had arrived on the shores of a wide bay, probably the one that the American Captain Robert Gray had explored in 1792. The Pacific was no more than twenty miles straight ahead, but the distance was made greater by the need to stick closely to the shore because of the waves.

This new information was a real letdown for Charbonneau and Sacagawea.

–How many more days to the great salted lake? the Shoshoni woman asked, somewhat disheartened.

–Don't know, and Charbonneau shrugged with a faraway look in his eyes.

During the next few days, it rained constantly, never stopping for more than a two-hour stretch. All the members of the expedition were wet through and through, cold and hungry, with nothing better to eat than some dried fish that was beginning to go bad.

The situation might have been tolerable if they had been able to move toward the ocean or find an adequate place to spend the night. But the wind was so fierce and the waves so tall that sailing was impossible, and they had to stay put for six days on that miserable sandy shore, washed over by the rising tide. They had their backs against a hill covered with pine trees, which left them only a narrow, pebbly surface to lay their mats down.

One night, as she examined her bedding that was rotting just like her clothes, Sacagawea asked Charbonneau:

–Do you think that we'll see Mr. Haley along the coast?

–I certainly hope so, otherwise, it'll be a damned long winter, he replied, squashing a bug between his fingers.

On November 15, 1805, the weather changed. When they woke up, the sun was shining brightly and the wind soon died down. The bay appeared in all its splendor.

–Get ready to leave, shouted Lewis.

All the men immediately got down to work in the best of moods.

Unfortunately, they had just finished preparations when a violent wind started blowing from the southeast, whipping up such tall and furious waves that it would have been suicidal to launch the boats. The captains were just as disappointed as their men, but they wisely decided to wait for better conditions. The windy day, however, was ideal to dry the clothes and bedding, repair the weapons, examine the ammunition, which kept the troop busy until the afternoon when the wind died down for good.

They hurried to load the canoes and left that awful place where they had been stuck for a week. The waves were not as tall as in the morning, but still strong enough to make Sacagawea as sick as a dog at the bottom of the canoe, as had happened in the first days of sailing in the Columbia estuary.

–You could at least do it overboard! scolded Charbonneau.

Looking greenish, Sacagawea gave her man a cold look.

–Keep your mind on your paddling.

Strangely enough, Charbonneau was not seasick. The man couldn't swim, but he had sea legs.

The troop went around a headland that jutted out into the water and reached a beach through which flowed a brook down from the hills. At the mouth of the brook, they found a village of thirty-six dwellings; its sole inhabitants, for the moment, were bugs. The captains decided to camp there, the coast not being very far.

When she got her strength back, Sacagawea took off her moccasins full of holes and walked into the bay with Jean-Baptiste in her arms. She cupped her left hand and brought some water to her son's lips. He made a face and spat it out, but still asked for more. Sacagawea licked her fingers and tasted salt. She stretched her arm out to the horizon and said to her child in Shoshoni:

–We have reached the ends of the world, my son, but you will go even further.

Later that day, the members of the expedition marveled at their first sunset over the Pacific. The sky was set ablaze by the glow of the reddish disk that slowly sank into the ocean, between Cape Disappointment to the north and Point Adams to the south. These two geographic points marked the entrance to the bay named by the British explorer George Vancouver.

Three days later, at sunrise, Clark set off on foot toward the coast with a detachment that included Charbonneau, Labiche, York, Sergeants Ordway and Prior, the brothers Fields, Shannon, Bratten, Colter and Wiser. As they were leaving, Charbonneau waved to

Sacagawea. She had a sulky look and she turned around without waving back.

Labiche had noticed her bad mood.

–What's wrong with your squaw, Charbonneau?

–She would have liked to come with us.

The men walked silently along a sandy beach. Seven miles later, they reached a small river; on its bank, they found a cabin with children and four women inside. One of the women was covered with ulcers, a condition that seemed to affect many of the Chinooks in that region.

-There's another woman Mr. Haley and his sailors must be very fond of, said Charbonneau to Labiche.

The woman clearly suffered from a venereal disease.

They crossed the water in a canoe paddled by two women. Clark gave each of them a fishing hook as a reward, after which the men resumed walking along the shore of the bay. After two miles, they discovered the skeleton of a beached whale. The Chinooks had probably stripped the animal of all its edible parts. It was nonetheless an impressive sight.

–It must be at least a hundred feet long, said Charbonneau who had never seen a whale before.

Labiche felt that the interpreter exaggerated a little, but was careful not to contradict him. He was planning to use his assessment to impress the men back at the camp.

After a meal of sandpipers and plovers they had shot on the way, the men reached a peninsula that stretched for two miles before them. It was Cape Disappointment, named in 1788 by the English merchant John Meares who was exploring the coast in search of a great river. Taking the Columbia estuary for a simple bay, he had been very disappointed indeed and had continued on his way.

While exploring the Cape that rose one hundred and fifty feet above the water, the detachment found the tree where Lewis had carved his name when he had been there two days earlier on the lookout for a sail. Clark carved his name too, together with the name of his country, the day, month and year. Many of the men did the same; when it was Charbonneau's turn, he took his knife and, knowing only two letters of the alphabet, carved his initials in the trunk. As long as the tree would stand, it would bear witness to the feat of Toussaint Charbonneau, the first French-Canadian to ever reach the Pacific by going down the Columbia River.

Lulled by the regular sound of the waves against the rocks of the Cape, Charbonneau gazed for a long time at the ocean. It unfolded its vast expanse to the west and washed up on the shores of countries the existence of which he was vaguely aware of, with names he didn't even know.

No matter how hard he scanned the horizon, he didn't see a single sail, no sign of this Mr. Haley who might have provided them with fresh supplies or take them back to the United States. Now that he had reached the furthest edge of North America, there was nowhere else to go except back. Toussaint felt depressed and thought of his country, Upper Missouri, with nostalgia.

Days went by without any ship appearing on the horizon. The possibility of a prolonged stay on the West Coast had to be contemplated. In the evening of November 24, 1805, the thirty-seven members of the expedition held a meeting on the beach to decide where they would spend the winter. Breaking once again with military tradition, Lewis and Clark had decided to put the question to a vote rather than imposing their choice.

They had three options: head up the Columbia as far as the falls; go back to the Sandy River, where the expedition had camped on November 3; sail across the bay and find an appropriate site near the village of the Clatsops, a friendly nation who lived on the southern shore of the bay.

Sitting around the fire under the stars that, for once, could be seen, one by one, each man expressed his opinion. Labiche voted for a return to the Sandy River, which flowed across a vast prairie and into the Columbia; he remembered fondly that place where, in just a few hours, he had shot fourteen ducks. Cruzatte chose the same site on account of the great variety of its trees.

Drouillard for his part opted for exploring the southern shore of the bay. According to what their new friends, the Clatsops, had told them, the region was teeming with wapitis. These animals would provide, not only food for the winter, but skins to replace their tattered clothes. Lepage agreed, and so did Lewis and Clark.

Six American soldiers, however, were not too keen on the idea of spending the winter in such a damp place; they expressed a preference for returning to the waterfalls of the Columbia, where the weather was drier. Furthermore, this choice had the advantage of bringing them closer to the United States: the men were beginning to be seriously homesick.

When it was Charbonneau's turn to vote, he abstained.

–Come on, Charbonneau, tell us what you think, said Drouillard, slightly impatient.

–Here or there, what difference does it make! It's going to be a damned long winter.

Drouillard shrugged his shoulders.

York voted next. He could tip the scales either in favor of the Sandy River or the south shore of the bay. Aware of the power he held, he took his time before speaking. He also appreciated the fact that he had a say in the matter, in the same way as the other members of the expedition.

–The southern shore, the slave said at last.

After York had voted, everyone looked at Sacagawea who could even the number of votes for the Sandy River and the southern shore of the bay. She blushed, torn between panic and euphoria; she also hesitated a long time. When she finally announced her choice, she offered a unique position.

–I'm in favor of a place where there are plenty of wapato roots, she said, smiling shyly.

Clark carefully wrote down her answer in his notebook; it most conclusively gave the majority to the option of the southern shore of the bay. The first truly democratic vote had just been held in America.

The building of Fort Clatsop was completed in late November. The work consisted of two parallel rows of small rooms on either side of a twenty-foot aisle closed off at both ends by sharply pointed logs.

Inside the room she occupied with Toussaint and Jean-Baptiste, Sacagawea kept repeating:

–I want to go!

–Captain Clark hasn't invited you, said Charbonneau, still lying in bed.

–It doesn't matter! protested the woman, pacing back and forth. I've come all this way and I haven't yet seen the great waters of the coast! I also want the chance to see the gigantic fish!

Surprised by her passionate plea, Charbonneau got up and dressed.

–I'll talk to the Captain, he said putting on his blue coat.

He went out, followed by Sacagawea who carried Jean-Baptiste in her arms. The fort was deserted. Fearing that Clark had already left, Charbonneau hastened his step to get to the Netul River, near which the expedition's winter quarters were set up.

The men were all gathered around two pirogues; Clark and twelve of them were about to start out on a two to three-day excursion to an Indian village to the southwest; according to chief Comowool, one of their Clatsop neighbors, a beached whale had been found nearby. The men were curious to see the sea monster and eager to get the oil and fat of the mammal before the local Indians did.

–Captain Clark! Captain Clark! called out Charbonneau, making his way to the canoes. Sacagawea wants to come along.

Drouillard translated, half-smiling.

–And why does she want to come with us? asked Clark.

–She says that she didn't come all the way here just to miss seeing the great waters from the coast, answered Charbonneau. She also wants to have a look at the whale. After all she's endured, she would find it unfair not to be able to go with you.

Clark looked at Lewis. His colleague merely shrugged; he didn't really care.

–All right, said Clark after thinking about it for a moment, she can get in.

–If she's going, I'm going with her, said Charbonneau, following his wife in the Captain's canoe.

With a smile, Clark gave the signal to leave. What kind of a trip would it be without Charbonneau, Sacagawea and Pomp, the little dancing boy?

Epilogue

The Heroes' Destiny

On October 11, 1809, three years and a few days after the return of the expedition, Meriwether Lewis shot himself through the heart. "He never got over the trip," said his traveling companion, William Clark, helpless in his attempts to bring him out of his despair, exacerbated by drugs and alcohol.

And yet, heaven knows Lewis and the other members of the Corps of Discovery were given a hero's welcome in St. Louis, with the exception of Toussaint Charbonneau and his family who had remained in Upper Missouri. Still wearing their leather clothes in rags, exhausted, sun-tanned and bearded, they came off their canoes on September 23, 1806, presenting to the local population the image of modern day Robinson Crusoes. They were believed dead, but they had completed their historic mission, which had lasted two years, four months and nine days, and covered more than eight thousand miles all the way to the ends of the continent and back. In the city's taverns and living-rooms, the explorers regaled trappers and merchants with stories of indestructible grizzlies, uncompromising or helpful Indians, impassable mountains and six-foot beavers at the confluence of the Yellowstone and Missouri Rivers, as well as at the Three Forks. They described the wonders of their journey of discovery, while trying to minimize the disappointments of their return.

After spending a rainy and gloomy winter at Fort Clatsop, on the banks of the Columbia, they had left on March 23, 1806, happy to be going home at last. In May, they had arrived in the village of Twisted Hair and the Nez Percés, who had looked after their horses as promised. They had been forced to wait until June 24 to start on Old Toby's trail because it was still buried under several feet of snow. Beyond the Bitterroot Mountains, whose crossing had turned out to be easier than the first time, the expedition had split up in two. Clark led a group of twenty-nine people, including York, Charbonneau and his family, down the Yellowstone. He had traveled at a phenomenal speed, thinking that he was the first White man to explore the mighty river that had its source at the foot of the Rockies and flowed, seven hundred miles further down, into the Missouri. In fact, this feat had been achieved a year earlier by none other than François-Antoine Larocque, the young voyageur from L'Assomption whom he had met during the winter of 1804-1805, at Fort Mandan.

In early August, Lewis had joined Clark at the confluence of the Missouri and Yellowstone Rivers. He was just back from a disastrous exploration of the Maria River. Accompanied by Georges Drouillard and Pierre Cruzatte, among others, he had had to flee across the plain following an armed confrontation with the Black Feet, which had ended in the death of an Indian, a blot on the reputation of the expedition. Then, he had been shot in the left buttock by Cruzatte who, being shortsighted, had taken him for a deer. Reunited with Clark and the rest of the troop, he had brooded for the rest of the trip home.

The news that the Corps of Discovery had returned spread right across the United States. The newspapers wrote enthusiastically about the feat of the two captains, the first Americans to cross the continent. In November 1806, after many celebrations in his honor, Lewis set off for Washington where Thomas Jefferson was waiting impatiently. The president had been reelected two years earlier and, like many others, had lost hope of ever seeing his protégé alive.

Lewis traveled from St. Louis to Washington accompanied by Clark and a numerous entourage which included Big White, a Mandan chief, the French-Canadian interpreter René Jusseaume and his family, Pierre Chouteau, a rich merchant from St. Louis, many soldiers and York. It was a long journey. In every city where the explorers stopped, the local dignitaries insisted on paying tribute to them. Lewis had not drunk any alcohol in months and had pushed himself to the point of exhaustion during the entire journey; he now drank to excess, never really quenching his thirst. The troop finally arrived in Washington on December 28. "Never has such an event aroused such rejoicing," wrote a journalist of the *Washington Intelligencer*. A well-known poet suggested that the Columbia River be renamed after Lewis.

At the White House, the Captain introduced Big White to Jefferson, praising the cooperation of the Mandans and the commercial possibilities of the West. Despite the recalcitrant attitude of the Teton Sioux and the presence of the Rockies, which put an end to the dream of a navigable route from the Mississippi to the Pacific, the United States would derive "enormous advantages" from Louisiana and Oregon, said Lewis.

Jefferson drank in Lewis' words and bombarded him with questions about the contents of the journals, the origin of the specimens, the accuracy of the data, etc. He asked him to have the journals and his scientific discoveries published without delay in order to inform the world of the wonders of the American West. Mistakenly thinking that the explorer was equally competent in every field, Jefferson named him governor of the Louisiana territory a few weeks later.

At the end of March of 1807, Lewis left Washington for Philadelphia, where he intended to have Clark's map published, as well as three volumes on the expedition. The first of the three, an account of the journey, was to be published on January 1st, 1808. As soon as he arrived in Philadelphia, Lewis recruited a botanist, a zoologist and an illustrator to prepare the scientific data of the expedition for publication. He did not, however, approach an editor to help him transform his journals into a narrative.

Crowned with glory, Lewis participated fully in Philadelphia's social life, attending all kinds of receptions in the hope of finding someone who would replace Maria Wood in his heart. He had dreamt of marrying the beautiful Virginian whose name he had given to the most romantic of the Missouri tributaries. Unfortunately, soon after his return to the United Stated, he had learned that Maria had married while he was at the other end of the continent.

One night, he made the acquaintance of Laetitia Breckinridge, "the most beautiful woman I have ever known," he confided to his brother Reuben. Mad about her, he tried to woo the young woman, but she rejected his advances, sending the alcoholic explorer back to his bottle.

Seven months later, when it was time for him to leave Philadelphia to fulfill his mandate in St. Louis, Lewis had not written a single line of his account of the journey, as he had promised Jefferson. He didn't do any better as governor of Louisiana where he incurred criticism for launching a commercial venture with Clark and his brother Reuben, among others. He invested seven thousand dollars in an expedition led by the French merchant Pierre Chouteau, whose main goal was to establish a trading post at the mouth of the Yellowstone on the Missouri River. The considerable sum was used to buy horses, barges and supplies, and to hire one hundred and twenty-five men to face the Sioux who were bound to stand up against the troop at the gateway of Upper Missouri.

Lewis wanted to become one of the first Americans to benefit from the fur trade in the West, but he had also entrusted Chouteau with a diplomatic mission: taking back Big White, the Mandan chief, to his village "safe and sound," as Jefferson had requested in a letter. The new governor had placed himself in an indefensible position. The money he had sunk in the commercial venture was not his own, but came from the government of the United States. He had eased his conscience by telling himself that Chouteau's expedition was carrying out an official mission by accompanying Big White home, but the new Secretary of State, William Eustis, refused to pay the bill that Lewis sent him, telling the governor to pay the seven thousand dollars out of his own pocket.

Eustis' decision mortified Lewis, who was already deep in debt. His serious addiction to drugs and alcohol added further to his financial troubles. Claiming that he suffered from malaria, he had opium pills of one gram each prescribed to him. He took one at bedtime, three during the night if he felt feverish, and two in the morning if he wasn't feeling any better. The rest of the day, he drank. He never looked at his journals, he didn't answer Jefferson's letters.

On September 4, 1809, in a sudden burst of dignity, Meriwether Lewis decided to go to Washington to explain himself and defend his reputation. He took a ship headed for New Orleans; from there, he planned to sail to the capital aboard another ship. Clark had made him promise, for the thousandth time, not to drink, and Lewis, full of shame, had sworn one more time to remain sober.

But as soon as he was on board, he got drunk, making such a nuisance of himself that the captain of the ship made him get off in Memphis, Tennessee. The major of Fort Pickering took him into his care and put him on an alcohol-free diet for three days. Once he had sobered up, Lewis decided to ride to Washington. On October 11, on the road to Natchez, he stopped at an inn and rented a room.

In the morning, the innkeeper found him lying on his back, shot through the heart, holding a pistol in his right hand.

Jefferson saw in Lewis' suicide the result of "the sensible depressions of mind" he had detected long before in his former private secretary.

Georges Drouillard, the highly skilled hunter, also met an untimely and tragic end. In 1810, he was slaughtered by a band of Black Feet at the Three Forks, in Upper Missouri, where he was involved in establishing a trading post on behalf of Manuel Lisa, a Spanish tradesman from St. Louis. The Black Feet had not forgotten their encounter with the Lewis and Clark expedition during which one of their warriors had been killed.

William Clark saw happier and more productive days, if one overlooks his treatment of his slave York. Three years after the return of the Corps of Discovery, he got married to Julia Hancock, the girl he loved. He pursued a political career that led him to the position of Superintendent of Indian Affairs in Louisiana and governor of this vast territory. He earned the respect and even the affection of the Indians, who nicknamed St. Louis, where he carried out his duties, "the City of Red Hair."

Up until the day he died, Clark remained attached to Toussaint Charbonneau. At the end of their journey, he tried in vain to persuade the French-Canadian to go with him to Washington to act as interpreter to President Jefferson. However, since no Hidatsa chief had expressed the wish to meet Jefferson, Charbonneau deemed his presence unnecessary in the capital.

Undaunted by his refusal, Clark offered to settle his friend and his family on a piece of farmland in the Ohio or Mississippi Valleys. He also committed himself to take care of Jean-Baptiste's education.

–We might go to St. Louis when the boy is old enough to go to school, said Charbonneau, while Sacagawea was nodding her assent.

On August 17, 1806, the expedition left Charbonneau and his family on the Knife River, near the Hidatsa villages in Upper Missouri. Clark paid the French-Canadian interpreter his wages, which came to five hundred dollars and thirty-three cents, including the price of a horse and a tepee. Three days after his departure, the Captain wrote a letter to Charbonneau in which he deplored the fact that he had been unable to reward the "woman who accompanied you that long dangerous and fatiguing rout to the Pacific Ocean and back..." He thanked the interpreter again for his contribution and closed with these words: "As to your little Son (my boy Pomp), you well know my fondness for him and my anxiety to take and raise him as my own child."

In 1809, Toussaint Charbonneau, Sacagawea and Jean-Baptiste arrived in St. Louis and Clark welcomed them in his home.

–I want my son to learn how to read and write, said Charbonneau to his friend.

The American hired a tutor to instruct the young pupil who had a keen intelligence.

Sacagawea enjoyed life in the increasingly cosmopolitan St. Louis where people of all nations mingled: French-Canadians, Spanish, French, Americans and Indians. She adopted the manners and dress of White women and was noticed for being sweet and kind. In 1812, she fell ill and expressed the wish to go home. Charbonneau had tired of the civilized life; they took a boat that was heading up the Missouri to Fort Manuel, a new trading post not far from the Hidatsa and Mandan villages. Sadly, on December 20, Sacagawea died at the fort, carried off by a high fever. She was only twenty-five. Charbonneau's tears flowed all the way to St. Louis, where Jean-Baptiste learned from Clark's lips that his Shoshoni mother had passed away.

Clark took over the planned publication of the expedition's journals, which came out in 1814 under the title The History of the Expedition Under the Command of Captains Lewis and Clark. The Philadelphia publisher had only one thousand four hundred and seventeen copies printed and the book did not sell very well. A version of Sergeant Patrick Gass' journal had been in circulation for a few years already, as were some unauthorized editions. The American press had lost interest in the expedition, having moved on to new endeavors and marvels, such as Robert Fulton's steamboat.

William Clark was a great explorer, an exceptional leader of men and a loyal friend, but he was never able to acknowledge York's humanity. In 1809, the slave asked his master to set him free, in recognition of his contribution to the success of their historic expedition. York wished to leave St. Louis as a free man and join his wife in Kentucky. Clark refused; he didn't even want to talk about it. And if York insisted, he threatened to settle the matter by selling him to a master from New Orleans who would treat him harshly.

York persisted in his request and he managed to drag out of his master the permission to go and visit his wife for a period of four or five weeks. He stayed in Kentucky over five months. Clark was furious and he summoned him repeatedly to come back to St. Louis, which York finally did, but taking his time and grumbling all the way. Between the two men, nothing was left of the good companionship of their childhood, nothing of the solidarity of the expedition, only a basic misunderstanding between master and slave. And yet,

Clark could never bring himself to sell York. For a few years, he hired him out to a tobacco planter from Kentucky. Then, in 1816, he gave him his freedom at last. York, who was grieving for his wife's death, tried to make a living as a wagoner in Tennessee, but he came up against the Whites' refusal to hire an emancipated slave. Nobody remembered the date of his death.

Dismissed by Lewis as a "man of no peculiar merit," Toussaint Charbonneau continued to work as a trader, guide and interpreter in the American West up until the early 1840's. In St. Louis, Clark always recommended the services of his old friend to those who were leaving for Upper Missouri. In the course of his long career, Charbonneau got to know all the great voyageurs of his day. In 1823, he met the German naturalist Paul Wilhem, Prince of Wurtemberg, who asked him to accompany him to the Three Forks. Charbonneau accepted on condition that his son be allowed to come along. Jean-Baptiste was then eighteen-years-old; after finishing his studies in St. Louis, he had gone to live with his father.

Jean-Baptiste amazed Wilhem, who never thought he would meet in the West such an accomplished young man, who spoke fluently French, English and many Indian languages; not to mention the fact that he could have taught many experienced hunters and trappers a thing or two. At the end of his stay in North America, the prince asked the boy's father permission to take him to Europe and introduce him to the old continent. Charbonneau accepted right away; he remembered the prophecy made by Sacagawea's mother, according to which Jean-Baptiste would meet crowned heads in faraway lands.

Thus Jean-Baptiste Charbonneau lived in Europe for five years. When he returned to America, he had command of two new languages, German and Spanish. He could have settled in St. Louis and become successful in business or any other field. Instead, he chose to return to the West, his native country. Without losing his genteel manners and his joviality, he became the best mountain man of his times.

In 1847, at the age of forty-two, he found himself in California, where he was named alcalde of the San Luis Rey Mission. He resigned his position a few years later to protest against the unjust treatment of the local Indians. He later took part in the California Gold Rush and invested in the mines with associates of dubious honesty, but fortune never favored him. In 1861, he worked as a cashier in a California hotel and, in 1866, took part in another gold rush in Montana, where he died of pneumonia on May 16. The major newspapers of the West published articles at his death, stressing his participation in the Lewis and Clark expedition.

Jean-Baptiste Charbonneau never forgot his father. When he learned of his death in 1843, he returned to St. Louis to settle his estate. Toussaint Charbonneau had left his son the appreciable sum of three hundred dollars.

When did the voyageur from Boucherville die? That remains a mystery. In the last years of his life, Toussaint Charbonneau worked at Fort Clark, one of the trading posts of the American Fur Company, a monopoly owned by John Jacob Astor, a rich merchant from New York. In 1834, he acted as interpreter to another German naturalist, Alexander Philip Maximilian, Prince of Wied, who showed up in Upper Missouri with the Swiss artist Karl Bodmer. The two men published a beautifully written and illustrated book on the Great Plains of the West, just before the arrival of the American settlers who wiped out the buffalo and a good portion of the Indian population.

During his stay at Fort Clark, Prince Maximilian had the opportunity to understand why Toussaint had been nicknamed the One Whose Man-Part Is Never Limp. On February 4, 1834, after one more day of waiting for him in vain, he wrote in his journal: “Charbonneau was still missing: this seventy-five year-old man is still chasing women.”

In 1837, the French-Canadian voyageur heard the last speech of the Mandan chief Mano-Topé, also known as Four Bears, whose warriors were dying of smallpox, as was he. For the first time in his life, Charbonneau worried about the future of Indians. Their numbers had dwindled and livelihood become precarious because Whites had brought that dreaded disease to the West, as well as alcohol and more advanced weaponry.

Addressing his warriors, Mato-Topé thus began his memorable and heartbreaking exhortation:

"My friends, all of you, listen to what I have to say. As far back as I can remember, I have liked Whites. I have lived with them ever since I was a child and, as far as I know, I've never done them any harm. On the contrary, I've always defended them against the insults of others, something they cannot deny. Four Bears never saw a White man starve without giving him food, drink and a buffalo skin to sleep on. I've always been ready to die for them. I've done everything a Red Skin could do for them, and what did I get in return? Ingratitude!"

Raising his voice, he continued:

"I've never called a White man a dog, but I must say to you that Whites have deceived me; they, whom I've always considered as my brothers, have now become my worst enemies. I have fought many battles, and have been wounded many times, but I am proud of the wounds my enemies have inflicted upon me. Today, I am wounded, and by whom? By those White dogs I've always treated as brothers. I'm not afraid of dying, my friends, you know that, but to die with a decomposing face, so bad that even the wolves will recoil from me while they say to one another: there's Four Bears, friend of the White man..."

After a pause, he went on with blazing eyes:

"Listen to what I have to say to you, for it's the last time you'll hear me speak. Think of your wives, children, brothers and sisters. In fact, all who are dear to you are dead, or dying, with their decaying faces, because of those White dogs. Think of all this, my friends: rise up together and don't leave a single one of them alive. Four Bears will do his part!"

Charbonneau was an old man; he didn't fear for himself, but he knew then that Mato-Topé's speech marked the beginning of the end for the Mandans, the Hidatsas and the French-Canadian voyageurs.

Notes

1 Device used by Native North Americans of the Great Plains for transporting their tepees and household goods. It consisted of two poles, lashed on either side of a dog or a horse, with one end of each pole dragging on the ground.

2 It was previously thought that Toussaint Charbonneau was forty-five. According to the book, *America,* written by Quebec historian Denis Vaugeois, Toussaint was thirty-five at the time of his meeting with Lewis and Clark. Denis Vaugeois found Charbonneau's birth certificate in Boucherville, Canada.

3 Big Bellies

4 On the road from pretty La Rochelle
On the road from pretty La Rochelle
Three lovely ladies did I meet.

We go where the paddle takes us
Far with the paddle we go.

5 Three lovely ladies did I meet
Three lovely ladies did I meet
I did not chose, but got the fairest

We go where the paddle takes us
Far with the paddle we go.

6 This journal entry, like many others, is filled with grammatical and spelling errors.

7 Pork eater; rookie voyageur.

8 On my way I met two ladies
Riding their mounts in style
Lon, lon, ...

9 Riding their mounts in style
One on her horse, the other one on foot
Lon, lon, ...

10 The North Country

11 Roving around, roving around,
Roving around the world.

Behind our house there is a pond
Roving around,
Three lovely ducks swam along
Roll, roll, rolling around.

12 I am killed.

13 White sausage

14 A *berdache* was a man who, in conformity with social convention, assumed a woman's role in every respect.

15 Tall Petticoat.

16 *The Red River Jig*

17 *Blind Man's Jig*

18 *The Hop*

19 *The Barber's Dance*

20 *Pretty Blonde*

21 *The Simple Great Jig*, also known as *The Red River Jig* and *Blind Man's Jig.*

22 Miss, will you dance
The hop with me?
Miss, will you dance?
The hop will begin.

23 Yes sir, I will dance
The hop with you
Yes sir, I will dance
I will accompany you.

24 Oh! sir, how I can dance
The hop with you
Oh! sir, how I can dance
Shall we begin again?

25 Oh! Miss, I can't go on
Hopping with you
Oh! Miss, I can't go on
Please, excuse me.

26 Here's the wind, the lovely wind
Here's the wind my love is calling
Here's the wind, the lovely wind
Here's the wind my love is waiting.

27 Behind our house there is a pond
Behind our house there is a pond
Three lovely ducks swim along

Here's the wind, the lovely wind...

28 See Note 19